Moral Materialism

Other Books by Ashish Dalela:

The Science of God
Time and Consciousness
Conceiving the Inconceivable
The Balanced Organization
The Yellow Pill
Cosmic Theogony
Emotion
Mystic Universe
Signs of Life
Uncommon Wisdom
Gödel's Mistake
Quantum Meaning
Sāńkhya and Science
Is the Apple Really Red?
Six Causes

Moral Materialism

A Semantic Theory of Ethical Naturalism

Ashish Dalela

SHABDA
PRESS

Moral Materialism—A Semantic Theory of Ethical Naturalism
by Ashish Dalela
www.shabda.co

Cover Design: Kit Foster
Interior Design: Ciprian Begu

Published by Shabda Press
www.shabda.co
ISBN 978-93-85384-02-8
v1.22(06/2021)

Dedicated to all those people who believe in free will and morality but could not find rational grounds for it.

Morality is of the highest importance—but for us, not for God.
– Albert Einstein

Contents

List of Figures

Preface

Why do bad things happen to good people? In fact, why do good things happen to good people? What is the connection between the goodness or badness of an action and the consequences of that action for its actor? These questions have traditionally been studied in philosophical ethics and have frequently run into three kinds of problems that prevent an objective understanding of morality.

First, questions of right and wrong are viewed as cultural and social issues, if not personal preferences; something may be right in one society or culture and wrong in another. How can there be an objective theory of morality if morals are what we agree upon rather than something that exists independent of us? Second, questions of ethics change with time, place, person, and circumstances, and the same action may be right in one situation and wrong in another, even within a given culture or society. How can there be any objective theory of morality when something is wrong at one time and right at another? This problem is aggravated by the scientific belief that nature is uniform: the same laws and material reality exist everywhere in the universe and these laws and material reality do not change with time. If nature is uniform but morals are not, then morals could not be natural. Third, we suppose that the causal connection between an action and its consequences exists for facts but not for the morality of those facts; for instance, if someone pulls a trigger on a gun, there is a causal connection between the trigger pull and the bullet emerging from the gun's barrel, but no causal connection between the trigger and whether the shooter's action is punished or rewarded.

The above three problems are closely related to questions of reality and natural law within science. Science treats reality as objects that exist independent of other objects but moral issues depend upon social, cultural, organizational, temporal, spatial, and circumstantial *contexts.* Science describes the effects of our actions but not their moral *consequences.* In fact, no action is right or wrong in science, and the effects of these actions can only be described as material transactions but not judged as morally right or wrong. A further issue is that science reduces the mind to matter, thereby eliminating a role for choice in nature. If there is no choice in action, then the consequences of those actions cannot be tied to moral judgments. Given these problems, moral consequences—e.g., why do bad things happen to good people?—are outside the scope of natural theories.

G. E. Moore in his book *Principia Ethica* rejected any connection between morals and nature as a *naturalistic fallacy.* He claimed that questions of morality are so ineffable that it is not possible to associate the facts of nature with their moral judgments. David Hume before Moore had similarly argued for a divide between *is* and *ought* claiming that nature only tells us what it is not what it ought to be. The early days of modernism thus led to the notion that scientific and ethical questions have to be dealt with separately. In one sense, this was necessary to separate science from the hegemony of the Church. In another, it was convenient to focus on natural problems that could be solved through observation and mathematical laws. By separating natural causes from moral judgments, philosophers condoned the existence of a moral God, though much limited in the scope of His control of nature. God, in this view, only delivers moral principles which are outside natural science. God may be the one who judges according to these principles, but they are independent of science.

Of course, the naturalists were not entirely convinced of this separation, because it left the loophole that God may still exist and deliver moral judgments, making humans accountable to God's view of morality. In recent times, therefore, several theories that hope to explain morality based on natural principles have emerged. These "ethical naturalists" counter the problems associated with the moral relativism of society, culture, time, or place, with theories that can be based on facts about nature. Evolutionists for instance claim that altruism is good for the survival of a species as a whole. Hedonism suggests that moral goodness is that which increases the pleasure of its actors. Utilitarianism claims that morality is that which maximizes the benefit and minimizes the loss for a group of actors.

The problem with ethical naturalism, however, is that it is not entirely natural—at least the way naturalism is understood today. For example, each of these viewpoints recognizes a role for choice (e.g., that we may or may not choose to follow ethical action, even at the detriment of our own existence) but how do we explain this choice? If 'collective good' is a natural concept, then 'individual good' must be a natural concept as well; however, how do we define this 'good' collectively except in relation to our intentions, which indicate a directedness in nature, when nature has no directedness? If pleasure is the measure of ethics, then what is pleasure?

An even more fundamental problem is that to define a contextual theory of ethics, we must recognize the reality of contexts, which depend on the idea of boundaries in nature—those which create *contexts* within which moral judgments are performed—although there is no natural explanation of boundaries in physical sciences. Materialists claim that objects exist in space-time and they randomly aggregate into structures, which appear as contexts; the context is, however, not real in itself; it is merely a collection of independent parts. But if the context is an epiphenomenon of the parts, then morals must reduce to the physical properties of objects. And that reduction takes us back to the original problem: physical sciences can predict whether the trigger pull will cause a bullet to be fired but not whether that trigger pull is right or wrong. To perform a contextual moral judgment, the context must be real and independent of the parts in it because then the contextual judgments would not reduce to the properties of the parts as they would be attributed to the whole.

The problem of ethical naturalism, therefore, reduces to the question of whether collections are materially real or merely epiphenomena of independent parts. Physical theories—as I will extensively discuss in this book—falter when they have to deal with object collections rather than individual objects, which suggests that there is a real role for a new kind of physical construct (boundaries) but such a role does not exist in current science. I will describe how the induction of this idea needs a shift in our thinking about matter from independent objects to contextually related symbols of meaning. The order and structure in matter, in this view, is an outcome of matter encoding meanings, rather than aggregating randomly.

This book describes an alternative view of matter. The cornerstone of this revision is that material objects are created, structured, and ordered by meanings. Meaning are therefore not just in the mind; they are also present in matter. The book extends some of my prior work that describes the problems of indeterminism, uncertainty, incompleteness, irreducibility, and irreversibility in physical, mathematical, and biological sciences. That work showed that the problems of incompleteness, indeterminism, and incomputability in physical theories can be resolved only if material objects were viewed as symbols of meanings. The world of symbols now has to be described using a hierarchical and closed notion of space and time, rather than the flat and open space-time of current science.

Once matter can encode meanings, it becomes possible to think about *theories* of nature also as material entities. In fact, we can now speak about a theory as a subtle form of matter which exists as our understanding of reality, quite different from the reality itself. Obviously, the theories would be associated with observers rather than with the external world. A direct consequence of this premise is that there are potentially as many real theories of nature as there are observers. All these theories exist; however, they may not necessarily be true, quite like false ideas can exist in our minds. There is, now, a profound need to understand how only one theory of nature is universally true, even though false theories also physically exist. It is also possible to speak about the evolution of theories quite like the evolution of material objects; the evolution of the theory would, however, arise due to its differences with the universal theory.

It is well-known that phenomena underdetermine the theory. There are many plausible explanations of a phenomenon, which would seem to work equally well. However, as newer phenomena are added, the number of plausible theories rapidly declines. Science progresses by incorporating newer phenomena into the same theory. A given theory—which was formulated to explain a given phenomenon—would be modified as newer phenomena are added to the list of facts that the theory must explain. To develop a perfect theory of nature, therefore, the theoreticians must consider ever more phenomena and try to explain them using their particular theory. Of course, this modification depends on the theoretician encountering newer experiences that compel him or her to modify the theory. If I have a false theory of nature and I always verify it against a single type of phenomena, which reinforces the theory, the theory can never be improved. To improve the theory, I must find phenomena that do not fit the theory and then find appropriate modifications to the theory. This is not always assured. For instance, how do I find the phenomena that will not fit the present explanation and modify it?

This is possible if we can speak about natural laws of interaction between reality and its theories. Science currently describes the evolution of material objects. Can there be a science that describes the evolution of theories? I will argue that this is possible when matter is conceived semantically as symbols of meanings. The interaction between a theory and phenomena will modify the theory. The law of nature will now describe how a semantic entity—i.e., the theory of nature—interacts with another semantic entity—i.e., the phenomenon—and that interaction modifies the theory of nature.

But what does the evolution of theories have to do with morality? I will argue that, if we adopt the semantic view, then the interaction between a theory and reality represents the choice of interpreting reality. The choice is in one sense free—we can choose arbitrary theories of nature to explain phenomena. But the choice is also compelled by the encounter with new phenomena. Whether to use a new theory to explain the newer phenomenon or leave the phenomenon unexplained as random behavior in nature, now becomes a choice. It is not a perfectly rational choice, so choice has to be separated from rationality. Once the role of choice is understood in the context of theory formation, we can speak about right and wrong choices; the right choice is one that adjusts our explanation of the world in terms of the newer phenomena, while the wrong choice just ignores it.

Since choice is a new type of fundamental construct involved in the interpretation of nature, we can conceive a new type of causal model for it. Unlike the material objects that are just involved in causes and effects, choices have effects, but also additional consequences. The interaction between theory and reality, therefore, produces a new type of logical-material entity which can be called the *entitlements* and *obligations* of the observers. If the theory is false, then its obligation is those experiences by which it can be corrected. If the theory is true, then its entitlement is those experiences that reinforce it. These entitlements and obligations determine subsequent experiences. As the observer undergoes new experiences, the theories may be modified, since the new phenomena may not fit the current theories.

For morality to exist in nature, free choices must exist prior because if there is no free choice then there is no responsibility, and moral consequences of choices cannot exist. But for free choices to exist in nature, meanings must exist even prior because choices are always made upon meanings. For example, a theory as an interpretation of the facts in the world is a type of meaning. In that respect, before a natural theory of morality can be formulated, a semantic view of nature must exist. This view describes the world as meanings and the observer as the theory of the world. The interaction between the theory and the world is now the ability to interpret the world differently and these interpretations must be responsible. The outcomes of such interactions, when they can be described naturally and when they have causal effects, can be used to understand morality.

This book argues that the universe has to be described in a way that contains both reality and theories about reality. Both of these can be material, but they are different kinds of matter. If, therefore, an observer has an incorrect theory of nature, the observer would be led into experiences that may cause changes to the theory. The evolution of objects is the physical theory of nature, while the evolution of theories represents the evolution of observers. When the evolution of the observer depends on their theory about nature, then false theories don't just have epistemological implications, they also have moral implications. In particular, a false theory will compel the observer to undergo novel experiences to correct the theory.

Morality and truth in this view are not separate judgments; they are identical. The judgment of truth involves the question of whether a theory is true. The morality of the judgment is that we are obliged and compelled to only adopt truth. Acceptance of falsity is immoral and has consequences that force repeated encounters with those experiences, which may then correct the theory. Nature is therefore goal-oriented. Its goal is to correct our understanding of reality.

This shift allows us to study morality in the same way that we study truth, and theories of morality can be theories of truth. Accordingly, there is a true theory that governs nature, and there are observer-specific theories of nature that materially exist although they may be false. The evolution of nature is governed by the true theory of nature and the evolution of the observer depends on their individual theories about nature. In effect, different initial conditions for observers create different trajectories of experiences. These observer trajectories are different from object trajectories; both object and observer trajectories are determined but they require different kinds of descriptions. In particular, the observer trajectory is based on moral judgments of the observer while the object trajectory is the material theory of objects. Objects and observers both exist in nature, but they are different kinds of matter: the observer is the theory about objects, which can potentially be incorrect. Questions of morality can thus be tackled in science by bringing theories, which are presently in the Platonic world, into the real world. The evolution of observers (as different from the evolution of objects) can thus be viewed as the theory of moral consequence and responsibility that arises from the discrepancy between reality and its theories. The morally correct action is that which follows a true theory of nature.

While a mathematical theory of ethical naturalism is outside the scope of the current work, *Moral Materialism* sets up insights that can be used to develop such a theory in the future. This allows us to see how ideas about morality could be understood in a scientific theory that describes material objects as symbols of meaning.

1

The Problem of Morality

A system of morality which is based on relative emotional values is a mere illusion, a thoroughly vulgar conception which has nothing sound in it and nothing true.

—*Socrates*

Free Will and Determinism

Determinism and free will are contradictory ideas, but they are necessitated by two equally important assumptions we carry about the universe. Determinism is mandated by the view that the universe we live in is a rational place because then we can predict the occurrences using logic and mathematical laws. Free will is essential because once we have the ability to predict the occurrences, then we should also be able to use these laws to manipulate nature for our benefit. After all, if we knew how nature works but could not manipulate this working, then the knowledge would seem quite pointless. Science discovers natural laws and technology manipulates nature using these laws, but most people do not see the contradiction between science and technology: scientific determinism is false if there is free will and technological freedom is impossible if there is determinism.

If there is complete determinism in nature, then we could not have goals and choices—not even of technological innovation. On the other hand, if we were completely free, then natural laws themselves would not exist, upon which the technological innovations have been built. The contradiction between free will and determinism is resolved by the postulate of morality: it performs the balancing act between extreme determinism and complete freedom. The balancing act suggests that our choices must have consequences; that we are free to choose, but we must also own the results of that choice. There is hence a free will in choosing between alternative paths, but there is determinism in the consequences of those choices. The real question, however, is: Can we describe the connection between choices and consequences in a rational manner? Or is that relation established by some divine judgment—e.g., the choices of God?

The problem of free will and determinism is essentially one of understanding if the rational place can also be a moral place; in fact, in some sense, the morality in the universe must also be identical to its rationality. This has seemed very difficult in modern times due to some peculiarities of modern science that I will shortly discuss. The problem stems primarily from the fact that the scientific model of rationality entails the ability to predict the occurrences in nature, but precludes the ability to choose between possibilities. Therefore, if nature is rational, then free will must be an illusion. If, however, free will exists, then nature's rationality must be false. I view this conclusion as a problem in the present scientific model of causality. For instance, can there be a causal model of nature where the cause-effect relation could be modified to include choices and consequences?

The contradiction between free will and determinism arises because determinism seems to entail that there is no free will. In a moral universe, the reward or punishment for our actions is due to the fact that we choose to act in different ways and those choices make us responsible for our actions. If we did not choose, then we would not be responsible, and if we are not responsible then we should not have to suffer or enjoy the consequences of our actions. Determinism, however, entails that if the universe is rational then we can predict everything in it, and someone's choices would not make a difference to what actually happens in the universe. If the universe evolves exactly how a deterministic law predicts its evolution, then free will is superfluous to the occurrences in the universe. If the universe is deterministic, then what happens in the universe had to happen. We have no choice in making something happen and therefore we are not responsible for our actions. Why are then some people rich and others poor? Why are some people successful and others failures? Why are some people loved and others ignored?

Two kinds of solutions are generally offered for this problem. The first one says that the universe is not deterministic. Of course, if the universe had no laws, then it would be impossible to make any predictions, and science itself would not be possible. Given the tremendous successes of science, it seems obvious to assume that nature is ordered and predictable. The critic of determinism, however, claims that although there is some order in nature, not everything in the universe can be completely predicted. This is because science is fundamentally incomplete and it would not be able to explain every possible phenomenon in nature. The things that cannot be determined by science represent the things we can choose from. So, scientific laws preclude many possibilities but they also include many possibilities, and free will is the ability to choose from them.

The determinist obviously disagrees with this solution. He or she would argue that science will eventually be complete, although there may be areas in which current science is inadequate. When science reaches its pinnacle of completeness, it would explain free will as the byproduct of chemicals in the brain. Since those chemical reactions can be deterministically predicted[1], it is wrong to suppose that free will is a fundamental causal agent. We might rather suppose that free will is an *epiphenomenon* of chemical reactions. Like the fluidity of water is an epiphenomenon of H2O molecules, we can suppose that properties such as consciousness and free will are produced through a complex structuring of atoms and molecules.

The conflict between free will and determinism, therefore, reduces to the question of whether science can be complete. If science can be predictively complete, then there is no free will. However, if science must be incomplete, then there is room for free choices in nature. Whichever way we answer this question, we would have lost one of the two equally important assumptions about the universe. If science would be complete eventually then the universe is not a moral place and claims of determinism will preclude free choices. If, however, science will always be incomplete then the universe is not rational; there will be things that we can know but can't predict. At this point, it seems that we are faced with a choice between a rock and a hard place: neither option is completely acceptable to us.

There is another profound problem in this debate, which cannot be ignored. Assuming science is incomplete and there is room for free choices, how would choices interact with matter? The problems arising in understanding the interaction between matter and free will have been debated for many centuries now. The point at which free will interacts with matter, free will becomes matter. The problem of the interaction between free will and matter thus leads to a reduction of free will to matter, returning us to the problem we started out solving—namely that science is incomplete and free will is supposed to fix it. If free will is supposed to fix scientific incompleteness and free will reduces to matter then we cannot fix the incompleteness.

It would therefore seem that even if science were incomplete, the postulate of free will would not fix the incompleteness because free will could not interact with matter without being reduced to matter. If matter exists only in a state of possibility, free will could not produce reality from it without itself being reduced to possibility. If free will also reduces to possibility, then the sum total of matter and free will are both in a state of possibility and there is no reality. The only consistent position that allows some reality to exist is that of determinism without free will. This might seem unintuitive, but the brief reasoning shown above leads us to that conclusion.

Finally, there are also some problems of moral responsibility which can be avoided only if the universe is deterministic. Suppose, for instance, that Max Planck (the inventor of quantum theory) had free will to change some part of the world and he used that free will to invent[2] quantum theory. The theory obviously created new possibilities for the development and use of technology that did not exist earlier, such as electronics and nuclear bombs. Since Planck created the atomic theory, is he now responsible for the things that are done using that theory? Obviously, we remember Planck as someone who started a revolution, and his ideas were adopted and subsequently extended by many others. As the originator of those ideas, is he responsible in some sense for the subsequent work of others?

Most of us would be quite comfortable crediting Planck with having a very important role in a lot of subsequent development in science.

But this question becomes problematic in two ways. First, if Planck is responsible for the good changes that came about using quantum theory, then is he also responsible for the bad ones, such as the atomic bomb (I will, for the sake of argument, assume that the atomic bomb is a bad thing, although some people argue that the bomb is good because it prevented future world wars)? Second, if Planck is partially responsible for the choices that other people made after him, then does it minimize the free will of those individuals? For instance, can we now say that our current choices are actually constrained by the actions that other people performed in the past? If that were indeed the case, then how could we be responsible?

The problem here is that if we attribute free will to individuals, by which they change the world, then their actions themselves seem to infringe upon other's free will and this makes the original actor responsible for the good and bad deeds even of later actors. On one hand, it would seem that an actor's actions could potentially stretch their effect far into the future, making him or her responsible for those effects. On the other hand, the same extension would rob others of their free will and if a sufficiently large number of such influences could be traced into the past, this would seem to deny free will.

Most commonsense thinking asserts that Planck is not responsible for what happens after him because the world of things itself does not determine how it is used because that use depends on our interpretation which is not in the thing itself. For instance, we might say that quantum theory is not good or bad; it is our choice to use it for electronics or atomic bombs that make it good or bad. But this line of reasoning is problematic because it entails that what happens in the world (electronics vs. atomic bombs) is governed by choices, and the choices must somehow interact with the world, taking us back to the problem of the interaction between the world and our free will. And if free will and the world can indeed interact, the outcomes in the world depend on our choices, and the actors must therefore be responsible for those actions, even if these actions are in the future and performed by other actors. Furthermore, if past actors' actions influence the present and there is a very long past behind us, then in what sense have we been left with choices that we can call our own? Aren't we simply predetermined products of choices in the past?

Whichever way we look at this, the idea of free will seems to create different kinds of problems. The interaction between choice and matter is problematic and entails that science is incomplete implying that nature is not entirely rational if it has to be moral. Furthermore, if nature is moral and there are free choices, any actor's actions could stretch their effects into the future, thereby encroaching on other actors' choices, making the original actor responsible for the outcomes that occur in the future. If this reasoning is extended, then one could argue that a moral God who created the universe did something that makes Him responsible for everything that subsequently happens. For, if the universe had not been created, the subsequent good and bad choices would not be possible either. As the creator of the universe, therefore, God must be responsible for all our choices.

Given all these problems, it appears that the only consistent and snag-free solution is to suppose that science is complete, nature is deterministic, and there is no free will. Indeed, a growing swath of scientists now thinks in this way. They claim that the experience of free will is an enigma of science—i.e., how material interactions produce experiences and the impression of free will—not a fact about the morality of the universe with free will and accountability. Furthermore, science is in principle complete, although we might not be currently in possession of a complete material theory of nature today. Progress in science will eventually produce a complete theory, which can then be used to explain free will as an epiphenomenon.

The Cosmic Drama

This book offers a solution to the above problem. In the solution, both determinism and free will are equally real. That is, science is complete and it can completely predict everything about the universe. And yet, we are also completely free to choose what we want. While the details of this solution—and how it would be grounded in the current problems and future development of science—will come in later chapters, let me try to sketch the solution through an everyday intuitive example here. I have often discovered that things that can only be understood through a very complex structure of reasoning are not very well understood.

Conversely, when things are well understood, they can be stated quite simply. So, let me provide a simple illustration of the solution.

Imagine that the universe is a cosmic drama whose roles and events are fixed *a priori* by the playwright, but its actors have not yet been identified because the play hasn't yet been dramatized[3]. The director of the play seeks to dramatize it and goes in search of actors to enact its roles, events, and dialogues. Assume that the director has access to a large pool of actors who could participate in the play. The director could choose actors based on a variety of factors such as their height, gender, acting talent, and suitability to play a certain role. The actors, too, have to agree to play a given type of role. They might sometimes be compelled to take on a role because other roles have already been taken by others, or simply because they are desperate to participate in the play in whatever capacity they can. If the play runs exactly as how the playwright wrote it, then the events in the play could be completely predicted even without watching it, or even without the play being enacted on a stage. The only difference between the playwright's version of the drama and the actual enactment on the stage is that some actors have been chosen to play certain roles. Ideally, we can assume that the play would not be different even if a different set of actors enacted the play, as far as the audience is concerned. The play with different actors would however be different for those actors participating in the play.

If the universe is a cosmic drama and its script is prewritten, then it is possible to know and predict everything that will happen in the universe deterministically. And yet, this determinism would not preclude the possibility that different actors could enact that drama. There can be complete determinism in the universe as far as the events of the universe are concerned. And there can be full freedom in the universe as far as the selection of actors is concerned. Of course, the freedom to choose actors for specific kinds of roles is not necessarily arbitrary; any good director expects certain traits and abilities in the actors to play certain roles. But these traits and capabilities do not fix a specific individual actor; we can imagine that another actor with the same ability could play the role as well.

It is also imaginable that the total number of roles and events in the play exceeds the total number of actors such that the same actors must enact several roles one after another. Some actors who play multiple roles would have to run backstage, change their costumes and makeup, just in time to be ready for the next role. The director also has to ensure that the roles and actors are planned in a way that the same actor isn't required to play multiple roles simultaneously, and there is an adequate lag between roles so as to allow an actor to prepare for the next role after having enacted the previous one.

When the universe is seen in analogy to a drama, it is possible to reconcile the determinism of events with the choice of actors. There are two ways in which such a drama with many roles and many actors can be described. The first description is about the occurrences on the front stage where the events of the drama are enacted. This is how the audience views the play. But there is also a second description of the drama about what transpires backstage where the actors change costumes and makeup. This is how the director views the play. These two descriptions of the play are complementary and underdetermined by each other. For instance, the same events of the play could be enacted by different actors, and the same actors could enact different events. The events and the actors are connected in a specific play, but the actors don't fix the play and the play doesn't fix the actors. When the playwright authors the play, he or she only defines the *roles*, although not the actual players in the drama. The events on the front stage are therefore the 'visible' component of the playwright's work. The events on the backstage are invisible to the audience but they are visible to the director. The playwright's work is a complete description of what happens on the front stage and the director's work is a complete description of what occurs on the back stage. Only a combination of the two, however, produces a drama.

The above analogy isn't yet rigorously grounded in any scientific ideas about matter, and it only represents a schema of how the free will and determinism debate could be solved. Subsequent chapters will try to identify the intuitions that can aid in the development of such a view of nature. My main aim in providing this suggestive picture here is primarily to illustrate that it is possible to conceive a reconciliation of both free will and determinism provided we can demarcate their respective functions. Determinism, in this case, is all that happens on the front stage in full view of the audience. The script for the play is defined in advance and it can be read by the audience even before they arrive for the show. If the play goes according to the script, there is nothing unexpected. The play is determined by the script. Free will here is the choice of actors to enact some role. The audience does not see and does not know how actors change roles. Knowing the script of the play itself does not determine the actors.

This picture separates the events from the actors in principle but connects the events to the actors in a play via a *role*. A role represents the events occurring in the play, while the actors represent those individuals who enact the events. This type of separation between roles and actors does not exist in current science; the actors are objects with properties and these properties, in turn, determine the events in the universe. Unlike the above picture of a drama where there are two things—a role and an actor—in current science, there is only one thing—actors. These actors are governed by deterministic laws, and therefore the actor has no choice to jump roles. Determinism and free will are therefore not inherently contradictory. Rather, the contradiction is created by collapsing the distinction between an actor and a role. If the actor is the role, and the actor is free, then the role cannot be predicted. On the other hand, if the actor is the role, and the role is fixed, then the actor is not free. The contradiction between free will and determinism is an outcome of trying to equate the actor with the role. If this distinction were reinstated in science, it would be possible to imagine a scientific solution to the problems described earlier, without compromising either the completeness of science or the moral latitude for accommodating free choices.

Newton's Mechanism

The current predicament in science is an outcome of Newton's conception of science. The picture of nature widely employed as the working hypothesis in science stems directly from Newton's theory of gravitation that fashioned the idea that nature is objects with possessed properties such as mass; these objects exist independently of the other objects and observers; their state changes are governed by natural forces such as gravity; their dynamics can be described deterministically by mathematical laws. In this picture of nature, the actor and the role are identical. The role played by a particle is fully determined by its properties (such as mass). You cannot say that the actor can play many other roles but is currently playing one of them. You must say that the particle is doing all that it can do. Properties like mass exert a force on the other masses, causing the particles to move. This motion can be drawn as a trajectory of the particle, thereby creating a picture of the role being enacted in the universe. However, the role and the actor cannot be separated because the particle and its behaviors (such as motion) are identical. The particle *is* the trajectory, and therefore the role is not distinguishable from the actor.

In the case of a drama, we can distinguish between the role (e.g., their actions and dialogues) and the actors because the actors are capable of playing other roles. This capacity to play other roles exists in the particle as alternative trajectories, provided we change the initial and boundary conditions of the particle. But this change to initial or boundary conditions becomes a choice that is eliminated in the real world. The world—once put into some initial and boundary conditions—evolves deterministically thereafter. Even if you change the initial or boundary condition, that change is also predictable. In short, the roles played by actors—i.e., the trajectories of the particles—are identical to the particles because each particle has a fixed trajectory, which makes the theory deterministic and eliminates choice.

If, for instance, Newton's theory had begun in the idea of *trajectories* as the primary constituents of the universe, and masses were selected to fit the trajectories, the distinction between the trajectory (role) and the mass (actor) would be obvious. It would also be obvious that the same mass could fit a different trajectory, creating the same indeterminism of the role-to-actor mapping that exists in a drama. But, this is not how classical physics describes the world. Since we cannot distinguish between a particle and its trajectory, we also cannot introduce the distinction between a role and an actor. In classical physics, the actor is the role; the trajectory is the particle.

The Need for Trajectories

The idea that particles are the primary reality in nature leads to a problem of particle conservation. If particles are real then they must also be immutable, and the total number of particles must be conserved. Reality in physics is tied to the idea of conservation; for instance, the property of momentum is real because momentum is conserved. The total number of particles, in Newton's physics, is not conserved. Rather, particles can split and combine, and while such changes would conserve other real properties such as the total momentum, they would not conserve the total number of particles. Since the total number of particles cannot be conserved, it is theoretically impossible to assert the reality of these particles in a physical sense. While we can say that momentum is real (since it is conserved) we cannot say that particles are real (since they are not conserved).

Of course, the problem of particle conservation also indicates that the trajectories also cannot be physically real because the total number of trajectories too cannot be conserved: trajectories can abruptly begin in object splitting and they can abruptly end in object combining. This is a contrast to the example of a drama, where the trajectories are preserved. For instance, if an actor fell sick and could not play a role, there would be a substitute actor in his place. The play would not change; the actors will be substituted by others. Therefore, the trajectories in a play are predetermined; they may not be conserved: e.g., a character can die, and his role would no longer be required, and his actions would no longer be visible. But there are many cases in which the actors can substitute for each other, so the distinction between the actor and the role is obvious. I'm quoting the example of object splitting and combining because it makes classical physics predictively *indeterministic*. The particle is still the trajectory, without the distinction between an actor and a role. A drama on the other hand is predictively deterministic—i.e., you can tell what is going to happen, but with a distinction between an actor and a role, because even if an actor fell sick, someone else would replace him.

What is then real in nature? In Newton's theory, mass, energy, momentum, and angular momentum are real, but particles and trajectories are not. If mass, energy, momentum, and angular momentum did not exist, particles and trajectories could not exist either. Particles and trajectories are therefore *constructions* from mass, energy, momentum, and angular momentum. That is, the universe begins in some total mass, energy, momentum, and angular momentum, which are then partitioned into particles and trajectories. Ideally, the goal of a physical theory should be to describe not just what is real (because it is conserved) but also how that reality produces phenomena (trajectories) by partitioning and combining that reality. One of the problems in modern science is that it can describe what is real but it is unable to predict how phenomena are produced from reality. That is, science can tell us which properties are conserved, but not how these properties are divided to create individual particles.

The genesis of this problem lies in the fact that while particles and trajectories are produced by dividing mass, energy, momentum, and angular momentum, there are infinitely many ways to divide them, thereby producing infinitely many sets of particles, which result in infinitely many sets of trajectories or phenomena. Each such way of dividing the conserved physical properties corresponds to the same reality although this reality appears to produce different phenomena. How can a single reality produce many phenomena?

It is worth illustrating this problem through an example. Imagine that there is a particle moving along a straight-line trajectory. This particle can abruptly split into two particles which then move in different directions. The split of the particle is consistent with Newton's physics for two reasons: (1) it obeys the laws of conservation of mass and momentum[4], and (2) the split requires zero total force. The split of the particle seems to violate Newton's first law of motion as often stated in textbooks, namely, that an object continues to move in a straight line path unless disturbed by forces. The law is violated because in the case of the split the object doesn't move along a straight-line path as it is split into two particles. This might lead you to believe that the particle can never split. However, this statement of Newton's first law of motion is a combination of two distinct ideas: (a) that momentum is a conserved property and (b) that the trajectory is the motion of an immutable particle. If the particle is not immutable, then the object can split without violating momentum conservation. Indeed, as we saw above, the idea of immutable particles is rather meaningless in physics because Newton's physics does not profess the conservation of particles as a fundamental principle of nature.

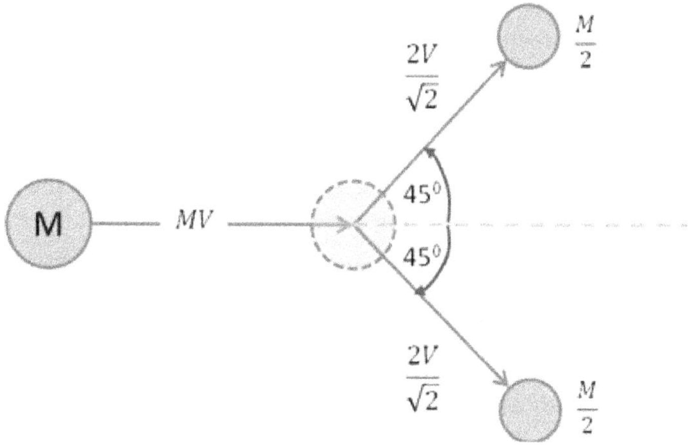

Figure-1 Particle and Trajectory Splitting

There is a sense in which Newton built the idea of immutable particles into his physics, although if we were to take this idea seriously then particles could not split and coalesce. Particles could only collide and maintain their identities or exert forces at a distance without ever being in contact. Coalescing and splitting would now be outside Newton's physics. Newton's theory is deterministic only if we prevent coalescing and splitting; this is called *elastic* dynamics. The determinism fails when material particles can coalesce and split; this is called *inelastic* dynamics. This fact is obvious in Newton's first law of motion which asserts two distinct ideas—momentum conservation and particle immutability—although only the first of these ideas is physically real. This is then the dogmatic aspect of Newton's physics: it uses the idea of particles and everyone who learns physics treats such particles as something real in nature, although the immutability or reality of such particles cannot be asserted in physics. The idea of a particle only supplies a realistic flavor to science, although in fact, we can only treat particles as phenomena, not reality.

A more accurate picture of classical physics is that it prescribes some fundamental properties such as mass, energy, momentum, and angular momentum, and these are real. Particles and trajectories are constructed from these properties by *dividing* or *distributing* mass, energy, momentum, and angular momentum into trajectories. There are infinite ways to divide the same total mass, energy, momentum, and angular momentum into such trajectories and there is nothing in Newton's physics that predicts it. This indeterminism is easily observed in the fact that there is no way to predict whether a particle will split into two particles: both split and non-split scenarios are consistent with all conservation laws. The only way to prevent the split is to assume that particles are immutable, which Newton subsumes in his first law of motion, but which is also an unphysical idea because the conservation of particles is certainly not true.

Newton's theory is deterministic only if we assume immutable particles. Each of these particles would move without changing their identities; the particles would never merge or split. The idea of immutable particles is implicit in Newton's theoretical formalism although it entails the conservation of particles which is never claimed. It is separately added to allow Newton's physics to portray a deterministic picture of nature where material objects are real and the universe exists as a collection of such immutable particles. If the particles are not immutable—and they are not immutable—then the universe is not deterministic. Newton's theory is consistent with many possible distributions of matter in space and time, even if we begin with a fixed initial condition. The evolution is deterministic only if the particles are immutable because then the total number of equations to be solved is fixed. As particles merge and split, the number of equations changes. While each equation may be deterministic, as the number of equations changes by the merging and splitting of particles, the total evolution of the universe becomes indeterministic.

I'm making this point because the supposed determinism of classical physics is false. This injects a new problem into science—i.e., recover the determinism in a new way. And that could be possible if we discard the Newtonian equation of particles with trajectories. The trajectories could be deterministic, but the particles may not be. That would in turn introduce a distinction between *objects* and *roles*. The trajectories would be the roles, and particles will be objects. The introduction of this distinction follows a problem—the collapse of determinism and the desire to reintroduce it in a new way. However, as we noted above, such determinism is compatible with choice.

When we allow a separation between objects and roles, then the picture of reality is deterministic, as far as the *events* in the universe are concerned, provided we look at these events from the 'outside'—quite like the audience views the drama on the stage. The determinism arises because the entire space-time structure (i.e., particles, their properties, and trajectories) has been chosen. However, a rather different picture of nature emerges if we look at the events from the perspective of the objects, if these objects are treated as observers. The difference is that when matter is distributed in space-time, there is only a consideration of *types* but no consideration of the *individuals*. For instance, two trajectories with mass *M* can swap the masses and the universe would be identical from the standpoint of the external observation but it would be different from the viewpoint of those objects if those objects were observers. This is because the two trajectories would pass through different events[5], and by swapping the masses, the respective observers will have different experiences.

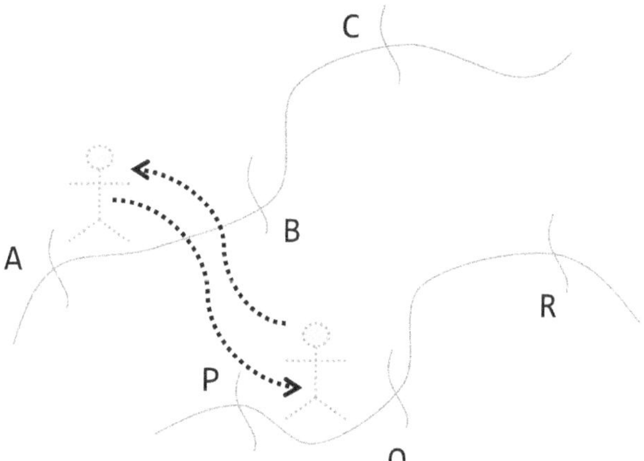

Figure-2 Particle Swapping Creates Indeterminism

The situation is now comparable to that of a drama being enacted by different actors. Two actors X and Y can play two roles U and W, and which role they play makes no difference from the standpoint of the audience but it does make a difference to the actors. As the distinction between a role and an actor in a drama, there is also a distinction between the trajectory and the material properties.

The Need for Objects

The problem of indeterminism doesn't go away by separating the physical properties like mass from the events associated with these properties. It is easy to assume that the mass is the particle, and when the mass splits, then the particle splits as well. After this split, we continue to speak about particles as objects which *possess* properties such as mass. The situation is akin to that in the drama, where an actor might be substituted by another with similar properties like height, weight, dress, looks, etc. Their behaviors are determined by the script of characters, the choice of an actor is decided by their suitability to play a certain role—e.g., their height, weight, looks, etc.—but they may still be different individuals or persons.

This compels us to distinguish between *objects* and *properties*. Given a certain succession of events, we can speak about different actors participating in them. But the requirement of a role doesn't specify the actor; it only specifies the *ability* to play a certain role decided by their properties. For instance, to participate in a certain event sequence, there must be a certain mass, but it could be a different particle that has the same mass. We might call this the *object*. In the drama, the object is an observer, who brings a coordinate reference frame into the picture, which is different from the events and the material properties. Coordinate reference frames must be tied to observers rather than properties or events. These observers will experience the same world differently with the same events, and the same material property distribution among these events owing to the differences in their respective coordinate reference frames.

At this juncture, it is important to distinguish between the observer and the object. Objects are conceptual entities, like properties. For instance, we can speak about a conceptual object like 'table' or 'chair'. These objects are not the observers to whom we can attach a reference frame. Similarly, particles in physics are not observers; they are conceptual objects quite like tables and chairs. We cannot attach a reference frame to the particle. A common illustration of this problem is that many reference frames can be associated with a particle as the origin; the particle doesn't fix the reference frame.

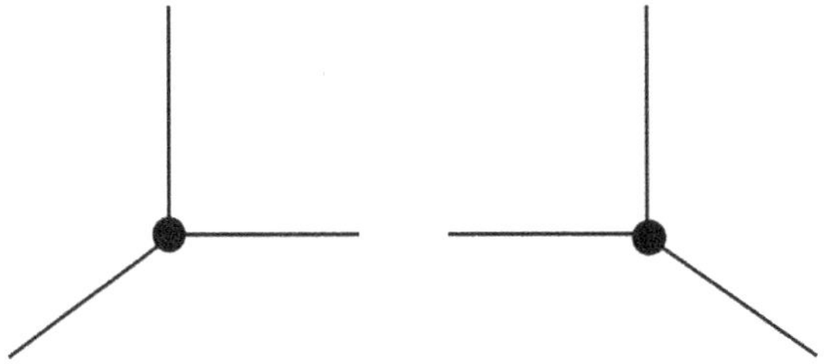

Figure-3 Particles Don't Fix Reference Frames

The observations carried out in classical physics are akin to the audience watching a play and these observations cannot distinguish between the cases when different players enact the same roles. The problem is that science only describes the *types* of objects, but not the specific *individual* objects. When you go to buy a car at a showroom, you care about the type of the car—e.g., you might be interested in a BMW 5-series car—but not the serial number on that car's chassis. Similarly, when science describes nature, it describes it as the type of object and not a particular instance of that object. The fact that there are many instances of the same type (just as there are many instances of the same BMW 5-series car) creates an indeterminism. This indeterminism is generally not noticed in physical theories because science has never been interested in describing the individual objects; science is only the description of certain *types* of objects.

We are therefore led to three kinds of categories. The first category is the events, which define the empirical observations. The second category is the material properties or types, which are used to explain these observations. The third category is the individual observers who connect the events into personal trajectories. A scientific theory deals in the types but these types (properties like mass) can split and combine. To maintain the continuity of experience, we must say that there is indeed an individual observer that goes through different experiences—including changing its properties and events. Newton's physics collapses these three categories into one. The observer is the particle, and we have no room to attach a coordinate reference frame to this particle. The entire universe must now be embedded into a universal space and time which means that the individual perspective on this world is lost. Even in relativity where the universe is described as the multitude of coordinate reference frames, these are not given a *physical* reality. The entire universe is described from a given reference frame, not individual frames, which exist simultaneously in the individual observers. Thus, we eliminate the role of the observer by collapsing particles into individuals.

To reinstate the observer into science, we must say that there are individual coordinate reference frames that allow the observer to interpret the same material properties and events differently. This difference amounts to a choice because the coordinate references can be varied, even if matter and events remain unchanged. In fact, we can now also speak about the evolution of the coordinate reference frame over time, which entails that the observer is not materially fixed in time; it can rather evolve its perspective. There is still an objective and universal space and time that pertains to the properties, but that reference frame of matter is different from the individual observer frames. Therefore, the meaning of relativity is not the rejection of the universal reference frame, but the *addition* of individual frames, and their recognition as something materially real.

The Problem of Indeterminism

There are hence three kinds of indeterminism in current science. The first indeterminism is that a given total amount of matter or energy can be distributed into trajectories in many ways. Therefore, even if there is a fixed amount of matter or energy, we cannot predict the events that will occur in the universe. Since these events constitute the observations of science, science cannot predict what will happen. The solution to the problem is that science must describe nature as a drama in which the event successions are fixed, even if actors are redistributed into these events. It involves the conceptualization of event successions as characters in a drama.

The second indeterminism is that even if there were a predictively complete account of the evolution of the universe, the theory would still be compatible with different *individuals* participating in the same events. The answer to this indeterminism is that they pertain to the choices of individuals, and a new kind of material reality that governs these choices must be postulated. By choice, I don't mean free will, which has no determination. By choices, I mean a reality that is subject to evolution and constitutes the reference frame through which the observer perceives and acts in the world. However, these reference frames are different from the material properties, which constitute the body and mind of the individual.

The third indeterminism is that each individual, or reference frame, can be associated with different material properties—e.g., the body and the mind. The body and the mind give us the ability to participate in different events. For instance, for someone to lift a heavy weight, they must have the strength to do so. A weak person cannot do it. However, a relatively weaker person with a strong determination to lift the weight may still be successful in doing so. In physical theories, the cause of an event may be one of the many properties such as mass or charge. So, a set of properties don't fix the events because they may not be applied to cause a change. And a trajectory doesn't fix the properties because one of several different properties may be used to produce the trajectory. Both properties and trajectories underdetermine each other and this is an indeterminism in science—which property defines which trajectory?

All three types of indeterminism appear many times in all physical theories, each time in different forms, and I will discuss the problem of scientific indeterminism in the next chapter. The indeterminism of all theories, however, takes on a common conceptual form, which remains invariant across various physical theories. This common form of indeterminism can be stated quite simply based on our prior discussion of the indeterminism in Newton's physics.

Scientific theories are causally incomplete because they describe many possible alternatives in nature, but do not pick out which alternative is *real*. As we saw in the case of Newton's theory, the theory is consistent with any number of deterministic equations, each pertaining to the evolution of a different number of particles. If we add other classical theories to Newton's physics—such as electromagnetism—then classical physics is consistent with one of multiple such properties producing the same trajectories. All physical theories permit infinite possible distributions of matter over trajectories, and different actors or objects occupying these trajectories, besides the objects possessing different kinds of properties. They do not single out a specific combination of object, property, and trajectory.

Given this indeterminism in science, the conversion of properties into trajectories and the conversion of trajectories into a world of events are attributed to randomness in nature. It is worth noting that randomness is different from probabilities; probabilities predict a certain likelihood of occurrence while randomness is a possibility without likelihood. In a randomness scenario, many things are possible, but we cannot predict (not even probabilistically) which one would occur. This is often less understood or not understood at all. Scientists emphasize the fact that the theory is deterministic although the initial conditions, boundary conditions, the number of particles or equations to be computed, all need to be determined, and they are uncertain. How the initial or boundary conditions are decided or how particles are determined remains outside the theory.

When faced with such problems of indeterminism, it is often rationally acceptable to suppose that if a theory explains many possibilities but does not pick a specific one, we might add a new kind of variable into the theory that makes this choice. While this approach is not *a priori* problematic, there are some reasons why it is not always as straightforward as it might initially sound. The reason is that often the theories in question have attained a form where it is impossible to add anything new to that theory because, upon such an addition, the theory will become either logically or empirically inconsistent. We always prefer a theory that is incomplete to a theory that is inconsistent. An incomplete theory makes some correct predictions, although it might not predict everything that is observable. An inconsistent theory on the other hand predicts things that will be false. We can live with an incomplete theory but we cannot live with an inconsistent one. Now, the problem is that the theories in question are incomplete, but if we tried to complete them by adding new variables, then the theory would become inconsistent. For instance, it might begin to make predictions contrary to observations.

The inability to add anything new to the theory often leads scientists to conclude that the theory is in fact complete. However, this completeness is arrived at not on the basis that the theory explains everything that can be empirically observed. It is rather necessitated by the fact that any attempts to add new ideas into the theory will make the theory inconsistent with observations or with other parts of the theory. Therefore, when we claim that the theory is complete, we only mean it in the sense that we cannot add anything to it, although we also know that it doesn't explain all observations.

A theory that doesn't explain all observations and which cannot be enhanced (because enhancements will make the theory empirically or logically inconsistent) can only be replaced by a new theory. The theory has reached a point where additions to it will not work. Now, if this were a problem with a specific theory, it might have been less perplexing. We could say that we don't have a complete picture of nature regarding a specific phenomenon, although such an explanation would be found by fixing the theory. However, this happens with all fundamental areas of science today—mathematics, computing, physics—and by implication to chemistry and biology. This makes the problem not just extremely serious but also incredibly difficult to solve. How can we replace everything we know today?

Note how the problem of indeterminism is quite different from the debate between free will and determinism. The proponents of free will can argue that there is room for free will because science is incomplete although it has been difficult to construct an explanation of how free will interacts with matter. In constructing such an explanation, free will reduces to matter, thereby taking us back to the original problem. Also, as we just saw above, it is not possible to add free will as a causal factor to the incomplete scientific theories because the addition of new factors would make the theories *inconsistent* either with observations or with other parts of the theory. Thus, we cannot add free will to complete the theory because the addition makes the theory inconsistent. Without such an addition, the theory is incomplete as it doesn't predict everything that can be observed. We must choose between inconsistency and incompleteness. This pattern of a choice between incompleteness vs. inconsistency repeats over and over in many areas of science including mathematics, computing, and physics, and I will elaborate on this in the next chapter. This pattern limits the possible pathways to a solution.

If science were only incomplete, we could think of adding new ideas to it without breaking its established structure. However, if adding ideas to science makes it inconsistent then there is no alternative other than to break the established ideologies in science. There are three important goals for such a remedial effort:

- Identify a description of nature that permits the distinction between actors and roles and establishes their interaction without the free will and matter interaction problems seen earlier.
- Separate the description of actors and roles from that of material properties, thereby creating three distinct categories—actors, roles, and material objects and their properties.
- The description of nature in terms of observable events should be predictively consistent and complete; i.e., it should be free from the matter distribution problems that lead to an untenable choice between inconsistency and incompleteness.
- The description of nature in terms of the choices of actors should be consistent with the essential notion about choices and should imbibe the basic intuitions of moral responsibility.

Most scientists today acknowledge the existence of many fundamental unsolved problems in science. However, scientists also claim that the *fundamental concepts* in science—the notion of objects, causality as forces, and laws as mathematical formulae that describe the motion of these objects, and the universality of nature, which were formed in Newton's time—are correct. The dominant view of scientific evolution is that science may find that objects of type Y are more fundamental than X, or a natural force of type F is better than G, or a mathematical formula P describes nature better than Q, and that should be determined by the progression of science. However, this progress will maintain the ideas about objects, forces, and laws. Furthermore, since the basic picture of nature in science will not change with its progress, and the notion of free will does not fit into this basic picture of nature, it will eventually be explained away.

I believe that when science has taken the remedial steps, the current notions about objectivity, forces, universality, and laws would themselves be changed in fundamental ways that we haven't yet foreseen. Let us presently turn towards such a possibility. While a detailed description of this solution will come later, an overview of the approach that I will be taking can be easily summarized here.

Fixing Indeterminism

From the previous section, we know about the need the fix three types of indeterminism—events, properties, and actors. The first problem requires the identification of a space-time structure without any material properties or actors. This space-time structure will indicate what will happen, but not who will do it, and how it will be done. The question of who will do it pertains to the actors, and the question of how it will be done refers to the properties that causally explain the event. This space-time structure is akin to the script of the drama which describes what will happen without some chosen actor, and the material qualifications that allow the actor to take the role.

The second problem involves a complete account of the properties themselves. For example, in atomic theory, the explanation of atomic particles is probabilistic and incomplete. The incompleteness is caused by the fact that we detect only the presence or absence of a particle rather than the actual effect of the particle. For instance, the presence of a property can create the sensations of smell, sound, sight, touch, and smell. It can also create the perception of some meaning, the judgment of truth, the feeling of like and dislike, and the perception of ideality such as beauty. If we simply measure the presence of a particle, but not the type of effect it produces—because the instruments are not sophisticated enough to produce that determination—then we cannot explain if the effect corresponds to one of the many possible effects, and the theory would be indeterministic. The answer to this problem is that we must define observations in terms of their sensory qualities, meanings, judgments, intentions, and ideals. This requires us to treat nature as meanings, which are organized in a hierarchy—e.g., 'blue', 'red', and 'green' are different shades of 'color'. Instead of measuring simply the physical presence, we must detect the type of the presence by its varied effects. We look at a squiggle such as '$' both physically and semantically. The two interpretations require no additional facts, but they require a new way of describing the facts. The indeterminism of physical theories can be fixed by treating material objects as symbols of meanings.

The third problem of actors participating in different actions using different properties requires a different material conception of the observer. The notion of observers that I will advance in this book is that the observer is a *coordinate reference frame* using which the observer organizes the world in that reference frame. However, in a universe where objects are representations of meanings, the reference frame too has to be defined semantically rather than physically. I will argue that this reference frame is the *language* in terms of which observers describe and manipulate the material universe.

By language here I do not mean the written and spoken tools of sound and sight by which we communicate. Thus, the word 'language' in this context does not signify English, Hindi, German, Spanish, or other commonly used languages. Rather, the term 'language' signifies the essential ideas or axioms of our worldview which we take for granted as presuppositions and use them to organize, order, and explain our experiences. These ideas may also be called *theories* in the specific sense that science uses the term. All theories involve axioms or presuppositions about the external world and the world is cast into the mold of the theory. Without a theory, we cannot organize knowledge or activity. Without a theory, the world is a puzzling morass of observations that makes no sense because we cannot predict or use it. Theories are features of observers using which the observers understand, order, and structure their observations.

Modern science has produced many theories such as physics, mathematics, chemistry, biology, computing, psychology, etc. Each such field of knowledge involves some types of objects and associated experiences. But the field of knowledge would not exist without a ground of axioms or presuppositions using which the world of objects is understood, structured, ordered, described, or predicted.

Immanuel Kant called this aspect of the observer *synthetic a priori*. It is synthetic because it is not logically self-evident (analytic) and it is *a priori* because it precedes organized experience. It is the 'goggles' by which we view the world. If the goggles were tinted, then the world would be perceived differently. The analogy to coordinate reference frames above is suggestive because science organizes the world by embedding it in a space-time. Newton's physics, for instance, postulated a homogeneous and isotropic space and time in which all locations and directions in space and time are identical. Classical physics postulates ideas such as mass, charge, temperature, etc. to describe the world of objects. The ideas in the theory are always abstract; they must be mapped to the world of things through experience. For instance, the idea of mass has to be connected to the visual of a pointer movement or the sound of a detector click.

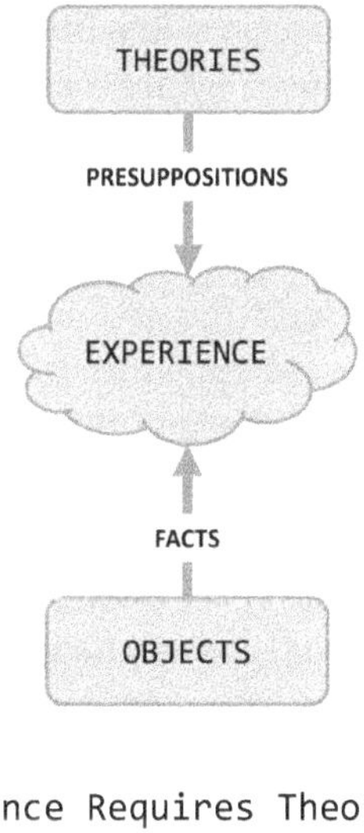

Figure-4 Experience Requires Theories and Objects

Science formulates theories and tests their validity in nature. But science does not treat these theories as a kind of reality that exists in the observer by which the observer perceives the world differently. Theories are rather viewed as abstract mathematical entities that exist somewhere in the Platonic world of ideas. Furthermore, while science admits only theories that are widely proven and logically consistent, most of us carry around with us a number of presuppositions that may not be mutually consistent and they might not necessarily have been confirmed against facts. In what form do these theories, axioms, presuppositions, assumptions, languages, or Kantian categories exist in the observer? I will argue that there is a real world of subtle ideas that we use to organize the conscious experience. I will argue that can be described in science as a coordinate reference frame of elementary ideas that shape experience.

These ideas are produced from past experiences and left behind as imprints of our experiential history. Unlike the external world which exists in the present, the observer is the past that exists in present. This past is not material objects that we can perceive through the senses. And yet, it is real in a sense that current science does not understand. The unconscious can be objectified as things or presented as experiences, just like we can signify a Euclidean coordinate system by joining three rods at right angles to each other. But, the three rods are not the Euclidean coordinate system; they are a *representation* of the coordinate system in an observable way. The coordinate system would exist even if the rods did not. In that sense, the coordinate system is real even if we don't perceive it. And yet, exactly how it exists cannot be explained in current science.

Unlike Kant, who believed that the *synthetic a priori* categories are universal and static, I will argue that the presuppositions in an observer are dynamic and personal. That is, each individual observer has different presuppositions which change with time. As logical and mathematical entities that evolve, science can describe their evolution. Their evolution is influenced by the interactions with the world. Observers with a worldview different from the world would not fit into that world. Either they would have to change their worldview or find a world compatible with their individual worldview.

Note how the ability to understand what the world tells us is in itself governed by our presuppositions. To decode the information about the world, we must know some language in terms of which to interpret it. If our language differs from the language the world is encoded in, then our interpretations of the world arrive at different meanings. We would now think that we have understood the world although that understanding is in itself based on presuppositions.

Indeed, post-modernists claim that understanding the true nature of the world is a hopelessly futile project because we can never overcome our presuppositions. Every experiment involves a theory by which the results in the experiment are interpreted. That theory is in turn built upon many presuppositions. How can an observer ever know the actual nature of the world if every experience is tinted with interpretations? The scientific solution to this problem is that to know if a scientific theory is correct the theory must be validated against an increasing amount of data. As the phenomena to be explained grow, the permissible theories dramatically reduce. Only a much smaller set of ideas can now be regarded as true, and knowledge has now progressed by a method of trial-and-error, by eliminating that which is not admissible. Of course, if the number of possible theories is infinite, then this project can take a long time.

For the moment, let us suppose that it is possible to discover the nature of reality by validating its tenets against the facts of the world. Science too evolves by bringing in facts. Often new facts that do not fit established presuppositions may be rejected and the scientists may hold their worldview. But, as the data piles up, and the scientist is rational and accepts the data, the worldview shall evolve, too. Refining our worldview to a point where our understanding of the world is just how the world is can be an arduous process. The observer's journey in the universe, in this view, is essentially the process to understand the universe. Different parts of the universe afford different experiences and therefore change the worldview in different ways. Once the world and the worldview are perfectly aligned, there is no more need to reject the world or move to a different part of the world more compatible with the worldview. In this state of true knowledge, the observer's evolution in the universe would halt.

Effects and Reactions

Until the world and the worldview are aligned, our knowledge and actions are incompatible with reality. The world and the worldview are, in effect, two different languages or semantic coordinate systems.

The interaction between the theory and reality creates experiences, which is the immediate effect of the interaction. Scientific theories—if they are not perfected—model limited parts of nature. The models of nature depicted in such theories partially explain nature when the effects of other parts are ignored. However, the neglected parts may not always be ignorable. When these parts cannot be ignored, they create effects that do not fit the predictions of the theory. That is when the theory must be modified. But, for such a modification to occur, the observer must encounter those phenomena that do not fit the theory. If the observer encounters the same phenomena that fit the current theory, then the theory can never be improved. How do we know that the observer will indeed encounter the phenomena that violate the theory so the theory can be improved?

For the observer to discover experiences that do not fit the predictions of the present theory there must be another effect of the theory-reality interaction, which we might call its *reaction* or *consequence*. The reaction, in this case, is that which causes the observer to move to a part of reality that is incompatible with the theory. The reaction to the theory is now an outcome of the difference between theory and reality and this difference is produced from the truth about the theory: if the theory is true no such reaction would be expected but if the theory is false the experiences that compensate the theory to bring it nearer to reality would be predicted. Such phenomena may modify the theory, and bring it closer to the nature of reality.

In a physical theory, too, there are effects and reactions to every cause although the effect and reaction apply to external objects. The above case, however, pertains to the interaction between the theory and the world. The theory is in the observer and the reaction to the theory represents the consequences of the theory. The reaction to a physical cause is immediate[6]. But the reaction to a false theory may not be immediate; in fact, if the reaction represents the observer's future experiences, then the reaction represents a cause that acts in the future. How do we conceive of causes that act in the future? What everyday intuitions might be used to model such kinds of causality in nature? After all, science is the refinement of ordinary experiences, and if science has to conceive new kinds of causalities, then it also requires us to delve into other parts of our intuitive experiences.

A causal model that acts in the future can be illustrated through the example of financial accounting and how it differs from the accounting in physical theories. Suppose that you have lent $100 to a friend. Your balance reduces by $100 and your friend's balance increases by $100. If this transaction were described in a physical theory, the increase in your friend's monetary status would be the effect and the decrease in your monetary status would be the reaction. The action and reaction are equal and opposite, and they occur simultaneously. However, the physical view of the financial transaction treats it as an act of *donating* rather than *lending* money. When you donate money, you don't expect it back. When you lend money, you expect it back. There is hence a difference in how these two types of transactions are accounted. Financial accounting needs additional mechanisms to account for loans. For instance, your balance sheet will carry a net positive 'account receivable' in the case of loans while in the case of a donation the balance sheet will simply deduct from your 'assets' without accruing anything to your 'account receivables.' The reverse would occur on your friend's balance sheet: he would have greater assets, but also greater liabilities. Physical transactions don't create an expectation of receiving the money back. Matter or energy is not an asset or a liability; there is nothing to receive after giving. Financial transactions, however, cannot work physically.

The 'account receivable' is a cause that acts in the future. That is, if your friend is honest, he or she would return the money at some other time in the future. You do not expect the friend to return the money immediately, because then the act of lending would itself be pointless. However, when the money is returned, it is not treated as another physical transaction of donating the money. Rather, the return of money is anticipated due to the 'account receivable' created in the original transaction of lending money. The 'account receivable' exists as negative money; we cannot observe or measure this money, but it acts as the cause of the reverse transaction in the future.

The moral notion of causality is like financial accounting rather than physical accounting. The physical transaction treats lending as a donation, while financial accounting does not. In the moral transaction too, if you give away money, you are also morally entitled to receive back money. In the physical theory, such an entitlement does not exist. This clearly highlights the conceptual gap in understanding morality in a physical theory. For a natural theory to describe morality there has to be some kind of material reality that represents the 'account receivable' which could not exist in the physical theory. The 'account receivable' has some similarities to the actual money but it is not actually the money; the 'account receivable' is the *absence* of money. We cannot measure this absence in the same way that we measure the object whose absence it represents. In that sense, this material reality cannot be observed and conceived in the traditional sense that we perceive and think about material objects. We have to rather think of a type of matter whose existence is non-existence.

This simple example illustrates that a natural theory of morality cannot be formed in the same way that we currently think of physical theories. This may not necessarily mean that we cannot form theories about morality. It only means that if we did form such a theory it would be based on intuitions about financial accounting rather than based on the physical effects that we can currently perceive.

Intuitions about this new kind of physical theory partly exist in current physical theories. Semiconductor physics, for instance, describes quantum objects not just as things but also as the absence of things. The theory of conducting materials for instance uses the concept of a 'hole' to represent the absence of an electron. If an electron leaves an atom, it is said to leave behind a 'hole' and physics speaks about hole mobility, in ways quite like how we speak about the motion of electrons. If we think of the world only as electrons, then the departing electron does not entitle the atom to receive back an electron. If, however, we think of a departing electron as leaving behind a hole, then this hole must eventually be filled. One of the reasons why physics can describe both electrons and holes is because atomic theory deals in possibilities and not in real objects. A real object appears at measurement and until a measurement has occurred, both electrons and holes are possibilities although not reality. There is hence no conceptual anomaly in thinking about the absence of matter in the same way that we think about matter. But there is a problem in how we distinguish these physically. For instance, if an electron was emitted, should we think of it as an evicted physical object, as a liability that was fulfilled, or as a credit that was borrowed?

Of course, semiconductor physics describes holes as physical entities and if we used such a notion for morality then the friend to whom you lent money would have to return the money in exactly the same manner in which he borrowed it. For instance, he would have to use the same currency and denominations to return the loan. He could not use different currencies or denominations. He could also not return the money by giving you another service or asset such a property, jewelry, or a prized possession. The reason is that a physical theory has no innate sense of meaning. The fact that some paper currency equals some amount of food cannot be described in a physical theory; it requires semantics. This problem can only be solved if atomic theory described objects semantically. For, then, it would be possible to speak about the act of giving some currency notes as a symbolic act of lending some money. It would also now be possible to speak about the loan being repaid through an altogether different set of objects. The physical notion of an electron filling a hole would not be the only prediction of such a theory. Rather, the theory would predict how other kinds of physical transactions could occur as a consequence of the first transaction. I will later describe how a semantic view of matter is entailed by problems in atomic theory and how the reactions to actions could also be described using atomic theory.

The semantic treatment of atomic theory is therefore not just a reinterpretation of its current formalism. Rather, it allows us to foresee new kinds of phenomena and predictions. The two types of matter—objects and holes—involved in the theory can be thought of as manifest and unmanifest realities. The unmanifest exists but it is not observable. Its presence can only be detected by its observable effects, such as the ability to receive back what was earlier lent.

This leads us to an interesting question: If some changes in nature can be described as the conversion of an unmanifest to manifest, thereby representing the act of returning what was earlier lent, then how would we distinguish between the acts of lending and receiving? For instance, should we say that the act of lending creates an entitlement for the lender to receive that money? Or should we say that the fact that the loaner receives money is in itself an outcome of some entitlement that the loaner has accrued through prior lending? In other words, is the receiver getting money because he is loaning it from a lender or because he is entitled to receive it due to some past instances in which he had actually loaned it to the giver?

This question is difficult because it requires us to trace the history of all lending-receiving transactions and find the 'original' transaction. That history cannot exist because with each transaction, some unmanifest becomes manifest and some manifest becomes unmanifest. While it is possible to scientifically speak about the current manifest and unmanifest, it is impossible to trace the history to the original material transaction because that history simply doesn't exist. Nevertheless, even for describing the current transactions, the unmanifest must be described semantically as the act of lending or returning. The act of giving money underdetermines whether the money is being lent in a new transaction or if it is a return of an earlier loan. That in turn means that if nature was semantic—and had to be thought of in terms of loans and returns—then the physical description of nature would be incomplete. In fact, as we have already seen, these forms of incompleteness appear repeatedly in science.

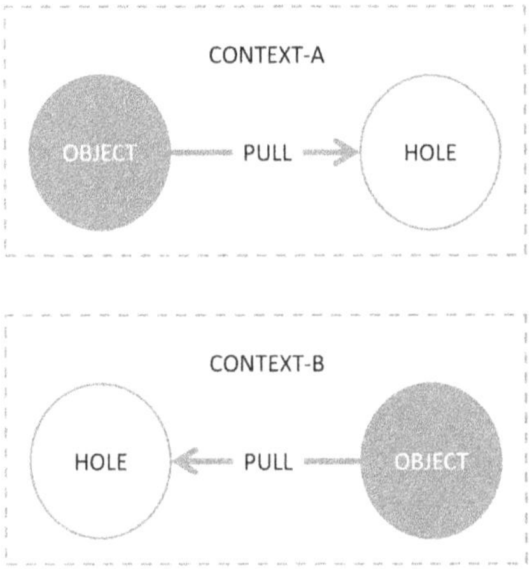

Figure-5 The Unmanifest Pulls The Manifest

The takeaway is that it is possible to speak about morality in a natural theory if we can speak about physical entities whose existence is the lack of another entity. These entities have to be described semantically as types rather than as quantities. The unmanifest pulls the manifest, thereby converting the manifest into unmanifest, in one context. In another context, the unmanifest (which was previously the manifest) reverses the original conversion. Every transaction would therefore be inverted, although there is a space-time gap between the original and the inverted transactions. This space-time lag can be easily described in a closed and hierarchical space-time theory. Essentially, in such a theory, forward and backward transactions would occur at semantically opposite locations and times[7]. The universe would oscillate and transfer matter into holes thereby creating new holes, which then absorb matter at another space-time.

In the context of theory evolution, this means that if a theory of cause and effect appears to work based on some observable manifest properties, it may not necessarily be because the theory is correct. It can also be because matter is being transformed due to some unmanifest properties which cause changes. Any theory based on manifest properties alone is false if the causality depends on the unmanifest properties. The theory of manifest properties can explain what happens *if* some matter or energy is moved from one place to another. However, it cannot explain or predict *why* such a change occurs. For instance, a theory of manifest properties can state the conservation of energy due to which the reduction in an object's energy must be compensated by the gain in another object's energy. However, such a theory cannot predict when the energy would be transferred and which objects would be involved in the energy transfer. In effect, nature is consistent with many possible energy distributions, but a specific energy distribution cannot be predicted. As I noted above, this is also one of the key problems of indeterminism in science.

Scientific theories can predict what happens *if* some energy is redistributed. However, they cannot predict whether that energy would be distributed. This problem appears in classical physics as the possibility to split and merge particles. It appears in even more sophisticated ways in other parts of physics, as I will discuss in the next chapter. This indeterminism cannot be bridged by adding more manifest properties to science, as adding these properties will make the theory inconsistent. The problem can, however, be solved by the notion of something that exists as the absence of an object.

In the new causal model, causality is not in the manifest properties which science currently describes. Rather, the causality is in the *reactions* to actions that produce further actions and reactions. All scientific theories based on manifest properties are incomplete; they can predict the outcome of an action but cannot predict if such an action would take place. As a theory interacts with phenomena, and models based on manifest properties are found inadequate, the theory can be modified creating newer models of nature. However, all such theories will remain predictively incomplete unless the notion of the unmanifest is incorporated in the predictive scheme. If the moral view is correct, then only a theory that incorporates the unmanifest can accurately predict the occurrence of all events.

The End of Morality

The moral view substantially changes the understanding of the conflict between free will and determinism. The conflict originates in the mind-body divide in Cartesian metaphysics. We suppose that matter is rationality—i.e., governed by mathematical laws—although the mind is not. Specifically, everything in matter is always true, but everything in the mind may not be true. For instance, our theories about nature could be false. Obviously, the mind-body divide creates problems in understanding how the mind creates false theories. If the mind is irrational then how do we rationally explain its creative activities? On the other hand, if it is rational then how do we explain the existence of false theories in the mind? The moral view collapses the divide between mind and body and treats both mind and matter semantically. The evolution of mind and matter must however require different kinds of models. Specifically, the evolution of the mind must arise due to the fact that its contents—the theories of nature—could be false. The evolution of matter is the evolution of facts while the evolution of the mind is the evolution of falsities. Some of the facts (e.g., the existence of theories in the mind) could be false, so the existence of facts cannot be evidence of their truth. If, however, the mind acquires the true theory, then its evolution must halt although the evolution of matter governed by the theory would continue. The mind's evolution thus needs an alternative kind of predictability.

In this new notion of predictions, nature evolves not because the next state is logically implied by the previous state but because the reality and its theory are inconsistent, and their evolution would produce a greater alignment between the two. The theory is the choice of the observer: it could be false. But if the theory is false, then there are consequences due to the falsity of the theory. The observer may choose an arbitrary theory but he or she cannot subsequently choose the experiences that validate the theory. Rather, if a false theory has been chosen, then nature would subject the observer to experiences that modify the theory until the theory and reality[8] are consistent. Once the discord between the theory and reality has been resolved, the theory's evolution can end. A true natural theory is consistent with all possible phenomena in nature, and the observer is, therefore, free to choose any experience because all experiences are consistent with the theory and no experience entails any other experience.

This leads us to a nuanced view of free will. Free will is not the ability to choose arbitrary views about the world, without a consequence. Free will—without a consequence—is the choice of the correct theory. In this sense, there is hardly any choice. However, remember that the observer is choosing a theory rather than an experience. Many experiences are consistent with the true theory and having chosen the correct theory, the observer is free to choose experiences. If, on the other hand, the observer chooses an arbitrary theory, then the consequences of this choice decide subsequent experiences. An observer's free will is thus not infinite. If we choose arbitrary theories, then we are constrained into some experiences. If we choose a fixed correct theory, then there is no limit to experiences. Our free will can extend to the choice of an arbitrary theory or an arbitrary experience, but, in a rational world, it cannot do both.

There is a simple definition of rationality in this view: rationality is the compatibility between theory and reality. If the theory and reality are consistent, there is free will of experiences. If, however, the theory and reality are inconsistent, then there is no free will. There is still choice although it always comes with its consequences. Free will and rationality are therefore identical in this viewpoint. This means that if we were rational, we would also be free.

This does not necessarily entail that the mind is always rational. We might have incorrect theories of nature, and laws of nature—by which we appear to be bound—would be byproducts of the difference between the true theory of the world and the false theory in the mind. If the mind had the perfect theory of nature, then it would also be rational in exactly the manner that the world is rational. Since the perfect theory of nature is compatible with every phenomenon in nature, it will allow the observer to partake in any experience in the universe. The choice of such phenomena is therefore not determined by the observer's theory; rather the observer is free to experience any part of the universe, unhindered by the natural laws.

This brings us to a new understanding of the nature of free will, which is that we are not free to interpret the world in whichever way we want. However, we are free to partake in any phenomena in the universe if we have the correct theory because such a perfect theory is consistent with every possible phenomenon, and each of the phenomena is produced from that perfect theory of nature. The perfect theory of nature is also the perfect rationality and the imperfect theory of nature is irrationality. Free will is therefore compatible with rationality and is in fact identical with rationality. However, free will is not equal to irrationality. In fact, an irrational theory of nature takes away free will or the ability to choose phenomena.

In the Cartesian mind-body divide, the mind's free will is its ability to interpret nature, including for instance to see the world in ways incompatible with the world. The ability to hallucinate, misperceive, have false beliefs, or distorted views of reality are all manifestations of free will. In the moral picture, however, the mind is not free in this sense because deviating from the true theory of reality forces the observer to partake in phenomena governed by some natural laws. The observers are not free to choose the phenomena, and they are not free to avoid the effects of such phenomena on their theories. What is viewed as free will in Cartesian metaphysics is thus determinism in the moral picture. On the other hand, what is viewed as determinism in Cartesian metaphysics is free will in the moral picture.

The purpose of the universal sojourn is the discovery of the true nature of reality. Ignorance of that nature causes the production of effects and reactions, which fix the observer's evolution. Implicit in this description is the idea that the causal evolution of the universe is entailed by a discrepancy between reality and its theories. If these weren't inconsistent, then the evolution of the observer would halt. The cessation of the deterministic evolution is the discovery of free will. There is an inherent connection between knowing the true nature of reality and the discovery of free will because knowing the nature of reality terminates the deterministic evolution. This observation gives us a simple test for knowledge: knowledge is that which sets us free from the laws of nature; knowing truth will free us. On the other hand, if we are not free of the laws of nature, we are also not in possession of the correct theory of nature. The order we observe in nature—and which science presently describes as the nature of reality—are not the real laws of nature, because they only tell us how we are bound by the laws. These laws are a form of irrationality which forces us to undergo phenomena without free will. The real laws, on the other hand, will free us from the natural laws.

In this view, the laws of nature—i.e., the sense in which we are not free—are the laws of morality producing effects caused by false theories. The real laws of nature allow us to choose the phenomena. If, therefore, we are rational, then we are also free. Determinism is a consequence of some defect in our view of nature, which causes the theory of nature to evolve by subjecting the theory to phenomena according to some predetermined law. There are laws of nature only so long as we have an incorrect picture of nature. The true picture of nature is lawful, but knowing that picture frees us from the laws.

The laws of nature are the moral laws of the evolution of theories. The laws of moral consequences stem from the misuse of free will to construct false and arbitrary theories of nature. Once such theories have been constructed, they must evolve deterministically and science can describe the determinism arising out of the mistaken theories. Neither the morality nor the false theories of nature are, however, permanent fixtures of nature. They are only consequences of the misuse of free will. When free will is corrected—by a true understanding of the nature of reality—free will is also recovered.

The Journey Ahead

I opened this chapter with a summary of the debate between free will and determinism and discussed the problems that arise from supposing that there is free will. I then showed that these problems can be solved by a separation between an actor and a role. Next, I traced the lack of distinction between roles and actors to the assumptions in Newton's mechanics and how that has become the mainstay in subsequent scientific thinking. I then demonstrated how Newton's ideas lead to three problems of indeterminism in science—namely that science can describe which matter distributions are possible but not which ones are real, that even if science predicted the matter distributions completely it would still not predict which observers participate in which events, and even if we did both of above, we would still not be able to predict the sequence of events in the universe.

I then described how overcoming the first type of indeterminism requires a view in which matter distributions are a representation of meanings. Since this still does not overcome the second type of indeterminism (of which observers participate in which events), I then described a materialist view of observers as reference frames and connected it to the notion of synthetic *a priori* categories in Kant's philosophy. The observer is, however, not static as in Kant's philosophy, and the evolution of the observer is connected to the evolution of theories. This evolution terminates when the theory is perfectly reconciled with reality, which also enables true free will. To overcome the third problem, I suggested that the world must be viewed as a predetermined script of a drama that decides all events. Matter and observers can be redistributed over these events, but they cannot change the events; in short, what will happen is fixed, but how it will happen, and who will do what, is underdetermined.

There is hence no conflict between free will and determinism, provided free will is defined as the rationality to choose the correct theory of nature. The conflict between free will and determinism arises when we define free will as irrationality. That irrationality forces a deterministic evolution of the observer robbing it of its free will. This notion of free will is consistent with everyday intuitions about free will: we are free so long as we don't misuse the free will. When the free will is misused, the free will is lost and is replaced by determinism. To recover the free will we must correct its use. This correction is achieved by the formation of a true theory of nature.

This chapter summary is roughly the summary of the book as well. The rest of the book provides more detailed arguments and rationale for these ideas and connects them to scientific problems, and to new theoretical ideas which can address these problems.

The first step in this journey is the recognition that scientific theories are incomplete. If they were complete, then there would be no point in trying to replace them. The second chapter surveys the problems of indeterminism in science—physics, computing, and mathematics. This survey is brief as I have described these issues in my earlier books such as *Gödel's Mistake, Quantum Meaning*, and *Signs of Life*. The interested reader may refer to those books for further details. The summary in this chapter is to expand upon the three kinds of indeterminism I referenced earlier and to show how they appear many times in scientific theories and why their solution is impossible in current science because attempts to complete the theory make it logically inconsistent with the predictions that make it true.

The third chapter describes in detail the semantic solution to the first problem of indeterminism, constructing it as a way to address the incompleteness in mathematics and incomputability in computing theory. The chapter illustrates how these problems require a hierarchical view of space and time, in which objects are also symbols of meaning. By the end of the chapter, the reader will see why a different view of reality is needed for a theory to be complete, computable, and non-recursive. This view can be converted into a mathematical theory of numbers and used to describe the material world, although such an effort is beyond the scope of the present work.

The fourth chapter applies the above-mentioned mathematical structure to the solution of physical problems discussed in the second chapter. The chapter outlines how the semantic view addresses the problems of indeterminism in quantum theory, statistical mechanics, and relativity. It also shows how the semantic view helps us understand deeply mystifying aspects of these physical theories and that the semantic view makes additional predictions consistent with observations but which are not adequately understood in the physical view.

Finally, the chapter illustrates how the three main pillars of modern physics can be reconciled into a single theory, which is currently the biggest outstanding problem in modern science.

The second, third, and fourth chapters, therefore, set up the essential insights for the semantic view, thereby solving the first and third problems of indeterminism—i.e., how can we predict all the events in nature? The fifth chapter attacks the second problem of indeterminism—i.e., how can we predict the evolution of the observers in the deterministic universe? While the first and third forms of indeterminism and their solutions have been discussed in my earlier books, the solution to the second problem—which involves a scientific notion of observers and how they evolve—is novel to this book. In particular, this chapter will revisit the discussion about the necessity to postulate a distinction between effects and reactions to convert a scientific theory of matter into an ethical naturalism.

The fifth chapter lays out a theoretical framework that can be used to develop a scientific theory of ethical naturalism in the future. Such a theory, the chapter illustrates, will predict the evolution of the observer in the universe. The evolution of the observers and that of the universe—which I earlier distinguished as roles and actors—form a single physical theory. The cornerstone of this theory is the idea that every theory has an entitlement if the theory is false. These entitlements determine the observer's evolution. However, if the correct theory of nature is known, the evolution terminates.

The sixth chapter undertakes a detailed discussion of free will and how it interacts with the world. How do we form false theories of nature? The chapter discusses how false theories are formed by filtering experience. These filters appear in science as the need to 'simplify' the study of phenomena by neglecting parts of the phenomena. The resulting theories may be adequate explanations of this simplified picture, but they become inadequate when the simplifications are no longer applicable. The evolution of theories is therefore the removal of all such simplifications. Nature is simple, but it cannot be viewed simplistically. As Einstein once said, "Everything should be made as simple as possible, but not simpler," the practice of simplicity in science needs a careful relook. As over-simplifying assumptions about nature are dropped, the theory approaches truth.

Science is the study of nature and it describes the evolution of matter. However, current science does not describe the evolution of theories because the effects or consequences of using a false theory cannot be described in science. The main thrust of this book is to show that when matter is described semantically, then it is possible to conceive of new forms of matter which can be called the observer's theories; in the semantic view, such theories will appear as the observer's semantic coordinate frames. Accordingly, the evolution of a false theory is the motion of such a coordinate frame in the universe. The semantic view not only produces a solution to the current problems in science, but also a new kind of science in which nature permits false theories but also forces their evolution. The mechanisms by which our incorrect theories are corrected can pave the way for understanding how the observer can find its free will.

2

A History of Uncertainties

The incomplete knowledge of a system must be an essential part of every formulation in quantum theory. Quantum theoretical laws must be of a statistical kind. To give an example: we know that the radium atom emits alpha-radiation. Quantum theory can give us an indication of the probability that the alpha-particle will leave the nucleus in unit time, but it cannot predict at what precise point in time the emission will occur, for this is uncertain in principle.

—*Werner Heisenberg*

Choices and Material Science

Evidence for choices exists everywhere in the human world, so we don't have to look very far if we actually wanted to study them. For instance, questions of choice appear in how the scientific laws are employed to develop technology. Everyday uses of science tell us that we have a choice to use technology in various ways. For example, every physicist knows that the laws of physics can be used to build a gun or a bicycle; physics does not dictate a specific use for its laws. To that extent, it should be obvious that the laws of physics are incomplete in predicting everything that occurs in nature. Nevertheless, the contradiction between the idea of a lawful nature and the idea of free choices has not been resolved so far. The scientist—whose freedom to inquire into the nature of reality depends on the possibilities for making free choices—undercuts that very freedom by claiming that deterministic laws hold sway over everything. Acknowledging that the laws of physical reality do not determine everything in the universe would appear to contradict the foundational assumption in science that nature is only material objects.

But I'm not about to launch into a discussion about how science does not explain the human mind. This, I think, is unnecessary because problems of choice also appear within scientific theories as limitations to the ability of modern science to predict the nature of reality. There are multiple issues about indeterminism and incompleteness of predictions in modern physical theories. These limitations have been discovered in the last century and they so deeply violate the picture of reality as painted in classical physics that most people—often many scientists—do not fully understand their implications. The dominant belief today is that these problems are perhaps temporary and will be overcome in a future theory when we will return to a picture of reality where the mathematical laws of nature can predict everything that occurs in nature. And when we get to such a picture of nature, there will be no room for choice.

This viewpoint is so pervasive and so mistaken that any meaningful discussion of the current status of scientific theories cannot begin without a closer look at their biggest outstanding problems. The biggest problem in modern science is that the picture of reality that is used as a working hypothesis to carry out scientific studies originated in Newton's mechanics where reality is comprised of objects, which have physical properties like mass, which exert forces on other objects, and which causes these objects to move in space-time. The laws of nature are mathematical formulae that help predict object motion after we measure an object's physical properties. This ideology about nature is taught in all introductions to science in schools and most of us grow up thinking of the universe as objects moving in space-time. Any doubts about whether scientific laws are true are quelled by reference to the pervasive technology around us. Since Newton's physics has no room for choice, we are compelled to unwittingly grant that there must be no choice in nature.

Of course, Newton's theory is now known to be false in many ways. Modern physical theories either do not make deterministic predictions or their deterministic predictions are one of several possible equally deterministic predictions. I will discuss these limitations of physical theories shortly. In modern physical theories, matter is not some *a priori* real objects that exist independent of observation; rather, objects appear and disappear randomly from space-time. Physical objects don't move forever once set into motion; they quickly settle down into stationary states unless energy is constantly added or removed. And given that there are limits to the divisibility of space and time in atomic theory, space-time continuity which was taken for granted in Newton's physics is now suspect.

With such a deep divide between Newton's physics and modern physics, it is very difficult to continue upholding the assumptions that were true in Newton's physics. And yet, the ideologies about matter, force, and physical law established by Newton continue to dominate the discourse in modern science. The reason is that the newer theories, which are known to be contradictory to Newton's physics, are so conceptually different from Newton's mechanics that their meaning is yet to be understood in most cases. There is little consensus today about how the picture of reality in Newton's laws must be modified and what the new notions about matter, space-time, causality, and lawfulness would be once this revision has been completed.

Meanwhile, there is also a strong academic resistance to any attempts to changing the Newtonian picture in any significant way. Especially problematic is admitting those ideas that might in any way, shape, or form seem like moving science closer to religious ideas. Modern physical theories, despite many revolutionary ideas, continue to think of reality in terms of objects, force as the cause of change, and laws of nature as mathematical formulae that predict the effect of forces. The picture of reality painted by Newton's physics is the central dogma about matter, causality, and natural law in science. Even though this dogma has been challenged by recent advances, attempts to change it are generally received with apprehension.

In what follows, I will begin with a discussion about the problems of indeterminism and uncertainty in physics. These are by no means the only problems within science. There are well-known issues in mathematics and computing which have an equally important bearing on the theories in physics. Subsequently, therefore, I will also briefly describe the nature of incompleteness in mathematics and computing. The reason for focusing on physics, mathematics, and computing is that these form the conceptual bedrock for other fields like chemistry and biology, although often shorn of much of the complexity in them. It is possible to formally and rigorously state the problems and demonstrate the reasons why the problems cannot be solved without a conceptual overhaul in scientific thinking, which is often harder in the case of other fields like chemistry and biology. Given these benefits, I will focus on the problems of indeterminism in physics, mathematics, and computing, although indeterminism is by no means the exclusive dominion of the formally stated fields.

I will, in the following sections, describe problems in three broad areas in modern physics—statistical mechanics, quantum theory, and general relativity. I will show how these problems are closely connected and pertain to a single conceptual shortfall in physics—namely the problem of dealing with object *collections* rather than with individual objects. While Newton's physics presented a deterministic picture of the evolution of individual objects, subsequent developments in physics such as statistical mechanics, quantum theory, and general relativity involve problems of indeterminism and incompleteness in dealing with object collections. The standard reductionist thinking in classical physics is that a collection is nothing but a combination of its parts. But, as the following discussion will show, this idea is false. To solve its problems, I will argue, modern science needs a theory that begins from collections rather than objects.

Of course, at first sight, this might seem quite unintuitive. How can we form a theory of collections without first forming a theory of the objects in that collection? But it can be understood if these collections are viewed as *conceptual types*. In mathematics too, sets were originally conceived as representing concepts. However, since it was difficult to define the set as some meaning (*intension*), the sets were defined as object collections (*extension*). When sets are constructed from objects, the object in the set can be treated both conceptually as an instance of a type and physically as a typeless entity. The latter notion of the object represents how the object exists outside the set and the former to how it is inside the set. Once a set has been formed, a problem of recursion quickly develops. For instance, think of a set of cars. Each member of this set is a car, but the notion of the car is defined only by aggregating the members in a set. Therefore, the type of the individual object depends on the whole set, but the whole set depends on the individual objects. Each member of the set must be a car before it can be collected into a set of cars, but the notion of a car is defined only after a collection has already been defined.

This recursive definition of sets and members leads to many problems in mathematics and computing, such as Gödel's incompleteness in mathematics and Turing's Halting Problem in computing. These problems arise because each object is both a type and an instance, but the definition of types is constructed from the instance although the instance cannot be individuated without defining the type. Contradictions now follow in mathematics and computing, rendering any theory of numbers either inconsistent or incomplete and any theory of computing unable to predict if programs are finite or infinite. The next chapter discusses how the problems of indeterminism and uncertainty in statistical mechanics, quantum theory, and general relativity can be solved by adopting a semantic view. The next chapter also shows that the solution of physical problems would require a prior solution to the problem of incompleteness in mathematics and to incomputability within computing theory.

Statistical Mechanics and Reduction

In classical physics, an object has physical properties, which create forces of nature, which in turn govern their motion. For instance, in Newton's physics, matter possesses the property of mass, which creates a gravitational force that causes objects to move in space-time. Newton's law of gravitation specifies the amount of acceleration an object will undergo if the masses of all the objects involved are known. If this is a true picture of reality, then every object must move according to deterministic laws of nature, and the universe as a whole must be governed by these deterministic laws. After all, what is the universe if not a collection of these independent parts?

The idea that the universe is nothing but a collection of independent parts had tremendous successes in explaining the motion of celestial and terrestrial objects, as long as the total number of objects involved was low. This idea ran into difficulties when physics tried to describe phenomena concerning the thermal behavior of gases, which are comprised of a very large number of molecules. It was noticed, for example, that the total amount of heat that can be *extracted* from a collection of particles is not equal to the total amount of heat that was *added* to it. Newton's physics held the conservation of energy as a basic law of nature and, therefore, the total amount of energy had to be the same whether or not we could extract that energy from a system. This was further confirmed by the fact that although we are not able to extract the energy from the system, the system still has a higher temperature. Therefore, it was natural to suppose that the system had energy, but we could not extract it. One way to theoretically explain this problem was to suggest that the reason we cannot extract the energy from a system has something to do with how that energy is *distributed* inside that system. For instance, if all particles in the system are aligned and moving in a single direction, then the total amount of extractable energy equals the total amount of energy. However, if these particles are randomly moving in different directions, then much of that energy is trapped in the interaction between the particles and cannot be extracted.

We could now call a system in which all particles move in one direction a highly 'ordered' system in contrast to a 'disordered' system in which particles move in random directions. Note that in the description of individual particles there is no notion of order or disorder. All particles are ordered because they behave according to classical laws of motion. But when we collect such particles, we are no longer looking at each particle individually. We are rather looking at all of them collectively and the notion of order and disorder emerges through a relative comparison between the states of motion of the various particles. The order or disorder is now not a property of the individual particles, although it becomes a property of the collection. The idea that a whole is nothing but a collection of particles is now false because the notion of order or disorder cannot be associated with the individual particles, and can only be tied to the collection.

While this reasoning is physically intuitive, it suffers from a mathematical problem that the laws of classical mechanics are *reversible* in time. So, if we start with an ordered system, and we find that over time it becomes disordered, there is nothing that prevents it from becoming ordered in the future. If, therefore, the amount of energy extractable from the system depends on the order or disorder in the system, then the extractable energy could change in time as the degree of order increases or decreases. This idea runs counter to observations. It is observed that once a system has been given some energy, the amount of extractable energy in that system does not change with time. Furthermore, it is practically impossible to compute the real particle states of motion in a large collection of particles, because the total number of equations that need to be simultaneously computed is far beyond the capabilities of any known computer. Therefore, the laws of physics cannot predict if all the particles in a system are perfectly aligned and moving in a single direction or randomly moving in different directions. While the notions of order and disorder can be intuitively stated, they are practically useless.

A new approach was now adopted in which the order or disorder was defined relative to the total number of *possible* states of the system. This idea is intuitively known as the possibility of one of the six faces of a dice turning up on a dice roll. Generally speaking, there are six possible outcomes of a dice roll (unless the dice stands on one of the edges, which is highly improbable). The total amount of uncertainty in a dice equals the total number of faces that could turn up on a dice roll; the uncertainty equals the total number of *possible* states of the dice. Similarly, if the particles in a system *could* be in some state then these possible states would represent a measure of the total uncertainty in the system state. The collection of particles was now described in terms of its *possible* states rather than its actual states. This description is based on the simplifying assumption that if the number of possible states in a system is very large, and it is practically impossible to predict which amongst those states is real, then we might assume that the system is simultaneously in all those states. This theory came to be known as classical *statistical* mechanics and it was successfully used to explain the irreversible phenomenon of heat.

Now, the statistical treatment of particles leads to a serious problem about whether we treat the statistics epistemically or ontologically. Should we say that nature is in fact in a definite state but we don't *know* which state it is in? Or should we say that nature *is* in fact in many different states simultaneously? If indeed the system is in a single state and statistics only pertains to our ignorance of that state then the predictions of the statistical description must be false. If, however, the statistical description of a collection produces correct predictions, then the total number of possible states has a *real* role to play in nature and the success of the theory would compel us to suppose that the system is indeed in many possible states simultaneously. Classically, we would have liked to believe that the system is in a single state but we don't know that state. However, given the predictive correctness of the statistical approach, we are compelled to suppose that the system is simultaneously in all those states.

This brings the conflict with classical physics to the fore. Classically speaking, the system is in a definite state, although it may be hard to predict it. Statistically speaking, our inability to predict that state has real empirical consequences. Are we to suppose that the system somehow knows that we cannot predict its state and therefore it behaves as if it is in an uncertain state? Or should we suppose that the system is in an uncertain state, even though we classically think that all systems must be in a fixed state? Some remarkable things happen when we shift our focus from individual objects to collections. The fact about a system here is that individually all objects are in a definite state, but collectively they are in an uncertain state.

How can a system have individual particles in definite states while the total system is in an uncertain state? This is an unsolved problem in classical physics. The problem is well-known as the irreversibility of thermal phenomena where systems appear to go from order to disorder, and classically speaking we cannot even define disorder at the individual particle level. The natural conclusion from this problem is that the theory that describes ensembles or collections must be different from the theory that describes individual particles. The world that appears classically deterministic becomes statistical for collections of particles. This transition from determinism to statistics presents a gap in explanation and it requires a new type of causal theory, even at the level of macroscopic objects.

The main reason I discuss statistical mechanics is to show that classical physics is causally incomplete even in relation to macroscopic objects when these objects represent particle ensembles. Classical physics is often said to fail in dealing with the extra-large and the super-small. This is not false. But what is generally ignored is that classical physics also fails for thermal phenomena, which are neither extra-large nor super-small. The root cause of this failure is still unknown. What we can say is that even if physics had not been revolutionized by quantum mechanics and general relativity, the classical physical picture of reality would still be very problematic.

The inability to predict the actual distribution of energy in an ensemble is a problem of computing and measuring the actual state. But the fact that the statistical approach predictions match observations also implies we don't have a problem of computing or measuring the state; rather, we have the even more profound problem that the ensemble isn't in any definite state. Each such definite state should represent a specific matter distribution and we cannot suppose ignorance about a particular distribution. Rather, we must suppose that matter is not distributed, or that there is energy in the system but it is not individuated into a specific set of particles.

This is a far more profound consequence of statistical mechanics than classical physics acknowledges. We suppose there is indeed a set of classical particles—molecules of gas or liquid—whose state is uncertain to *observers*. The more accurate interpretation of statistical mechanics is that there isn't a set of molecules into which the total energy is divided unless a measurement is performed. When we perform a measurement, the act of measuring requires the addition of information that creates particles. The fact that we see particles upon measurement—and which in turn implies a definite state—is not how reality exists prior to measurement. Rather, measurement creates a definite state, but the state is otherwise uncertain.

The problem of not knowing the exact matter distribution in statistical mechanics results in the conclusion that the material particles are not real until a measurement is done. The measurement provides the necessary information to 'create' a set of particles. Statistical mechanics tells us that the system has only energy, but not *a priori* real particles. Particles are outcomes of a measurement and are produced by the information added during measurement.

This problem can be considerably demystified if we treat the ensemble as information rather than as physical particles. The ensemble prior to measurement can be said to exist as *abstract* information, which upon measurement becomes *detailed*. For example, think of the hierarchy of the classification of species. A 'mammal' is abstract information, a 'dog' is more detailed, and an 'Alsatian' is even more detailed. If we haven't specified that the ensemble represents a dog, and only defined it as a mammal, then it could be any of the mammals, such as cats, dogs, horses, cows, etc. So, in the abstract state, the ensemble exists in *all* possible states of refinement. However, if we refine the ensemble by adding information—e.g., converting the mammal into a dog—then the state of the ensemble is more definite. This process of refinement can continue almost indefinitely because we can pack more and more information into the ensemble. For example, we can say that the Alsatian has long, brown, hair; specify the length of its teeth and tail, the weight of its body, the color of its eyes, etc. At each step, we are refining the definition, by adding more qualifiers and that excludes other possible descriptions of the ensemble.

In the same way, we can say that an ensemble is some energy, but the distribution of this energy into individual particles is underspecified. Therefore, the system exists in all possible states of distribution. In this state, the information is abstract. However, if we perform a measurement, such as by shining light to cause a diffraction, then in the process we are adding information through the experiment. We will then find individual particles because we are making the state of the system more certain in the act of measurement. When we observe, we see the particles, and the state is indeed definite. When we don't observe, the state is uncertain not because we cannot predict it but because the particles to be known do not exist.

This viewpoint equates the statistical uncertainty to missing information. A classical statistical ensemble is not just epistemically uncertain but also ontologically uncertain. Our observations provide the information that fixes the epistemic and ontological uncertainty. That also implies that information must be real and objective. With the information, the system is classically definite. Without that information, the system is classically indefinite. Since definite and indefinite systems produce different predictions (reversible and irreversible phenomena) information has a real role in nature. The role is simply that energy can be distributed into material particles in many ways, which cannot be predicted upfront. The exact distribution of energy into particles represents a system uncertainty, and that uncertainty leads to non-linear behavior in thermodynamics. The extent of uncertainty can also be equated with the amount of information that can be encoded into the thermodynamic system.

Non-linearity in classical physics entails the inability to separate the system into individual parts. The cause A depends on the effect B, which in turn depends on A, creating a circular causality. These causal loops in material systems imply that we cannot distinguish between the interacting parts. It is, therefore, necessary to say that the system is in fact not individuated into parts. Only linear systems are totally distinguishable; non-linear systems are not distinguishable. Classical physics is linear and distinguishable but statistical mechanics is not, which creates a difficulty in understanding macroscopic systems within classical physics. The difficulty arises because we would like to think of the world as individual particles governed by linear theories, but experiment shows that the system is non-linear. The only possible resolution to this problem is to discard the idea that the system is *a priori* divided into parts although the parts are deeply entangled due to non-linearity. The resolution would entail that there is a system although it is not built up of parts; that there is energy but that energy is not distributed into classical particles.

The reversibility of fundamental physical theories and the observed irreversibility of macroscopic phenomena represent the essential paradox of classical reduction. If reduction is true, then thermal systems must be reversible. Problems in statistical mechanics illustrate the connection between reduction and reversibility; they demonstrate that the only correct way to think of macroscopic non-linearity is to discard the idea of physical reduction and embrace informational divisibility in nature. That is, nature is not *a priori* divided but it can be divided at the point of a measurement. The manner in which nature is divided depends as much on the reality being measured as it depends on the measurement procedure.

Quantum Indeterminism

Quantum theory inherits some problems from statistical mechanics and has some new problems of its own. In statistical mechanics, we cannot know the state of the system as a whole, because the system is simultaneously in many possible states. This problem exists in quantum theory as well. But, in addition, in quantum theory we cannot know the state of individual particles even if we knew the state of the whole ensemble. This problem is new to quantum theory.

The quantum counterpart of the inability to know the state of the entire system is that a quantum system is described by an eigenfunction basis, which represents the state of the entire system, and there are many possible eigenfunction bases, which describe the ensemble of particles equally well. The difference between statistical and quantum mechanics is that statistical mechanics supposes that there is indeed a fixed set of a priori real particles which only change their states of position and momentum but in quantum mechanics, the particle and the state cannot be distinguished. Therefore, we cannot say that there is indeed a real set of particles whose state we cannot know. We must rather say that we cannot know which particles are real, and therefore which states are real. The quantum indeterminism is a more profound kind of indeterminism because we cannot know the *identity* of particles. In classical physics, when a particle moves from position A to B, it is the *same* particle. In quantum theory, particles at positions A and B are different particles. The uncertainty in the state of a quantum system means that the theory cannot tell which particles exist in an ensemble. The identity of the particles can only be known together with their state. And since the state of the entire ensemble is uncertain (due to the eigenfunction basis being undecided until a measurement is performed), the same ensemble can be described in terms of different sets of particles (eigenstates).

But which amongst these different sets of particles is real? Quantum theory does not say which particle set is real, but one amongst many possible particle sets can be picked during a measurement. In the quantum slit experiment, for instance, one particular eigenfunction basis (set of particles) is picked out by choosing the number of slits in the experiment. This creates difficulties in understanding the nature of reality in quantum theory. The choice of the number of slits is only an experimental arrangement. How can changes to experimental arrangements change the nature of reality being observed? How does reality *know* about the manner in which it is being measured to adapt to these changes? It is clear that the selection of an eigenfunction basis involves a choice. This choice has empirical consequences but they are not predicted by quantum theory. For instance, two eigenfunction bases predict different position measurement outcomes, but the theory does not predict which of these alternatives is real. The total energy in the ensemble can be refactored into many different sets of particles, and the theory does not say which of these sets of particles is actually real. Quantum theory only speaks of the total energy in a system but not its distribution.

One way to illustrate the quantum problem is to consider what happens when we draw some money out of a bank ATM. If I withdraw 1000 Rupees from an ATM, I do not *a priori* know if I will get this money in denominations of 1000, 500, 100, or 50. The bank only guarantees that I will get 1000 Rupees but not their denominations. There are many ways in which the same money could be delivered into currency notes. In the same way, quantum theory says that when describing an ensemble, we do not know which particles are real. Like some money can be accrued from different currency denominations, the total energy in the ensemble can also be constructed from many different particles with different energies. Which currency denominations you actually get depends on some 'choice' in the ATM. Similarly, how the total energy in the ensemble is cut up or distributed amongst individual particles depends upon a choice. The theory is consistent with all such choices but does not pick out one specific division. As a theory of reality, this creates serious problems for the classical view of nature because it means that the total energy somehow exists but particles of that energy do not exist *a priori*. If you check your bank account, you will see the total balance, but not the actual denominations in which that balance would be paid out. But as a theory of reality we like to think that there are real individual particles. Quantum theory tells us there is a whole but it is divided into parts only when someone performs a measurement on it.

In classical physics, the whole is made up of the parts. The parts are real but the whole is not until the parts are combined. In quantum theory, the whole is real but the parts are not real until the whole is divided into some parts. If the parts are individually real then the whole is automatically fixed. But fixing the whole does not automatically fix the parts. There is a choice or indeterminism in how the whole is cut into parts. But this means that the whole exists in some form even if the parts don't. In this case, it means that the energy exists but material particles do not. In what form does this energy exist? Quantum theory describes matter and radiation. Matter exists in stationary states and radiation moves at the speed of light. If energy exists as material particles then the parts are fixed, and the theory should not permit many eigenfunction bases to describe it. If, however, the energy exists as radiation then it would have already escaped the system. This creates a paradox about reality in quantum theory. There is energy and it exists neither as radiation nor as material particles. It is not material particles because that would fix the eigenfunction basis. And it is not radiation because that would have already escaped. How do we conceive such a form of energy?

Of course, the problems of quantum theory do not end with the choice of eigenfunction basis. The basis only tells us which *denominations* we get when we make a draw, but it does not tell us the *order* in which those denominations will arrive. The bank ATM can, for instance, deliver 1000 Rupees as 500, 100, 100, 100, 100, 50, 20, 20, and 10 Rupee notes. Other ways of delivering the same money are also possible. Therefore, even if we fix the denominations in which the ATM will output cash, there is still uncertainty about the order in which those Rupee denominations would be delivered.

Finally, assume that there are many people withdrawing money from the ATM, and simultaneously being delivered cash. Assume for the moment that the ATM gives out only a single note at a given instant in time. Everybody gets their cash in due course of time, but they have withdrawn different amounts, and the ATM is delivering these amounts in different denominations in different orders.

How do you predict which user will get which denomination at which point in time? A single user will get many denominations at different times—as they are delivered in some unpredictable order. But collectively, there are many users who receive the cash in different orders at different instances of time. If we assume for the moment that all the currency denominations are of the same size and weight, each user—if he is illiterate, and measures only the physical properties of the note—will register an event of reception. He cannot distinguish—because he is illiterate—which denomination he received, although he can say that he did receive a note. The note is a symbol of currency—because each denomination has a different value. But if you are illiterate you would not know the currency denomination, *if* all those denominations had the exact dimensions, weight, etc.

This is the central problem of quantum theory. In a measurement, the different users are the different detectors. They register individual measurement events, which correspond to the ATM delivering a note. But they only measure the physical property—e.g., dimensions of the note—rather than what is imprinted upon it. Therefore, for them, all the notes are identical because the symbolic content is lost in the measurement. Furthermore, they cannot know which denomination will arrive in which order, because this order depends on the past denominations, the total amount you have asked for, and the calculus in the ATM that decides to deliver notes from certain denominations in some order. If we combine this problem with that of multiple users drawing from the ATM simultaneously, and we are a neutral party just observing the ATM deliver different notes, we will say that user X gets 10 notes, user Y gets 20, user Z gets 30, etc. And we can draw up probabilities of how often each user will get a note. But we would miss two key things: (1) we will not know the denominations of the currency, so we don't know the total amount of money delivered; we would just know the total number of notes, rather than their value, and (2) we will not know the order of delivery because we don't understand the internal calculus of the ATM.

Quantum theory describes this problem partially—the part that ignores the value of each denomination, and simply measures the number of notes received by a given user. Since X gets 10 notes, Y gets 20, and Z gets 30 notes, you can assign a *probability* of each user getting a note a certain number of times. The quantum state is also defined in relation to the user—i.e., the measuring instrument—disregarding the denomination of the note. In short, we don't treat the particle as a symbol that encodes some currency value, but as a piece of paper that has some physical properties like size, weight, etc. Once the symbolic meaning is disregarded, and the order of denomination delivery is unpredictable, quantum theory arrives at a measurement outcome in which we can only measure the probabilities of observing a note in the hands of a certain observer (measuring instrument).

Quantum theory calls this limited description of the problem a wavefunction 'collapse' where the possibilities of a note arriving in a user's hand are 'collapsed' at the point of the note being delivered. Quantum theory is recognized to be incomplete because it does not predict the order in which a note will arrive in a different hand, but it isn't currently considered incomplete due to its inability to distinguish between different denominations. As we noted earlier in the case of statistical mechanics, the problem becomes intractable unless we treat it as a problem of information. In the same way, the quantum problem is intractable without inducting a role for information. In this case, for instance, we must say that the probability of receiving a currency note does not imply the total amount of money received. You could get just one note that was 1000 Rupee denomination. Or you could get 100 notes each of 10 Rupee denominations. What does the differing frequencies of receiving of a note by a user really mean, unless we understand the denominations being received?

The right way to solve this problem is to treat the slits in the experiment as determining the denominations. We can suppose that there are many denominations of the currency, but some denominations have the same *size*. The slits fix the 'size' of the slot through which currency must be delivered, and thereby indirectly fix the denominations. If we change the number of slits, we indirectly change the denominations. So the number of slits has a role in deciding how the money is *represented* in terms of currency notes. But this is only one part of the problem. The second part of the problem is that each user has drawn a different amount of money and would receive the denominations accordingly. We cannot just measure the number of times a note has been delivered without knowing the denomination being delivered; in short, we cannot treat the measurement event physically, disregarding the symbolic content of the note. Finally, there is also a third part of the problem, namely, that the ATM has an internal logic by which it delivers the notes in a certain order. It might deliver higher currency notes before the lower currency notes, or vice versa. It might also deliver them in some other order. If we don't know the internal logic of the ATM, and we disregard the symbolic content of the note, it is just a piece of paper—i.e., an event.

Current quantum theory treats the entire situation physically, rather than informationally. So, it measures the frequencies of note delivery but has no account of which user has drawn how much money, and the internal logic in the ATM to deliver it. Since the ATM is delivering cash to many users simultaneously, and we observe all these users at once, we only observe the frequencies of notes but have no understanding of *why* a particular user gets notes more often—is it because they drew a lot of cash, or because the representation of cash in notes (depending on the size of the slits) entails that the money has to be delivered more often in smaller denominations? The problem entails that we can never measure the entire ATM at once because it delivers notes one by one. Should we say that the reality—i.e., the notes—is hidden inside the ATM and it manifests itself one after another? That would make it patently inconsistent with classical physics where we could measure everything at once.

And yet these problems of quantum theory are conveniently discarded when the sub-atomic particles are combined to form atoms and molecules. It is incorrect to assume that reality exists as some fixed set of atoms and molecules. It is rather more correct to say that there is some energy, which could be divided into atoms and molecules in many ways. There isn't a fixed set of atoms or molecules out there. Rather, which atoms and molecules exist is a choice of observation. Furthermore, even if a certain eigenfunction basis of atoms and molecules has been chosen, it cannot be assumed that all these atoms and molecules exist simultaneously. It would be rather more correct to assume that they appear at the point of observation and do not exist at any other time. This would however undermine the idea that molecules are formed when atoms enter stable bonds. If the atoms (and sub-atomic particles) in a wavefunction do not even exist simultaneously then how can they be said to form stable bonds? Chemical bonding depends on the idea that sub-atomic particles exist simultaneously although quantum theory says they don't.

Another problem in quantum theory is the idea of change. In classical physics, if an object has momentum then the position of that object is changing. In quantum theory, if an object has momentum then its position is fixed. To change this fixed position, the energy of the object must be changed, and for that to occur the object must be placed in a changing energy field. This changing energy field must be caused by another changing field, which in turn must be caused by another changing field, etc. The problem is that once you suppose that objects must be in stationary states if their energy is constant, then state change requires a change in energy, which must be caused by an external agent. But that agent too is in a stationary state unless its state is changed by another agent. The universe of classical physics is in a state of motion. But the universe in quantum physics is in a stationary state. Due to this difference, the universe in classical physics naturally circulates energy but the universe in quantum physics requires energy to be moved around by an external agent. Quantum theory predicts the effect of a changing field but does not explain how the universe in which all objects tend to go to stationary states will stay in a state of perpetual motion. While classical physics described how the universe once set into motion would always be in motion, quantum theory tells us that the universe has to be constantly made to move by transferring energy from one system to another.

Quantum causality is consistent with everyday notions about causes, although it violates ideas of causality in classical physics. To understand this better, consider how the laws of science are used in everyday life. The laws of science tell us that *if* two chemicals are mixed, then a chemical reaction will take place. *If* we take medicine we will be cured. *If* we refrigerate water, its temperature will fall. The laws of science do not indicate if chemicals will be automatically mixed, if medicine would be automatically consumed, or if water will be automatically refrigerated. There is a choice in everyday actions, which determines if the correct state preparation procedure is performed to observe the outcomes. Classical determinism discards this choice and claims that state preparation is nothing but the previous state. Quantum theory, however, restores the choice of state preparation. Now, when an energy field is applied, a change will occur. But whether the energy field would be applied is not predictable.

Quantum and classical physics view the same world in two different ways. Classical physics studies a system from the 'outside' and models the forces of nature between objects into motion of objects based upon aggregate properties of objects. Quantum physics studies a system from the 'inside' and models the forces of nature between objects into stationary states. Classical physics is incomplete when the theory about the aggregate property behaviors is applied to describing the parts in that aggregate. Quantum physics is incomplete when the theory about parts is used to describe the behavior of the aggregate. This difference between classical and quantum physics lies at the root of the inability to unify these theories. The theory of the aggregate and the theory of the parts are separately incomplete. There is a need for a theory that describes the different kinds of behaviors of the aggregate and the parts using a single formalism.

Before such a theory can be formed, we need to recognize the unique role that aggregates play in science. The aggregate in this case is energy which can be distributed into particles in many ways. These ways are described by the theory as different eigenfunction bases, and the theory does not predict which eigenfunction basis is real. Since all these bases represent different particles, we cannot claim that there is an *a priori* real set of particles that exist prior to observation. We can however claim that there is some reality that can be described in many ways although not in arbitrary ways. Since particles are no longer real, the only reality underlying the observation is the ensemble which must be treated as being more real than the particles themselves. The indeterminism of quantum theory is that a total amount of energy can be distributed in many different ways, and each of these ways consists of many particles which cannot be observed simultaneously. The choice of the eigenfunction basis and the choice of the eigenfunction order in that basis is indeterminism in quantum theory. Furthermore, the theory only predicts the consequences of state preparations but does not predict whether some state preparation will occur. That is another type of indeterminism, which corresponds to the question of whether someone will draw money from the ATM, which cannot be predicted by the theory.

Choices in General Relativity

General Relativity was created by unifying two classically deterministic theories—Newton's theory of gravitation and Maxwell's theory of electromagnetism. So, it might seem counterintuitive that the theory involves indeterminism. The element of surprise in relativity is also higher because indeterminism in relativity is not as well-understood as in the case of quantum and statistical mechanics.

The indeterminism in relativity is not conceptually different from that in statistical and quantum mechanics. Relativity is a deterministic theory when the individual particles and their states are fixed. By fixing the individual particles and their states, the total energy of the universe is also fixed. When Newton described gravitation, he assumed the existence of individual particles, their masses, and their initial states of position and momentum. However, when Einstein created the general theory of relativity, he began with the idea that there are space-time events and energy needs to be distributed over these events. In classical physics, we begin by assuming particles and their energy. In quantum theory, we assume total energy, which is used to compute particles. In relativity, we assume energy and *events*. The indeterminism in relativity is based on different assumptions, although conceptually it is similar. It assumes events, which quantum theory does not, but does not assume particles as classical physics does. The indeterminism of relativity is that there can be different particles with the same events. The determinism of classical physics is missing in relativity, although the theory is more deterministic than quantum theory because it *a priori* assumes the existence of space-time events, so the outcomes are assumed.

The goal of Newton's gravitational theory was to describe the motion of objects, not the origin of these objects. However, Einstein showed through general relativity that matter is produced from space-time curvature. The primary reality in relativity is therefore space-time. But how do we define space-time? To create objects from space-time curvature, space-time had to be defined as events.

A formal statement of the indeterminism in relativity was originally formulated by Einstein as an argument about why general relativity is impossible. This argument has now come to be known as the Hole Argument. The argument hinges on the fact that for any differential equation, there are many possible solutions. The first-order differential equation is underdetermined by a constant, the second-order differential equation is underdetermined by a first-order differential, and so forth. These solutions to a differential equation represent different matter distributions, in which some quantities are constant, but others are changed. In general relativity, the total energy, the total number of particles, and the metric distance between events are constant while the changed quantities include the space-time coordinates of events. If we begin with a specific matter distribution, then the field is automatically fixed. But if we begin with the differential equations, then there are many possible solutions to that equation, which correspond to different matter distributions.

The Hole Argument specifically states that the field equations can produce two solutions that are the same everywhere except inside a 'hole' where they differ. There can also be two solutions that are identical till some t=T and different afterward. This seems to imply an indeterminism if you subscribe to the idea that there is a fixed space-time container in which the events occur. For, it seems that the theory is unable to predict the exact location and time at which some event will occur. Indeed, Einstein worried about this problem for several years while working on formulating the theory of general relativity because he thought that general relativity was impossible unless there was a clean solution for this type of indeterminism.

Eventually, however, he withdrew the Hole Argument based on a positivist viewpoint that Erich Kretschmann had promulgated earlier. Kretschmann had basically claimed that the empirical content of a space-time theory is exhausted by observations, which in general relativity are represented in the intersection of world-lines (trajectories) rather than space-time coordinates. The essence of Einstein's reversal lay in the idea that the observable quantities of physics are those that remain invariant even after coordinate transformations. This includes the total energy, the metric distances between events, and the total number of particles. The things that change in a coordinate transformation are coordinate values but these values have no empirical significance without an absolute space-time. The idea that there is an absolute space-time is called Space-Time Substantivalism as it treats space-time as a container or substance in which events occur. If such a substance exists then we could detect the consequences of different matter distributions. If, however, such a substance does not exist, then the various matter distributions are empirically identical although they seem to be theoretically different.

The idea of a space-time substance had been refuted earlier in special relativity based on the observation that the speed of light is constant even for moving observers. Therefore, it naturally follows that there is no absolute space-time, and the absolute values of coordinates are empirically meaningless. The empirical content of relativity theory is limited to the events and no matter how much you stretch or contract the space-time these events will still be intact. This is because space and time are defined as event coincidences.

One simple way to visualize Einstein's position is to think of space-time as a tennis net. The strings in the net are object trajectories and the points at which these strings intersect are events. If you stretch the net, the intersection points on the net move farther apart, and this constitutes a different way to distribute the matter in the tennis net. But this does not change some fundamental things about the net, namely the total number of strings (particles), the total mass of the net (energy), and the number of points at which the strings intersect (all the events). Only if you think that there is indeed a space-time in which the net is 'contained' can you actually talk about the fact that the points of intersection on the net are now farther apart. Einstein's argument amounts to the idea that when the net is itself the space-time then there is no other space-time in which the increased distance between the knots on the net can be described. We can speak about the points of intersection, the particles, and the total mass of the net, but not the space-time that holds this net.

Einstein's argument is now called the Point Coincidence Argument because the only observationally real entities in this view are the points of intersection of world-lines. This argument is taken to oppose Space-Time Substantivalism in which the events in the universe are supposed to exist in an absolute space-time 'substance.'

The Point Coincidence Argument, however, ignores a particular type of symmetry in which objects of identical mass are exchanged. Let's suppose that there are two trajectories with identical masses—e.g., 65 kg. These masses are in different locations and they are materially different particles. However, we can think of matter redistributions that swap these objects. The swap will not cause any detectable change from the standpoint of gravity. But the situation will be different if we take into account the *identities* of objects. For instance, if these two objects were different *observers*, then their swap will preserve all physical invariants, but it will change experiences. If the first object passes through events A, B, and C while the second object passes through events P, Q, and R, by swapping the objects, the first object will go through events P, Q, and R while the second object will go through the events A, B, and C. From the standpoint of general relativity, nothing has truly changed. The total mass, space-time metric, and point coincidences are all the same. But, from the standpoint of the observers, the events they experience have changed.

The rationale behind the Point Coincidence Argument is that the invariants of relativity are all the observables, and if these invariants are not changed then nothing is empirically changed. This view of the universe looks at space-time from the 'outside,' because when identical masses are swapped, there is no observable difference if the observer is outside the universe. But if the objects in the universe are themselves observers then swapping matter between events would be consistent with relativity but observationally indeterministic. The Point Coincidence Argument fixes the events, but it does not fix the matter that passes through the events. If the observer is outside the universe, then the events are unchanged, regardless of what matter passes through the events. But if the observer is in the universe as one of the objects, then the events in the universe are different from the standpoint of those observers. Now the fact that each point coincidence represents an experience and matter can be swapped between these points itself represents a change in experience without a change in the events themselves. Matter swapping transforms now represent choices of events that an observer passes through. Relativity would now imply that observers cannot change the events in the universe although they can change their experiences.

General relativity is *what* deterministic but *who* indeterministic. That is, it predicts what will happen in the universe but not who will experience it. This indeterminism needs theories about object *identities*. Both classical physics and general relativity are matter preserving but not identity preserving. When two objects with some mass collide, their masses could potentially be exchanged. Classical physical theories cannot distinguish between the cases when the masses were and weren't exchanged. The problem of general relativity is it has no notion of object *identity*. We can measure physical properties and physics is defined around physical properties and not identities. Observers have a sense of identity and when the objects in the universe are equated with observers the indeterminism is palpable.

These issues raise questions about the nature of trajectories. In classical physics, a trajectory is the path of an object. In general relativity too, the trajectory is a path, although this path can now be traversed by many different objects with the same properties. We should now think of a trajectory as an 'actor' who constitutes the 'object' that passes through various events. When matter is redistributed over events, the causal explanation of the events changes because the same event is explained by a different matter distribution. Similarly, when the observers are distributed over the events, different actors have different experiences as they pass through different roles. An actor can perform different roles, so which actor performs which role is not decided neither by the event nor by the material properties.

Summarizing the Physical Problem

The problems in physics can be summarized through the drama analogy I discussed earlier. Quantum theory has three problems: (1) it appears that while some drama plot has been conceptualized, its exact actors and scenes have not been defined; the actors (quanta) are defined only when someone comes to watch the play (i.e., when a measurement is performed), (2) it is not clear whether anyone will come to watch the play, and therefore whether a play will be enacted on stage cannot be predicted in advance (i.e., we cannot predict if some system will transfer energy), (3) even if the play is enacted, the order in which the actors will appear and the dialogues they will deliver cannot be predicted; it seems that while the roles have been defined, the actual script for the entire play has not been defined.

Of course, it still seems that the play has been finalized in some form, because if nothing was definite then there would be no predictions at all. In this case, we could say that the play exists as some kind of conceptual entity, and when someone comes to watch the play (a measurement is performed) some set of actors are quickly defined based on the taste of the audience (eigenfunction basis is selected based on the number of slits in the slit-experiment) who then appear on stage in some particular order (quantum order) and while we cannot predict the exact order of events on the stage (the scenes), we can predict that some actors will play lead roles and will therefore have more scenes (will appear more frequently) than others.

The problem of quantum theory is that in classical physics we thought that the drama and the actors were identical and they were defined even before the play was enacted on the space-time stage. Quantum theory tells us that much of what happens on the stage is defined based on what the audience wants to see (only if they want to see), and there is no fixed script that the actors will follow. However, there is still some sense in which the play has been defined, although overall, the play is just an idea, which is improvised on demand. If you have grown up thinking that nature existed and behaved independent of its observations, then that picture is shattered.

The picture in statistical mechanics is different. Here, we begin by assuming that there is an *a priori* real drama troupe, which can enact different plays (that there is an ensemble of *a priori* real particles). The troupe is supposed to enact some play over the next few days, but unfortunately, the play hasn't been announced yet (we don't know the exact evolution of the particles in the ensemble). You happen to know that the troupe is currently rehearsing the play inside the theatre behind closed doors. Therefore, if you were curious about which play is being rehearsed, you might try to snoop on the sounds coming from inside the theatre (perform measurements on the ensemble from the outside). However, the troupe has taken great care to hide their secret from such potential snoopers; the sounds from the theatre are muffled, and you are unable to decipher the play from these sounds. Now, the normal thing to do for any snooper would be to admit his inability to figure out which specific play was being rehearsed although there must indeed be one specific play that is being rehearsed. But our snooper is not going to admit his failure. He rather presumes that if he is unable to figure out which particular play is being rehearsed, then it must be because the troupe itself has not finalized the play. Rather, due to its indecision about which play to rehearse, the troupe is rehearsing all possible plays at once.

Furthermore, our snooper may presume that the troupe is able to simultaneously enact all the plays because they have a lot of energy; the actors are very enthusiastic about performing and so they are acting out all the plays at once. The snooper may suppose that over time, they will get tired of doing many plays at once, and they would then settle down into one play, and that's the play that would eventually be enacted. So, he allows the actors to drain their energies (extracts energy from the particle ensemble as a whole) and keeps snooping on them. However, when the actors have become tired, their voices go down and the sounds coming out of the theatre are even less audible. If it was hard to decode the play from the earlier sounds, the situation is now worsened. Using such muffled sounds, even more numerous interpretations of the sound are possible, and rather than reduce the number of possible plays, the reduced sound further increases the total uncertainty about the actual play.

The problem of statistical mechanics is that in classical physics we assumed that there is only one definite reality, which exists independently of whether we observe it. But reality appears not to be definite. We are trying to measure the aggregated sounds coming from the theatre and this aggregated sound underdetermines the actual play. Furthermore, in classical physics, if we reduce the total energy, the particles move slower and we might assume that this reduction of energy would help us increase our certainty about the state. But quite the reverse happens. Rather than increasing our certainty about the state, the energy reduction further decreases it[1]. In classical physics, we could observe each individual particle's state. In a large ensemble, however, we can only look at a collection from the 'outside' and the 'outside' view underdetermines the 'inside.'

The bigger problem in statistical mechanics, of course, is that if we are unable to determine the system's state then the system behaves as if its state was actually uncertain. There are two ways to interpret this uncertainty. First, we might suppose that the system somehow 'knows' that we are unable to determine its certain state, and therefore it behaves uncertainly, but this would require the system to be 'aware' of our ability to know its state, which is problematic. Second, we might suppose that the system is indeed in an uncertain state which would contradict the classical theoretical view that all classical systems are in fact in a real and deterministic state. Whichever way we look at it, the ensemble of particles does not behave in the way we suppose it should according to classical physics.

The problems of general relativity are even more puzzling. General relativity has two problems, which can be understood in the drama analogy. First, the playwright of the drama begins with a pen and paper (time and space) and there are so many ways in which he or she can spread the pen's ink on paper (i.e., draw the trajectories), thereby producing many different plays, all consistent with the total amount of ink remaining conserved. These correspond to innumerable ways in which matter or energy can be spread in space-time to create many different histories of the universe. Second, even when the play is completed, and a deterministic flow of events has been identified, the specific actors in the play have still not been determined. The conversion of the play into an actual dramatization of the play requires the selection of actors, which would require a director. The same play can be enacted by different actors and the same actors can enact different plays. Therefore, the play underdetermines the actors and the actors underdetermine the play. The theory is unable to predict which plays and which actors would actually be real.

The deeper problem in relativity is that physical theories do not describe matter as individuals; matter is described as quantities. The same property quantity can exist in distinct individuals. The property specification, therefore, underdetermines the individual; we might say that science describes a *type* of object (although these types are different from the types used in everyday language). The role in a play is a type of character, but many actors can enact the same character. Current physics equates the actors with the characters, and thus it is indeterministic about the actual actor distributions.

The problems in modern physical theories arise due to their differences vis-à-vis classical physics. Classical physics began with the idea of objects, space, and time as separate categories. Problems in this view of nature begin when the starting assumptions are changed. For instance, if we cannot suppose that there are *a priori* real objects, but only a total energy that needs to be distributed, then the same energy can be distributed into many different objects leading to indeterminism. Similarly, when matter is created from space-time structure, differences in space-time structure itself create indeterminism—i.e., which space-time structure is the real structure of the universe? Finally, problems in thermodynamics illustrate that the actual state of the system is incompletely defined, even though we suppose that the system must be in a classically definite state.

If we begin with the idea that there is space, time, and objects, then physical theories are deterministic. If, however, we begin with space, time, and energy, or with space-time events whose structure represents objects, then scientific theories are indeterministic. Finally, if we collapse the distinction between space-time and matter, then the space-time structure itself becomes indeterministic.

These forms of indeterminism can be viewed as *choices*. A role for choice did not exist in classical physics but it exists in modern physics because of the indeterminism. The role for choice, therefore, emerges in science not because we would like to believe that we are free. It rather appears because physical laws do not predict everything in matter. Choices become necessary because science is incomplete, not just because we would like to believe we are free.

Of course, it is possible to interpret the indeterminism in science as indicating a role for conscious choices, but I don't believe this is the correct approach for the simple reason that how these choices interact with an underdetermined reality is itself problematic. The correct approach is to first define matter as information, which can be abstract or detailed. A matter distribution is now the expression of meaning through symbols and material objects are those symbols rather than meaningless things. The widespread belief today is that the world is meaningless and the mind gives it meaning. Therefore, the idea that meanings can objectively exist in matter itself requires a profound understanding of the problems of indeterminism in physical theories. Once we recognize that matter is itself symbolic meaning, then the interactions between such objects must be modeled as interactions between meanings. Similarly, the reference frame through which these interactions are perceived and understood must be viewed semantically as axioms, theories, and worldviews.

Incompleteness in Mathematics

Physical theories are of course not alone in being incomplete. Rather, there is a deeper problem of incompleteness—called Gödel's incompleteness theorem—which makes any theory of numbers incomplete. I have separately surveyed this problem in my previous writing[2]. In the following paragraphs, I will try to paraphrase that discussion through examples. The crux of the problem is that numbers can be treated in three different ways—as things, concepts, and names—but it is not possible to maintain this distinction in mathematics. The inability to maintain the distinction between things, concepts, and names results from the fact that these are semantic categories while mathematics treats numbers as quantities. When we treat numbers as quantities, the distinction between things, names, and concepts is lost. The same word can denote a name, thing, and concept. Therefore, if the distinction between these categories were dropped, words meant to signify one category can be interpreted to denote another category, thereby creating contradictions.

The distinction between things, names, and concepts exists in all ordinary languages. By this distinction, a word is sometimes a thing (a physical token of meaning), sometimes a concept (when it represents a class of such individuals), and sometimes a name (if the word refers to a specific individual). If we only viewed the word as a physical token, then we could not derive its meanings—i.e., that it denotes a class of individuals or a specific individual in the class. The loss of this distinction results in contradictions, which Gödel interpreted to entail the incompleteness of all number theories. Gödel's theorem can be summarized as the problem that if numbers represent things, concepts, and names, then number theory is inconsistent; however, if numbers are only things, then number theory is incomplete.

To illustrate how Gödel proves the inconsistency vs. incompleteness choice, let us take the example of the word 'nobody' and understand the different ways it can be used in English. These uses can now be used to arrive at logical contradictions if we fail to make the necessary categorical distinctions. Consider the following three sentences using the word 'nobody':

- Nobody has six letters
- Nobody is perfect
- I am nobody

In the first statement, the word 'nobody' is a thing, or a physical aggregation of six letters. In the second statement, 'nobody' represents a name that refers to people. In the third, 'nobody' represents the concept of insignificance. Ordinary language is replete with such uses of words. If we used these words interchangeably, we can come up with conclusions such as the following two shown below.

- Nobody is perfect. I am nobody. Therefore, I am perfect.
- Nobody is perfect. Nobody has six letters. Therefore, perfect has six letters.

In the first case, we arrived at an erroneous conclusion but it is not logically flawed. In the second case, we have arrived at something that is logically incorrect, because the word 'perfect' has seven letters rather than six. We don't need to be linguists to understand the source of these paradoxes. The problem here is that the word 'nobody' can denote things, concepts, and names. To use language consistently, the user must respect these categorical distinctions; when that distinction is not honored, paradoxes inevitably arise.

In mathematics, the categorical confusion appears when numbers are interchangeably used as objects, names, and concepts. The number '5' for instance can be treated as a *thing* or a token. It can also be treated as a *name* when we have ordered objects in a collection and labeled them by numbers; for instance, we can call someone 'Employee #5.' The number also represents the concept of fiveness, which exists in all collections that have five elements. Mathematics can talk about each of these meanings, but not talk about them at once. In separate contexts (or theories) mathematics can formulate and describe ideas about numbers as things, names, and concepts. But when the same theory employs all these categories at once, there is potential for paradoxes. Gödel's incompleteness is not the only instance of such a paradox. Similar paradoxes arise even in set theory when a set is used both as a *class* and an *instance*; the former denoting a concept and the latter a thing. Bertrand Russell also produced a paradox in set theory by including a set within itself; the including set is the class or concept, while the included set is the object. If we lose the distinction between these categories, contradictions arise.

Mathematical paradoxes point to the fact that mathematics lags behind ordinary language in its ability to deal with linguistic categories. To deal with these categories, it should be possible in mathematics to treat the same number as a thing, name, concept, program, algorithm, problem, and perhaps other things. We might say that a number is a physical thing or a token that has several different kinds of meanings. These meanings are sometimes called *models* of a symbol and they represent different interpretations of the same symbol. In the formal study of models in mathematics, a *theory* is a collection of sentences whose truth is decided by the syntax of that sentence. A *model* on the other hand is a domain of objects that satisfies the statements of the theory. For instance, we can formulate a theory of numbers that describes the outcome of addition and multiplication operations. Such a theory will make claims such as:

IF A AND B ARE NUMBERS THEN A + B IS A NUMBER
IF A AND B ARE NUMBERS THEN A * B IS A NUMBER

The claims of this theory are satisfied for different kinds of number domains such as natural numbers, integers, rational numbers, and irrational numbers. These domains are called the *models* of the theory. If we had to explain the theory, we can concretely demonstrate it first by showing the addition and multiplication of integers. Then we can show that it works even for rational and irrational numbers. These different models are various ways to *understand* the theory, but the theory is different from that understanding. Inherent in mathematics is therefore the separation between the statements of a theory and the *meanings* to be attached to the statements.

Generally, we assume that the various models or interpretations of a theory are mutually exclusive. That this, different interpretations of a theory are true if we keep these interpretations separate. This assumption is false for ordinary language where various categories are present in language *simultaneously*. Thus, for example, we don't use different contexts for things, concepts, and names. Rather, we talk about things, concepts, and names alternately within the same context. This leads to paradoxes because claims made about a thing can be applied to its name which is then interpreted as a claim about a concept, resulting in a contradiction. For instance, Gödel framed the sentence "P is False." This statement was now named "P" and the name was interpreted as the idea that P is False. Now it appears that statement P claims that P is false, which is a logical contradiction.

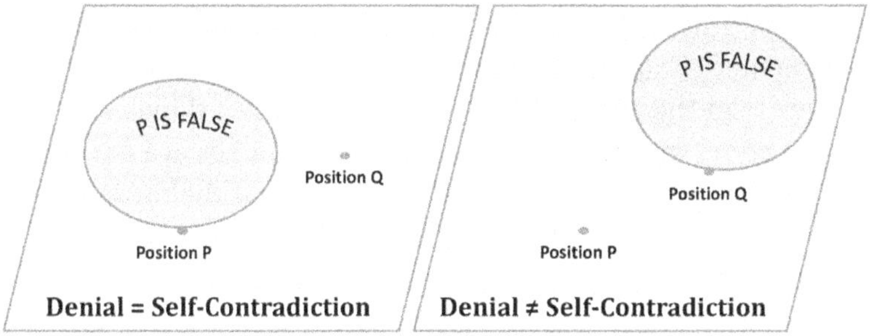

Figure-6 The Conflict Between Meaning and Naming

This problem would not arise in the following two cases. First, if we could maintain the distinction between names, things, and concepts. Second, if we could prevent "P is False" being named as "P," because then even the dissolution of the categorical differences would not lead to contradictions. Neither option is permitted in current mathematics. The ability to apply the first option results from using mathematics like ordinary language. As ordinary language permits categorical distinctions but maintains the difference between them, mathematics too can be used with categorical differences, but since the distinctions cannot be maintained in mathematics the result is logical contradictions. The second option is forbidden because mathematics measures meanings using the syntax of statements rather than their semantics. In this approach[3], it is impossible to know that the meaning of the squiggles "P is False" is that the statement P is false. When a statement is syntactically analyzed, its meaning is not evident. When the meaning is lost in syntactical analysis, the proposition can be mapped to a semantically opposite meaning, which results in a logical contradiction between the name and meaning.

This brief survey of problems in mathematics is by no means exhaustive or even rigorous. But, hopefully, it shows why it is *logically* impossible to even construct a *representational* account of meaning using current materialist theories. A representational theory says that material objects *denote* meanings through symbols but that does not reduce meaning to those symbols. The impossibility of achieving this in current mathematics is given by the fact that any representational theory of descriptive meanings will need to incorporate the categorical distinction between things, concepts, and names to avoid contradictions. That is, the symbol and its meanings are not identical (because then the categorical distinction between things and meanings will not exist) and the symbol and its meanings are not separate (because then we will not be able to speak about the meaning of the symbol in the same theory that we speak of the symbols).

Mathematical paradoxes illustrate that mathematics needs to hold categorical distinctions (i.e., differences between various classes of meanings) but it is not capable of holding meanings as long as it describes symbols physically. We can also conclude that any theory that describes reality in terms of physical tokens will be either inconsistent or incomplete if those tokens are also required to denote meanings. If the theory is consistent, then it will be incomplete because it cannot incorporate categorical differences. However, if the categorical differences are incorporated in the physical model, then the theory will become inconsistent. This is a far bigger indictment of physical theories than what scientists acknowledge. The limitations are not just about number theory. They are problems for any scientific theory that describes reality as physical properties.

Turing's Halting Problem

While Gödel had shown that number theory would be incomplete, there wasn't yet a clear example of a specific kind of problem that is undecidable. Alan Turing supplied the first instance of such a problem[4]. Turing was a pioneer in computer science and he formalized the notion of an algorithm through his Turing Machine that reads instructions and modifies inputs into outputs. An algorithm is considered finished when the Turing Machine comes to a halt. However, it is possible that a problem is unsolvable and then the Turing Machine would continue indefinitely. Since there could be complex algorithms that take a long time to finish, it is important to determine whether an algorithm will ever halt. There is no point in expending a computer's energy in trying to solve a problem that is essentially unsolvable since no amount of computation could ever prove or disprove its statements. The question of whether or not an algorithm will stop is called the Halting Problem and it tells whether a machine that tries to compute a solution will ever come to a halt.

Turing proved that the Halting Problem is undecidable, an example of Gödel's unsolvable problems within arithmetic. Turing's proof means there is no procedure to decide if a program will meet its intended goal and stop. The only way to know it is to run the program on the computer and find out if it actually terminates. The essence of Turing's limitation can be illustrated by the following simple program:

```
INSTRUCTION 1: GO TO INSTRUCTION 2
INSTRUCTION 2: GO TO INSTRUCTION 1
```

The casual examination of these instructions shows an infinite loop between them. The first instruction asks the computer to go to the second instruction, which puts the execution back on the first instruction. A computer can never exit this infinite loop because there is no instruction that tells it to stop. If you run this program on a computer, the program will run forever and it is advisable that we avoid starting a program that is never going to conclude. Turing's proof of the Halting Problem means that there are no formal procedures to distinguish programs that halt from those that don't.

In short, computers can never stop even when the problem is unsolvable and Turing formalized this in the Halting Problem. A problem might take a hundred years to solve, so it is worthwhile to know that the problem indeed has a solution before we spend a hundred years trying to solve it. It would be futile to spend a hundred years and then abort the attempt because the solution wasn't found thus far. Humans have the ability to abort intractable problems and Turing proved this to be impossible for a computer. The Halting Problem is an example of the kinds of unsolvable problems that Gödel's theorem alludes to but did not explicitly identify. The machine that attempts to answer such a question for a program that never halts will also run forever since coming to a stop means determining that the program being analyzed must also come to a halt.

Note how Turing's problem hinges on the use of infinite loops. A program with a finite loop is not problematic, but one with an infinite loop is. But how do we know if a loop is finite or infinite? There are two possible ways. First, we look at the program as a whole and then determine if it has an infinite loop. Second, we can execute the program and go through its steps one by one. In the latter case, there is no way to know if the loop is infinite because every number—if it can be counted—is a finite number. The computer can keep counting the steps in the loop and never conclude that the program is infinite. The only way a computer can know if a program is loopy is if it can process the program as a whole without actually executing it. But this processing is tantamount to knowing the meaning of the program and machines cannot know or represent meanings.

A further problem is that even if a program halts, it might be malicious. A growing number of computer programs today are malicious. Ideally, if a computer could know the meaning of a program, then it could also know if the program is useful or malicious. But since knowing the meaning is itself impossible, it is also impossible to know if the program is malicious. There are hence two problems of meaning related to Turing's theorem. First, we cannot know if a program will halt because we cannot know if it is meaningful. Second, we cannot know if the program that halts is useful or malicious. If we could solve the first problem, we would also solve the second. But the solution to the first problem is impossible in a physical theory.

Summarizing the Mathematical Problem

The essence of the mathematical problem—as seen in Gödel's and Turing's theorems—is that numbers cannot denote meanings. To denote meanings, numbers have to be viewed as *types*. However, current mathematics describes numbers as *quantities*. In the case of number theory, the quantitative treatment of numbers results in the loss of the distinction between things, concepts, and names, and thereby leads to Gödel's incompleteness. In the case of computing theory, the quantitative treatment of numbers results in the inability to know if some finite number represents an infinite procedure; an infinite procedure is not a valid procedure, and therefore the quantitative treatment is unable to decipher if some number is also a valid procedure. We could also construct syntactically correct but semantically invalid statements—e.g., "colorless green ideas sleep furiously"—and these statements can be encoded as numbers, but a computer would not know if such a statement is meaningless. In short, the conversion of programs and statements—which have meanings—into numbers (when these numbers are described as quantities instead of types) results in a loss of meanings. Once meanings have been lost, the categorical type distinctions are gone, the semantic correctness cannot be determined, and a logic that operates without meanings potentially creates many logical contradictions.

The deeper problem in mathematics is that it tries to construct meaning from objects, which is impossible. For instance, mathematicians treat a set as the representation of a class or concept. Think of a collection of cars. For a car to belong to the set of cars, we must already know that it is a car. But the definition of car depends on the set, which is formed after collecting potentially all the cars. So, to form the set of cars, we must already know what a car is; in short, the concept must be defined prior to its being defined. This creates an infinite regress and makes the definition impossible. The lesson from this problem is that we cannot construct concepts from objects. We can however invert the process and construct objects from concepts. For instance, a 'car' would be a refinement of the idea of a 'vehicle'. A specific type of 'car'—e.g., a sedan or SUV—would be a further refinement of the idea of 'car'. You can keep refining this definition and construct a very accurate definition of a certain type of car. If we begin with the definition of a car, we face no problems in constructing an individual type of car. But if we start with individual cars, we have a problem of recursion in constructing the definition from objects.

This requires us to invert our thinking. We must view an actual car not as a material object, but as a conceptual construct; even things are concepts. They are just different *instances* of a concept—e.g., there can be many instances of a certain type of car. So, the individual car is a combination of a universal and an individual. The individual is a coordinate reference frame—that denotes the individual's 'perspective'. There are as many such reference frames as there are objects. This reference frame is also conceptual and hierarchical; the abstract axioms are logically prior to the details which follow.

The indeterminism in physical theories and the incompleteness in mathematics both point towards the same problem. The problem is that science is defined as the study of independent objects contained in universal space and time, and the collection is supposed to reduce to those individual objects. The problem is that you cannot define the class and the object in this manner. You can define the object from the class—by refining it—but you cannot construct classes from objects. If, however, you do treat the class as being logically prior to the individual—as in the case of physics when we begin from the ensemble of total energy and matter—then without the agency that refines the class and constitutes a matter distribution, the theory becomes indeterministic. So, the mathematical problem is that it begins in the objects and is unable to construct the collections. The physical problem is that it begins from collections and is unable to construct the objects. Both these problems can be attributed to the fact that we are treating the objects and the collections physically when we should be treating them semantically. Since science evicted the role of meaning from the study of matter, the problems are inevitable.

The remedy to the situation is that both collections and objects are real, but they are both semantic. The collection is an abstract idea and the individual is a detailed idea. We construct the object from the collection; the collection is logically prior to the object. However, this is only the first step. The next step is realizing that the collections and individuals are of three distinct kinds—material events, material properties, and objects, individuals, or trajectories. Just as we construct a hierarchy of objects and collections, now, with three categories, we must construct three kinds of hierarchies of collections and individuals. In any observation, there is an individual object, some material properties, and an interaction or event. The event is the observable, matter is the causal explanation of that event, and the individual is the observer participating in the measurement of the event. Therefore, the three categories must be combined in all situations.

3

A Type Theory of Reality

If you have to prove a theorem, do not rush. First of all, understand fully what the theorem says, try to see clearly what it means. Then check the theorem; it could be false. Examine the consequences, verify as many particular instances as are needed to convince yourself of the truth. When you have satisfied yourself that the theorem is true, you can start proving it.

— *George Pólya*

The Notion of Boundaries

Scientists generally cringe at the discussion of mind and meaning within science, because science has progressed under the Cartesian divide between mind and matter. In the Cartesian view, the world of material objects exists independent of the mind, and the mind only provides *interpretations* of the world. Even in mathematics, there is a separation between a theory and its models as we saw earlier.

While the induction of the mind in science appears as the introduction of some non-material substance inside the world of matter, it doesn't have to be so. As we saw in the last chapter, meanings become necessary when we must deal with object collections, rather than independent objects. Since the class definition involves circular recursion, we are compelled to suppose that the class is a concept that logically precedes its members. The members must now be defined as refinements of this class—conceptually. They must also be defined as individuals that instantiate that class. So, the object becomes a combination of the universal and the individual. To combine these two, even the individual must be treated conceptually.

The problem of meaning, therefore, appears in science not in trying to induct a non-material mind into matter. It rather appears in the attempt to describe object collections as sets of individual objects. However, this problem overhauls the philosophical underpinnings of materialism; nothing is material anymore; it is all meaning. The meaning exists, however. So, we must redefine matter as meaning. It is objective and real, and it interacts with other meanings. So, the laws of interaction must be defined as those governing meanings.

This formulation of the problem of meaning is essential to the progress in science because attempts to induct a non-material mind into the world of matter are unlikely to succeed. The problem of object collections is entirely physical in one sense because the collection only presents itself as a boundary in space-time. However, it is also unphysical in another sense that the boundary is not material. The main question then for the progress of science is: Can a non-material boundary in space-time be viewed as a physical entity? Can there be physical constructs in science that are not material objects?

Note the difference between *physical* and *material* properties. By physical, I mean things that exist within space and time. A scientific theory describes what happens inside space and time by postulating some material properties such as momentum, energy, angular momentum, etc. which can be measured through some experiment. But a scientific theory also postulates other properties such as mass, charge, and force which cannot be directly observed except through their *effects* on the measurable properties such as momentum, energy, and angular momentum. For instance, we cannot measure mass, except when it causes other objects to move or change their path of motion in space-time. While observable properties such as energy, momentum, and angular momentum are material (in the specific sense that they can be observed), notions such as mass, charge, or force are physical although not material (because they cannot be directly observed). The primary job of a scientific theory is to explain the material properties based on the physical properties.

In this regard, Willard van Orman Quine's view about scientific beliefs is quite instructive. Quine believed that the sum total of our knowledge is like a web of interconnected ideas which touch our experience only at the periphery. That is, ideas at the periphery of the web of knowledge can be experimentally verified. There are also other ideas at the core of the web which cannot be directly verified by experience, although they lend necessary support to the web as a whole. Quine's point was that it is misleading to speak about the truth of a single scientific statement in isolation because the truth of these statements doesn't stand by itself. A scientific claim only lives within the web of many such statements and a theory—as a collection of various ideas—is either collectively verified or refuted.

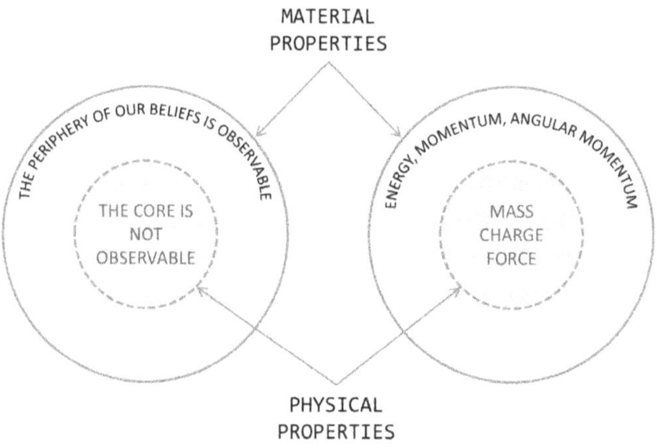

Figure-7 Physical Properties vs. Material Properties

The distinction between physical and material properties is like the distinction between the periphery and the core of scientific beliefs. In physical theories, momentum, energy, position, time, angle, and angular momentum are material properties and they lie at the periphery of a theory because they can be measured. Ideas such as mass, charge, force, field, etc. are physical properties because they too live in space-time, although they cannot be directly measured except through their effects on the material properties, and they are therefore at the core of the physical theory. In fact, the idea of space and time is also a physical property although not a material property because we cannot directly measure space and time (or properties such as the curvature of space-time) except through their effects on material properties such as position or speed or acceleration.

Quine also held that the core of our belief system is underdetermined by the periphery and several cores can be used to explain the same periphery. In other words, the causal explanations of material properties such as momentum, energy, position, time, angle, and angular momentum—which are currently based on ideas such as mass, charge, force, field, etc.—could be changed if there were other types of causal notions that better explained the phenomena.

The idea of a space-time *boundary* is one such idea. It is not a material property because it cannot be observed. However, in that respect, it is on par with other physical concepts such as mass, charge, force, and field which also cannot be directly measured. If this idea were to be made mathematically rigorous and then used to explain the material properties, then it could augment or replace other physical properties such as mass, charge, force, field, etc. The role of the boundary would now be in creating collections that are given meaning, following which the parts in those collections also become meaningful, although this meaning is defined after that of a set.

The Problem of Recursion

The key conceptual difficulty in defining a boundary, a set, or a collection is that it leads to a problem of recursion. Suppose that we are trying to define the idea of a car by collecting various objects called cars. The definition of the car depends on there being a finite number of such objects being available. To collect cars into the set of cars, we must be able to define cars before collecting them because without a definition we would also be collecting shoes, chairs, or houses into the set of cars. But how do we define the idea of a car? Ostensibly, the idea of the car is only expressed by the set of cars. This set is created only when all the objects that can be called cars have been aggregated into the set. To aggregate the cars into a set, we must define the idea of car, and be able to apply this definition of the car to individual objects, because otherwise we would not know which objects to collect.

The problem of recursion is that the idea of a car depends on many individual cars, and to know that each object is a car we must define the idea of a car before we collect. The set of cars, therefore, depends on each individual object being a car, but each individual object can only be a car if the set was already defined. The problem of recursion is the recursive dependence between concepts and objects. Of course, the concept of a car is only one of the concepts. The same problem exists for every type of concept, including numbers

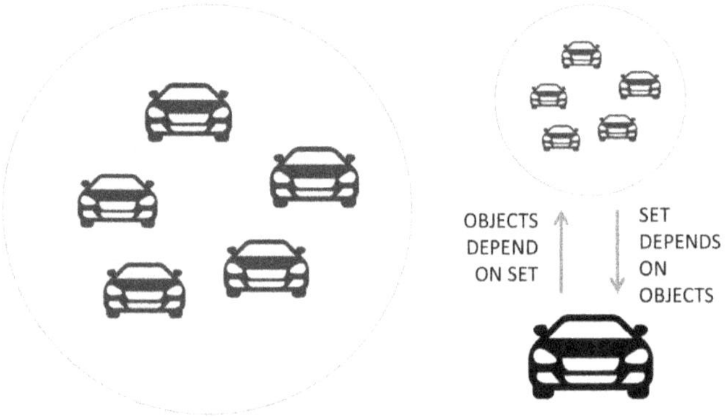

Figure-8 The Problem of Recursion

Set theory in mathematics avoids this problem in one of two ways. First, it defines sets in some *a priori* manner without reference to any objects and then goes about finding the objects that will belong to the set. The problem here is that we assume that the idea of a car can be defined regardless of any physical car. If this notion was extended as the foundation of mathematics, then we would have to suppose that ideas must exist even prior to objects. Of course, most mathematicians are Platonists, so they have no problem in acquiescing to this stand about ideas. The Platonist grants that there is an original world of ideas of which the world of objects is but a poor imitation. However, how this world of ideas is reflected in the world of things remains an unsolved problem of Platonism.

A mathematical Platonist does not worry about this problem because he or she is only interested in the world of ideas and never the world of things. However, it helps to remember that mathematics is not necessarily about ideas; it is also about mathematical statements which must be expressed as symbols. Indeed, when Gödel proved the incompleteness theorem, he wasn't dealing with pure ideas. Rather, he created statements about statements, where both the referring and the referred statements are expressed physically, and their meanings are computed based on this expression, not based on the idea. As we previously saw, mathematics becomes incomplete when it must deal with the distinction between things, names, and concepts, and therefore, while the Platonist would like to think that mathematics is not about the world of things, that isn't true. Things enter mathematics when mathematics deals with the meanings of propositions. Mathematics has no way of expressing pure ideas; it expresses ideas through symbols, which are physical tokens. To speak about the meaning of a theorem mathematics must use the physical expression of a theorem. This is the kind of problem that leads to Gödel's incompleteness when the meaning of a proposition is derived from the physical expression (symbols) of that proposition.

Second, set theory can also suppose that the objects being aggregated don't have a type; they are just objects or individuals, and the set—having collected these individual things—does not denote a concept. For instance, we can draw a boundary around the things in some geography and call that boundary a city. The city is not an idea or type. It is just a physical aggregation of things, which do not have any types either. While this view of sets works perfectly fine, it precludes any ideas or concepts being permitted in mathematics. Members of a set are physical things, and the set is a physical aggregation of such physical things. At no point does the set become a concept and the members of this set, too, are not instances of any concept. When we go by this approach—which is logically consistent—we end up with incompleteness in mathematics as we saw previously.

The incompleteness is a consequence of the fact that many sets in mathematics—such as when numbers are defined using sets—cannot be treated as physical aggregations of things; they must be treated as ideas. If you treat a physical collection of 5 objects as the number 5, then every time you say that you have 5 objects, you must refer to the first set of 5 objects that you defined as the number 5. To claim that another set also has five members you must map its members to the members of the set one-to-one. This is a viable solution to the problem, except that we must go back and ask: How did we know that there were five and not six members in the original set? We must have had the ability to distinguish the objects before we collected them. But how did we distinguish them? Obviously, to distinguish things we need properties—e.g., shape, size, position, color, etc. Counting follows the distinguishing. But now to define the idea 5, we need to define all the other ideas like shape, size, position, color, etc. And to define these latter ideas, we would need even more ideas, and the problem slowly expands to innumerable definitions.

The definition of a set is therefore not as straightforward. The idea of a set is highly problematic for the following reasons:

1. If you think that both sets are ideas and objects are examples of such ideas, then this leads to a problem of recursion—i.e., which idea comes first, as they depend on each other?
2. If you think that sets must be defined as *a priori* ideas, then you must admit a Platonic world and how that world interacts with the physical world remains problematic.
3. If you think that objects are *a priori* real, and sets are only physical aggregations, then mathematics becomes impossible as it requires infinite properties before counting.

When I look at these three alternatives, I arrive at the conclusion that approaches 1 and 3 cannot be mended. Recursion creates a logical difficulty in defining anything and infinite regress in defining ideas makes definition impossible. The 2nd approach can work if we mend the problem of Platonic interaction between ideas and things. The 2nd alternative assumes an *a priori* definition of sets as ideas, which entails that ideas must exist prior to things, and things are selected to belong to the set based on the idea definition. To select the objects based on the idea, the objects themselves must be instantiations of the idea. How are ideas instantiated into things?

The Platonic Interaction Problem

There are two kinds of problems in the Platonic interaction. First, we need to define how ideas exist when they are not embodied into specific objects, and this has been very difficult because it requires us to first define the space in which these ideas can exist, and how locations in that space could individuate such ideas. Note that all physical objects can be individuated simply by their location in space (if these objects are not evolving); location suffices to individuate an object. If ideas similarly must be individuated, then there must be a space in which these ideas exist. The Platonic ideas define a 'world,' and if such a world had to exist, then it would require a space for ideas.

Second, if ideas have been defined in some idea-space, how do we use these ideas to individuate objects? Each idea has some properties, and the same properties must be used to determine if a thing is an instance of that idea or not. Take the idea of length. If a set of all lengthy objects must be defined, then the property of length must be used to determine if the objects in question have the property of length before they can be admitted into the set of lengthy objects. Now we have the following problem: How did the Platonic idea of length become the length of an individual object?

The standard physicist response to this problem is that length is not an idea; it is a physical property—i.e., a quantity—which requires a measuring instrument. However, if you extend this thinking to all other concepts, then all concepts will require a measuring instrument. You will not solve the problem of defining concepts; you can only shift the problem from defining the concept to defining the measuring instrument. Now, you must say that only a few properties will be entertained in science; all others are 'epiphenomena' of those few properties. That entails the rejection of most concepts. The task of reducing the rejected concepts to the accepted concepts becomes infinite, and in practice, you can never complete it. But it still leaves the question of how those few admitted properties must be defined. They too are concepts. For instance, if we decide to admit 'length' into our repertoire of concepts, how do we define length?

Again, the physicist's response is that we are never going to define the property. We will simply pick a measuring instrument that can measure the property. The property is in fact the measuring instrument. In short, to solve the problem with Platonism—i.e., how the concept is instantiated—you reject *all* concepts, and you discard the idea of instantiation itself. You end up with a world of objects, divided into two categories—standards of measurement, and the rest. Those standards are arbitrarily chosen in most cases, just for the convenience of converting the property into a number. For instance, if you say that length is 5 meters, the meter as a standard is arbitrarily chosen. You cannot say that it *has* the property of length. You can however say that it *is* the property of length. In short, you must convert all ideas into physical things, and whatever cannot be converted in this way must be rejected, with the hope that its description can be reduced to the output of the few chosen measuring standards.

When this reduction—called physicalism—is done, we lose most of the expressive power of language because objects can no longer be treated as *names* and *concepts*. We cannot refer to things, and we cannot express their properties in terms of concepts. Essentially, we cannot form any propositions. This now leads to Gödel's incompleteness because language can in fact use names and concepts, but when it is reduced to individual objects, contradictions can be created, as the categorical distinction between things, names, and concepts disappears. In short, the physicalist view of the world is provably incomplete, although it is logically consistent. To get completeness and consistency, we need to seek another approach.

The Semantic Tree

The notion that concepts can be reduced to physical properties also runs into difficulties when we speak of complex ideas such as a car. How do we measure or analyze the carness in an object to know if it can belong to the set of all cars? We might say that a car is a complex idea in turn built from other simpler ideas. For instance, we can deconstruct the idea of a car into the idea of a chassis, wheels, steering, headlights, seats, engine, axle, transmission, etc. But this deconstruction is itself not very helpful, because the deconstructed ideas are themselves still quite complex. So, we might further deconstruct each of them into even simpler ideas. For instance, we can deconstruct the idea of a wheel into something that is circular, is made up of elastic material, and has a rough surface to grip the road, etc. The problem, however, does not end here. We must further define what we mean by a circle, elasticity, roughness, grip, road, etc., and these attempts at reduction can go on potentially infinitely.

We generally suppose that this reduction of the idea of a car can eventually be completed to find a perfect definition of a car. Once such a project has been completed, we could then apply the definition of a car to decide if some object is a car or not. But this supposition is false. As you start to reduce the idea of a car to other simpler ideas, you will come across a peculiar problem—you must have a specific car as the standard of measurement for all cars. Remember that physicalist reduction works only by adopting standards. To apply this in the case of cars, you will have to define a specific car. For instance, is the car a 4-wheel drive or a 2-wheel drive? Does the car have leather seats or fabric seats? Does the car have a stereo system or not? How many rows of seats exist in the car? What type of storage is available in the car? What color should it be? What is the diameter of the car's wheels? Is the car stick-shift or automatic drive? What type of fuel does it use—petrol or diesel? What's the horsepower of the engine? And these are only high-level questions about the car. Each of these can further be refined into even more specific questions.

As we try to answer more and more of these questions, we find that we are beginning to describe a specific car: it may be the car that stands in my garage and which I think is the canonical car!

Once we realize that more and more accurate definitions of a car will potentially leave out many other things that might otherwise also be called cars, we will likely stop trying to refine the idea of a car. But what exactly is this point where we stop refining the idea of a car to a greater and greater level of detail? Should we just say that a car is something that has 4 wheels, a steering, and an engine? Or should we keep providing ever more details of a car? The problem is that too ambiguous a definition would permit even trucks and buses. Similarly, too refined a definition would leave out many types of cars. There is no point at which you can stop refining the idea of a car and be completely content that you have accurately defined a car. You can only assert that what you have is a provisional or tentative definition of a car, which can be made more abstract by omitting some details or made more concrete by adding even greater details.

It is not difficult to see that the attempt at refining a concept constructs an inverted hierarchical tree of differentiation. In this tree, abstract concepts are near the top while specific details are at the bottom. If we are trying to describe an object, and an approximate description suffices, then we can use concepts near the top or the middle of the tree. This description would not be *incorrect*, but it would be *incomplete*. That is, the approximate description would leave out some details about a specific object. As we add more and more details, we preclude some objects from that description and thereby define other objects more accurately. The definition of a specific object, therefore, comes at the *expense* of other objects. If we have completely described one specific object, then we would have completely excluded all other objects. At this point, the distinction between the Platonic world of ideas and the real world of things has been collapsed. That is, the complete description of an object is also a Platonic idea, but it can also be said to exist within this world.

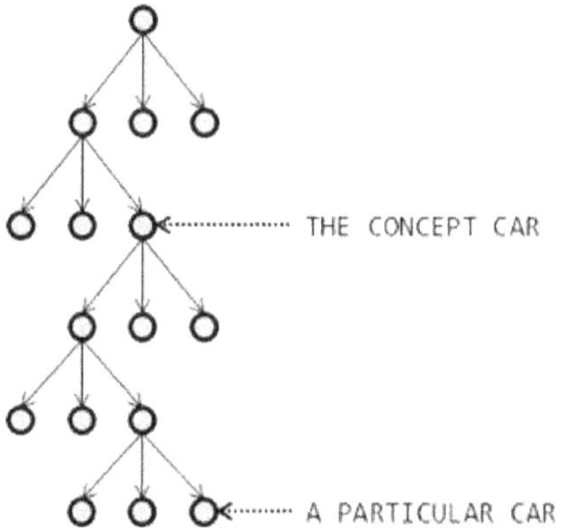

Figure-9 The Hierarchy of Concepts

Two things follow from here. First, the form of ideas and the forms of things cannot be different because that would make the application of ideas to this world impossible. For instance, if some ideas only existed in the Platonic world they could not be applied to objects and we could never, therefore, understand such ideas. Similarly, if some properties could not be conceptualized then they could not be in the Platonic world, and we could never use these properties in a physical theory of nature. The form of a thing must be the form of the idea if ideas are used to describe the world. Second, the separation between ideas and things exists only when we are speaking about abstract ideas. Through abstraction, we describe many things simultaneously, but at the expense of describing each thing incompletely. The point at which we describe a thing completely is also the point at which we describe only one thing. Therefore, the Platonic separation between ideas and things as two separate worlds is false. We see the separation only if we look at the top or the middle of the conceptual tree. At the bottom of the tree, ideas are in fact things—now the universal is no longer a set; it rather an individual object. Or we might say that the set has only one member—a specific object.

We saw in the previous section why starting with ideas and then using them to determine whether an object belongs to the set is the only viable scheme that avoids Gödel's incompleteness and the recursion problem. In this section, we now saw how objects are refinements of ideas because this refinement can be taken to a point that the idea describes one object. If we have constructed such a conceptual tree, then to determine if an object belongs to a set we only have to traverse upwards from the object or downwards from the concept. In fact, if we had a complete description of an object, we could also know all the sets it belongs to because the object's description would itself be the method of its construction by abstract sets.

The hierarchical construction is free from Gödel's incompleteness because the object, its name, and its meaning are all identical, although numbers would have to be defined as types rather than as quantities to avoid the contradictions in Gödel's proof. The proposition not-P can never be mapped to the number P in this scheme and the contradiction that leads to Gödel's proof cannot be constructed. It is also free from Turing's Halting problem because there are no loops in a tree. Any program constructed using a hierarchical division methodology would always be loop-free. The hierarchical construction is free from the Recursion Problem because the set comes logically prior to the object instantiated within that set. The object, therefore, depends on the set, but the set does not depend on objects. Finally, the scheme is free from the Platonic interaction problem between things and ideas because things are refinements of ideas. All things are also ideas, but all ideas may not be things. Even ideas that are not present as things are present *within* things as an incomplete description of that thing. Therefore, every idea is either directly a thing or it is indirectly present within a thing. The purported interaction between ideas and things is unnecessary.

The World as Symbols

The Cartesian mind-body divide separated the world of things from the world of ideas. Once we collapse this distinction through a hierarchical construction, the world of things is a world of *symbols*. All things are constructions from ideas and they are ideas. A complex idea includes a simple idea within it, and the complex ideas are therefore representations of simple ideas. Since all material objects are complex ideas (as they sit at the bottom of the conceptual hierarchy) they are also representations of ideas. As such, all things (except the root of the semantic hierarchical tree) are a symbol or representation of the next higher ideas on the semantic hierarchical tree. Every symbol in isolation appears as a thing. The same symbol, when examined within a hierarchy, is the representation of an idea. In the semantic tree, the higher-level node in a tree represents a collection.

When the symbol is produced from a set by elaborating the idea of that set using additional ideas, to know the symbol we must know the set from which it was elaborated. For instance, if we aim to describe a specific car, which has many more attributes than the generic notion of a car, we must understand the idea of car first. The notion of a car in this case is something from which all other cars are derived. Therefore, a good understanding of the individual car requires the understanding of all the other cars that are like it. And if we must invoke the set in an understanding of an object, then we cannot study the object in isolation. We must study it only in relation to the set. Note that in this case, the car is defined *a priori* as a type of meaning rather than as the collection of things. The specific car in question is also an instance of the meaning, although it embodies additional meanings over and beyond those included in the idea of a car.

In this view of nature, the universe does not begin in the smallest physical particles which are then aggregated to form complex things. The universe rather begins in simple (and therefore abstract) ideas which are then divided to produce complex ideas. The division of abstract ideas to create contingent ideas can employ the abstract ideas, quite like complex words are created from a smaller set of alphabets. The smallest sub-atomic particles in the universe are therefore the most complex ideas while everyday objects (like tables and chairs) are relatively simpler ideas. The universe as a whole—which is the idea of space—is the simplest idea, and this idea is divided over and over again to create all the locations in space. For this to be possible, the dimensions of space have to be viewed as elementary ideas which are combined to create all the individual locations in the universe. The universe is now an inverted semantic tree of ideas, which begins in elementary ideas and ends in the most complex ideas.

The fact that there is a limit to the smallest objects in the universe (indicated by Planck's constant in atomic theory) entails that there is a limit to the complexity in ideas. We cannot forever divide the universe into parts; there is a limit to this division, which is attained when the smallest sub-atomic particles have been created. Indirectly, the smallest particle and the universe as a whole present the conceptual limits to the most complex and the simplest ideas.

The semantic notion of complexity overturns our approach to reduction in nature. In the physical notion of complexity, the smallest parts of nature are more primitive because we believe that small is simple. Physical reductionism, therefore, begins with the smallest parts and tries to build larger things by aggregation. The aggregation gives the impression that the whole is reducible to parts, although physical theories are unable to carry out this reduction because the whole indeed has a logically prior existence. Since the whole is abstract, and the parts are contingent, the study of the whole makes the system under study seem indeterministic. This could be solved if the objects were symbols and were in turn produced from ideas.

In the semantic approach, the world is not things whose combinations are perceived by the mind as ideas. The world is ideas whose combinations produce things. In the Cartesian mind-body divide, both mind and matter are substances. In the semantic approach, both mind and body are ideas. There is no material substance, and there is no mental substance either. Rather, both mind and matter can be described in a single theory of ideas. The mind is a simpler idea relative to the meanings or other ideas that it produces. Like a complex idea can be produced from simple ones, thinking or thoughts can be created from the mind. The mind, therefore, does not have a special position in the pantheon of ideas; the mind is just another idea. It happens to be a relatively abstract idea as compared to the ideas which can be generated from the mind. But it is not necessarily the most abstract idea; the universe is the most abstract idea.

Similarly, the senses of observation and action are ideas, too. These ideas are less abstract relative to the idea of the mind, but more abstract relative to the external objects that they perceive.

All these abstract ideas can be detailed through material objects we can observe. For example, the idea of mind and senses will exist as detailed physical entities—e.g., in the brain. A neuroscientist who studies the brain's electrical activity can conclude from this that the mind and the senses are indeed in the brain and this conclusion would not be entirely false. However, the matter in the brain itself has to be treated semantically if the theory of senses and mind has to be complete. For instance, a neuroscientist can identify a certain region of the brain to be responsible for color perception. However, which specific neuron in the brain would fire to represent the color red or yellow cannot be predicted in a universal manner. In different brains, different neurons will fire for the same type of color perception. Similarly, the color perception region in the brain would not be exactly identical in all brains; the regions of color perception will vary in different brains. Likewise, the brain areas associated with other aspects of experience such as emotion, music, language, decision making, analytic thinking, or kinesthetic activities such as painting, swimming, or cycling would slightly vary in different brains.

The problem here is not that the senses and the mind are not represented in the brain. All aspects of our experiences can potentially be represented in the brain and the neuroscientist can also study them. The problem is only that if we treat the brain physically then we would be unable to *accurately* predict the part of the brain responsible for different types of experiences. The specific neuronal activity—e.g., that neurons A, B, and C represent the perception of red color—also cannot be predicted without treating the brain semantically. Neuroscience without semantics would be predictively incomplete, although it would make probabilistic predictions. As the brain architecture changes—for instance, as the neuroscientist studies brains in different species, or even in different individuals of the same species—the same experience would involve different parts of the brain, and different neuronal activities would be observed.

To increase the accuracy of predictions, the neuroscientist would have to study how the different parts of the brain are interconnected into wholes, which are then parts of larger wholes, etc. This will expand a type of perception into all types of perception, then expand the perception into the study of the entire body, and then the interaction of these parts and wholes with the external world. As we strive for more accuracy, more aspects of the body must be considered and woven into the neurological predictive theory. At each point, we will find that we have increased the accuracy of prediction, but the predictions are still inaccurate. The problem lies in the fact that all these aspects about the person are present in the brain as symbols of meanings but unless we study the brain as a symbolic representation of meanings, it is impossible to know which molecule, neuron, or electrical activity represents what experience.

The symbolic view also entails a radically different view of the inanimate material objects. Just as the brain can represent the qualitative experiences about the world, the external objects too must be symbols of the qualities that the brain attributes to the world. In other words, if the brain sees a red apple, then the redness and the appleness of the sight could potentially also exist in the external object. The brain and the apple are both physical objects. But if the brain can denote ideas then the external world too can be ideas.

This view has historically been highly problematic. In the early days of science, empiricist philosophers—such as Descartes—drew a distinction between primary and secondary properties. Primary properties include length, mass, speed, temperature, etc. while secondary properties include color, taste, smell, sound, touch, etc. Descartes viewed the separation between primary and secondary properties as essential to the development of science because it was obviously very hard to describe the external world if it comprised of qualities.

Descartes, however, also rested this divide between primary and secondary properties on the divide between matter and mind. One distinction followed from the other and it was impossible to claim the primary and secondary property distinction without committing to the mind-body divide. Critics of this distinction—such as Leibniz and Berkeley—argued that the idea that the world is primary properties, can never be known because we can only know the world through secondary properties. However, the distinction stuck and has been the bedrock of modern science. Over time, however, science has dissolved the distinction between mind and body by showing that the brain can encode the properties of the senses and the mind. It should therefore follow that the distinction between primary and secondary properties must be dissolved as well. But, if we commit to this dissolution, then we must describe the world as apples, chairs, and houses rather than mass, charge, force, fields, temperature, etc.[1]

The reduction of mind to matter is an advance in scientific reductionism. But its implications are inadequately understood. The implication is that if some material arrangement in the brain can denote color, smell, taste, or touch, then similar arrangements in the objects being observed must denote these properties as well. It is important to note that the chemical activity in the brain is not directly taste, touch, smell, or color; these arrangements are material *representations* of these perceptions. Therefore, it is not necessary for the apple to have the qualitative feel of redness or sweetness. The apple only needs to *represent* redness and sweetness like the brain represents these ideas during perception. To view the apple as a representation of ideas rather than as physical properties constitutes a remarkable shift in the way we think about material objects: we would have to describe these objects as symbols instead of things.

An ordinary example can perhaps better illuminate this way of thinking. Think of what happens when we read a book, such as a travelogue. The travelogue can be described as a collection of squiggles—shapes, sizes, etc. But, in addition, the words in the travelogue also denote meaning. Of course, the squiggles are not identical to the experience of meaning. However, they are representations of the experienced meanings. By reading a travelogue, we *know* about an author's experiences of travel, although we don't experience the travel itself.

The symbols in the book thus represent objective *information* about the traveler's experiences, although reading the book isn't the same as traveling itself. Of course, we could imagine those experiences, but our mental reconstruction of an author's descriptions of travel may differ from the experiences of the author, and certain things in the author's experience may never be reconstructed.

Current science can measure the height, weight, and speed of the travelogue, but it cannot measure the meanings in that travelogue. However, even if science were to measure the meanings, there would still be a difference between the reading of the description and the experience of traveling. A neuroscientist studies the brain like we read the travelogue. She can infer from the brain knowledge of what the brain's owner is experiencing, if the brain is described semantically. However, there would still be a difference between knowing someone's experiences and having those experiences. A semantic understanding of the brain will give insights into the person's mental state. However, the mental experience is not identical to the brain; the difference is between knowing about the travel and traveling.

The derivation of meaning from physical states is seen in the appreciation of art or music where artistically savvy people understand meanings while others do not. And yet, there are at least two ways in which we can view the perception of meaning. We might, for instance, say that the meaning of art and music resides in the observer's mind, but not in the musical and artistic works. Or, we might say that the meaning really exists in the work of art and music, although its perception depends on the observer's ability to decode the meaning.

Which of these positions is true? By committing to the former idea, we lose the ability to assert that some object is a book, music, or work of art because the meaning is only in the observer. In this view, there is no such thing as a work of art or music; it is only our perception that makes it so. In other words, objects have no meaning because meanings are created by the mind. But if artistic or musical objects do not encode aesthetics, then how can the brain encode those experiences, since the brain is also a material object? This problem is unsolvable except to say that all experience is an illusion. The notion, therefore, that music or art only exists in the mind leads to the conclusion that there is no mind and hence no art and music.

The symbolic view would instead state that meanings are objectively in the book or music. We cannot understand these meanings if we look at individual frequencies or squiggle shapes. We can, however, understand them if we view the frequencies or squiggles as representations of meaning, governed by some language. The words in the language are organized in a hierarchy, and the context of the description is a higher node in the hierarchy. Therefore, the meaning of the words cannot be understood without understanding the context. For instance, words such as 'force' and 'field' have a different meaning in a physics book than the meanings in common discourse.

The comprehension of meaning begins in the comprehension of the context before we comprehend the individual parts. We must know that we are reading a physics book before we can accurately interpret the words in it. Meanings are therefore not in the individual squiggles. Meanings are in the relations of these squiggles, to the higher-level semantic entity. Generally, the title and subtitle of the book, the name, and background of the author, and the description on the cover fix this context. This is meta-information about the book which helps the reader know the meanings of symbols in it.

The symbolic view of nature entails some dramatic shifts in science: (1) objects are not things; they are symbols, (2) the symbols represent the same types that we can potentially perceive and conceive, (3) the symbolic meaning arises from the relations between the symbols to a higher level (more abstract) symbol, (4) the meaning is hence fixed by the context as a whole, (5) for the context to have a meaning, it must again be a symbol, whose meaning is determined by the relation to other contexts, which reside within a larger context, (6) the nesting of symbols inside contexts, and then treating contexts as symbols within larger contexts leads to a hierarchy of meanings, (7) this hierarchy must terminate at some point in self-evident ideas, which can be called the *axioms* of the theory and of the world.

Hierarchical Space-Time

The scientific counterpart of the above philosophical view is that space and time in the universe must be described as closed and hierarchical domains rather than open and linear domains as in current physical theories. To illustrate, suppose we are trying to describe a specific type of rice as the ordered hierarchical tuple of attributes: {species, plants, grasses, rice, basmati}. Each such attribute represents a set, and if the universe were symbols of ideas, it would comprise closed hierarchical conceptual domains, such as those in the case of basmati rice. Each such domain would be defined through a distinction in a larger conceptual domain, and so forth, until we reach the most elementary ideas.

As we saw earlier, in a conceptual hierarchy, the name, concept, and thing are described identically. That is, we use the same words to describe names, concepts, and things. We cannot, therefore, call a grain of basmati rice as a grain of soya bean. The identical description of name, concept, and thing avoids the problem of Gödel's incompleteness, which arises from a contradiction between names, things, and concepts. If names, concepts, and things are described by identical words, then the contradiction between these categories will never arise even if we interpreted the name as a concept or a concept as a thing. If this grain of rice was a computer program, it would be loop-free since it has been constructed using a hierarchical tree and tree structures are loop-free. Such a program would always halt. The tree structure avoids the recursion problem as well, since the higher-level concept is defined before the member objects are defined. The hierarchical definition is, therefore, free of all logical problems.

Examples of hierarchical addressing are quite common in the everyday world. Two well-known examples include postal addresses and Internet addresses. A postal address is defined hierarchically using the name of the country, state, city, area, street, and building, with each successive entity nested inside the previous one. An Internet address is similarly described by dividing the Internet into subnets, using a dotted decimal notation such as 234.567.90.1, and using ordinary language hierarchical names such author.blog.company.com.

In current addressing schemes, however, there is a difference between an entity's name (the postal address or the Internet address), its conceptual meaning, and the entity's physical identity. For instance, the postal address itself may not indicate whether the building in question is used as a house, a school, an office, or a shop. By knowing the Internet address, we cannot always know if the computer given that name is a file server, a printer, a laptop, or a robot. Even knowing the domain name is often insufficient to know the purpose for which the individual or the institution uses the domain. It is not obvious, for instance, that www.google.com is a search engine, and companies develop 'branding' strategies to map their name to their functions. Likewise, a certain Mr. Porter may be a professional barber, and the name doesn't indicate his profession.

These differences generally work in the everyday world due to our ability to distinguish between names, concepts, and things. A name is not identical to the concept (and may sometimes be opposite to the concept), and the concept doesn't uniquely identify the thing. Since we do not equate names with concepts and with things in ordinary language, the use of language does not lead to confusion. However, for the separation between names, things, and concepts to work, there must also be mapping schemes that allow us to convert names to things and things to concepts. These mappings are provided by various techniques and procedures. For instance, the mapping between Internet addresses and Internet domain names is provided using a Domain Name Service (DNS) that converts a name such as author.blog.company.com into its Internet addresses. A postal address must similarly be mapped to a property through a legal process of registering the property with the government, obtaining a legally unique name, and then marking the property with that name. Mapping allows us to retain the differences between things, names, and concepts while allowing us to discover one using the other.

Time is similarly described hierarchically in the everyday world. For instance, we can call the current moment 1/1/2015 10:45:23, which nests seconds inside minutes, minutes inside hours, hours inside days, days inside months, months inside years, etc. This description of time is semantic, and it exists in conjunction with physical notions of time such as the total number of seconds elapsed since January 1, 1970, which is used in computers to measure time. The physical time in the computer is mapped to clock time using conversion schemes. These times may be mapped into a space-time evolution diagram for prediction of some physical phenomena in a theory.

Possibility vs. Existence vs. Truth

While the various branches of the semantic tree are created and destroyed, the root can never be created or destroyed. While the various branches of the tree exist sometimes and they may be true at times, the root must always be true. The truth of the branches and that of the root are therefore different. This difference pertains to the distinction between *proof* and *truth* in mathematics. All the branches of the semantic tree can always be—in principle—constructed. However, they are not always constructed. The potential to construct the branch at any time represents the fact that these branches are provable. However, the fact that they are only occasionally constructed represents the fact that all such provable things only occasionally exist. Furthermore, all the things that exist are not necessarily true, because even false beliefs and theories can also exist in nature.

Only the root of the tree is always provable, existent, and true, whereas the other branches are provable, although they may not be existent or when existent they may not be true. Many things exist in the universe, but they are not eternal, and they are not true. The root of the tree is the axiom from which realities are created at different instances of time. These realities were always possible, but not always real. Time, therefore, has an important role in converting possibilities into reality. The semantic tree is all the statements that can be produced from the language. The method by which each such statement is produced represents its *proof*. However, not all such provable statements are always true. The statements which can be proven but which presently do not exist can be called provable but non-existent statements. Furthermore, the statements that have been proven but are different from the nature of reality must be called false. The provable statements are the possibilities; time converts them into existents; some of these existents are true while the others are false.

The semantic view thus changes our approach to the question of truth; specifically, all that is possible does not necessarily exist, and all that exists is not necessarily true. Truth is the subset of existence and existence is the subset of possibility. The fundamental particles in nature are always possible. When they create propositions, something exists. Some of these existents are true. The unchanging root of this tree must exist for the duration of the universe. If the universe is created and destroyed, space-time is itself being created and destroyed—not just at Big Bang and Big Crunch, but at every moment of change. The unchanging root is however eternal as it exists as long as time exists, and it is unchanging as long as space exists.

The semantic view also creates some problems which don't exist in the physical view of nature. The key problem is that all meanings are produced from distinctions or oppositions. There is 'hot' only because there is 'cold,' 'bitter' only because there is 'sweet,' 'up' on because there is 'down,' etc. Different locations in space and time are therefore also semantically different. The root of the tree—and the origin of space-time—therefore must be defined as the state of the universe without distinctions from which all distinctions are produced. The state without distinctions is semantically unknowable in the conventional sense of oppositions, although it still exists. This unknowable state is in a sense 'nothing,' although this nothingness must be defined in a new, semantic rather than a physical sense.

Imagine that we were to count all propositions in the universe and label them with numbers. The elementary ideas would be labeled with small numbers and the complex ideas would be labeled with large numbers. Since the semantic universe contains opposite ideas (such as 'hot' and 'cold') the numbers denoting these ideas would also be positive and negative. The positive and negative numbers here should not be thought of as quantities; we must rather think of numbers themselves as types, such that a simple idea is a smaller number and a complex idea is a larger number. All objects that can be known in terms of such oppositions would be labeled by some positive or negative number. The number zero however cannot be described in terms of these positive or negative numbers. Zero represents the *origin* of the universe from which other opposite signed numbers can be created (zero is recreated when opposite sign numbers are collapsed and zero can recreate the number with opposite signs).

We saw earlier how the universe can be produced from a singularity if time divides this singularity into a particle and anti-particle pair. The particle and anti-particle pair will represent opposite meanings, because they exist in time with opposite directions. The singularity is without distinctions of space and time. It is the zero from which all other numbers are produced because of time, which creates opposite time directions and hence opposite meanings.

While the different positive and negative numbers can be created and destroyed by the effect of time, the number zero remains unchanged. It is, in a sense, the origin of all other numbers. And yet, even when all the numbers are destroyed, zero still exists. Zero can therefore represent the unchanging and fixed truth in the universe. It is that which remains absolute and unchanging. All other positive and negative numbers are defined in relation to zero. Zero is also the origin of space-time, when it is understood semantically. This origin is both physical and semantic because zero is a name, concept, and thing. It exists physically, it can be called the original object and it means the origin. Thus, the origin *in* space-time is also the origin *of* space-time. Nature is a space-time with a fixed origin, which is the singularity from which the universe springs. This singularity, however, is not the infinite concentration of matter. It is rather the most abstract and non-dual idea—the idea of nothingness. Nothingness does not entail non-existence. It only entails the non-existence of all *dual* things which must be described in mutual oppositions.

While the zero is always true (because it exists prior to the creation of a distinguished space-time), everything else which differs from zero is relatively false. All such falsities can be proven; however, they will not always exist. The smaller numbers—which are 'closer' to zero—would be truer than the numbers which are 'farther' away from zero, because they would exist more often. Obviously, this means that the simple ideas are closer to the truth and the complex ideas are not, even though all such ideas are provable. The bigger the number and the more complex the semantic object, the farther it must be from origin and truth—i.e., it will exist less frequently.

Of course, the simplest idea, in this case, is *nothingness.* All other ideas spring from this elementary idea. However, this nothingness is not emptiness, non-existence, or non-being. Equating nothingness with non-existence assumes a physical notion of nothingness. Semantically, nothingness is the idea from which all other ideas spring forth. This nothingness can be called the number zero. The number is neither empty, nor non-existent, nor non-being. However, it is different from everything else we call existent, meaningful, and being. If all other existents are created by distinctions or duality, this nothingness is the state of non-duality from which duality can spring.

Absolute vs. Relative Space-Time

In a linear and open space-time, the mapping between names, concepts, and things is arbitrary. For instance, in Newton's physics, any particle (thing) can be at any coordinate location in space-time (name). The ability to map any object to any location number in space-time is also called *coordinate transformations* by which we retain the particles but change their names. Similarly, any location in space-time (name) can have any physical property such as mass (concept). In the previous chapter, I identified this ability as the root cause of various kinds of indeterminism in science where a theory predicts various possible matter distributions but does not identify a specific matter distribution. For instance, the gravitational theory does not predict which mass would be at which space-time location; given some total matter and energy, there are many equivalent ways to distribute matter and energy over space-time events[2].

Coordinate transforms (CT) and matter redistributions (MR) are two standard ways in which scientific theories change the mapping between names, things, and concepts. Indeed, as we saw previously, Gödel constructed the proof of incompleteness by mapping a proposition not-P (concept) to a number P (name) and then interpreted the name as the concept (since the distinction between names and concepts cannot be retained in mathematics) creating a contradiction. CT and MR are possible in an open and linear space-time, and this leads to the incompleteness of all number systems. It also leads to the problem of mapping vocabularies across the three worlds of observation, reality, and mathematics, as seen in the previous section.

The existence of CT and MR in linear and open space-times creates the impression that a coordinate frame or matter redistribution is a *choice* in a scientific theory. All such choices are equivalent in relativistic theories and they cannot, therefore, determine which of these choices is real. The MR choice represents the possibility that the universe will have different events while the CT choice represents the possibility that the same events can be described differently. The universe is indeterministic in the former case and a deterministic universe is incommunicable in the latter. For the universe to be deterministic and communicable, CT and MR should be forbidden.

Of course, since CT and MR are possibilities permitted in relativistic theories—which are empirically confirmed at various levels—forbidding CT and MR would seem to entail a violation of the relativistic principle, and thereby appear to empirically falsify the theory. However, I will later discuss why a universe in which CT and MR are forbidden can still permit these types of alternatives without breaking semantic principles. Additional scientific concepts are required to forbid CT and MR and yet allow them; these alternatives—I will show—correspond to a specific choice being the 'right' choice in the universe which, however, does not preclude other 'wrong' choices. The 'right' and 'wrong' choices are not identical in terms of their consequences although they are equally allowed. The differences between these choices can form the basis of a moral theory, provided some additional physical concepts have been inducted.

Prima facie we know that a universe where CT and MR are allowed cannot be free from Gödel's incompleteness, Turing's Halting Problem, and the problem of recursion. Therefore, if the universe has to hold meanings, then forbidding CT and MR is necessary. This view has to be subsequently enhanced to address the other problem of explaining why some arbitrary choices are permitted in nature, and how the various kinds of choices could be distinguished. In later chapters I will discuss how the relativistic principle—namely that all CT and MR choices are *equivalent*—is false, although, in principle, all such choices are *permitted*. Two additional physical constructs will help us distinguish between the 'right' and 'wrong' choices.

A hierarchical space-time structure forbids CT and MR. The words used to describe a name, concept, and thing are identical. This space-time is absolute and not relative. While any open and linear space-time will permit CT and MR transforms, thereby mapping any name to any concept to any thing, a hierarchical space-time permits only one view of nature. This view of nature represents what we might call *reality*[3]. It includes material objects—animate and inanimate—but also material representations of experience. Indeed, since both mind and matter are described using the same language, science can decode the observer's subjective states from the study of the material brain. The subjective states would not be identical to the brain, but they would be described using identical words. However, the words used in such descriptions would not be the words of current science. They would rather be the words of subjective experience. Thus, for instance, we will not say that the brain has some electrons which have mass and charge, and which experience natural forces. We would instead say that the brain has symbols of meaning and the meaning of the symbol is that it describes the subjective experience. The brain would be the mind's travelogue; the travelogue is written in space-time and can therefore be observed by other subjects. The ability to express the subjective experiences in space-time allows the subject to communicate with other subjects, but this does not equate the subjective experience to the communicated symbols.

In the absolute space-time, material objects are identical to space-time. There aren't two distinct types of entities—material objects and space-time. Rather, material objects are space-time. This fact is like the relativistic notion of matter being identical to the space-time structure, although space-time, in this case, is absolute rather than relative. Furthermore, since the space-time locations are representations of meanings, all locations are conceptually distinct. A distinct location denotes the name by which the object is called. That name is also the meaning of the object. And the meaning is also the physical constitution of the object. Therefore, as we change names of locations, we also change the types of objects. Objects at two different locations must be different types of objects. Accordingly, space and time are not homogeneous and isotropic. Rather, all locations in space and time are distinct and it is not possible to substitute one location or direction of space or time with another.

The Conservation Law Problem

The idea of space-time homogeneity and isotropicity underlies all material property conservation laws. For instance, the homogeneity of space is responsible for momentum conservation; the homogeneity of time is responsible for energy conservation; the isotropicity of space is responsible for angular momentum conservation. Therefore, a space-time structure that breaks the homogeneity and isotropicity of space-time would also break conservation laws.

The conservation laws stem out of a notion of change that depends on *motion*. In conservation, matter or energy is never created or destroyed; it is only transformed from one form to another. In the case of semantics, however, information can be created and destroyed. The creation, destruction, and conservation of meanings are therefore three distinct types of phenomena. If material objects are symbols of semantic information, then these objects can be created and destroyed by adding and removing information. The construction of the hierarchical tree itself implies that more concrete ideas are produced from abstract ideas by adding information. Similarly, it is conceivable that information can be removed thereby collapsing the hierarchy. Since objects are identical to the space-time structure, the addition or removal of information pertains to the creation or destruction of the space-time structure. However, it is not necessary that a space-time structure that creates and destroys information would also violate the material property conservation laws.

Let us examine this idea in the context of energy conservation. Energy conservation is based on the homogeneity of linear time. In the hierarchical space-time, however, time is cyclic, which causes the production and destruction of information. If we look at opposite points on a time cycle, the information is always conserved. But if we look at the immediately next or prior moments in time information is created or destroyed (depending on which part of the cycle we look at). Accordingly, the conservation laws would appear to be violated to various extents at various points in time, *if* we look at a single time-cycle. However, we don't have to look at a single time cycle. In a semantic space-time, time instances are constructed through semantic distinctions. The origin of the universe is also the origin of time; time (and by this, I mean the phenomenal experience of passing) did not exist prior to the origin of the universe. The origin of time therefore must be looked at in a semantic way as the creation of a distinction.

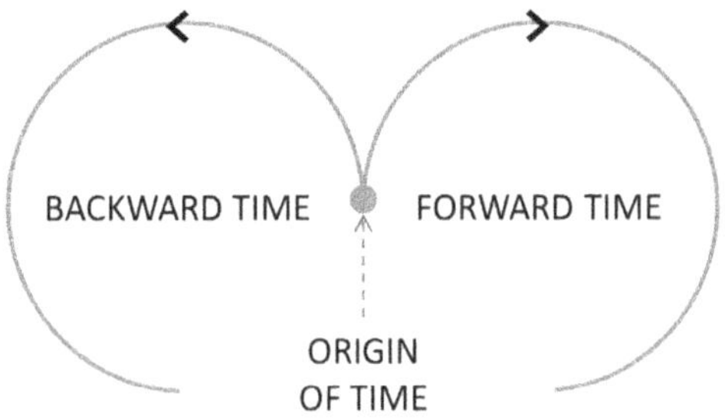

Figure-10 The Origin of Time

In the case of time, this would occur as the creation of opposite time cycles, which can be called the forward and the backward cycles. These cycles will create and destroy information but at opposite instances. For instance, the instant at which the forward cycle is creating information, the backward cycle would be destroying information. This production and destruction of information can be correlated to understand energy conservation. For instance, when the forward cycle gains information, there can be a corresponding loss of information in the backward cycle. The opposite cycles would appear to emit and absorb information at opposite points in time; the time at which the forward cycle absorbs information would be the time at which the backward cycle would emit information. The emission and absorption event cannot, therefore, be random. Rather, these events must be synchronized by the *type* of time in different cycles, and by the fact that the time cycle was originally created in a synchronized manner from a state of the universe where time did not exist.

The production of time from a state of timelessness is problematic when time only moves in one direction, but it is unproblematic when a timeless state produces two opposite time directions. Semantically, meanings are always defined through oppositions, or not at all. There cannot be hot without cold, sweet without bitter, or up without down. Likewise, there cannot be forward time without backward time or information creation without information destruction. If these two cycles are synchronized, then the creation and destruction of information would not violate the conservation laws of information. Therefore, even when time is not linear and local energy conservation is not true, the universe can still conserve energy. This view of conservation comes at the cost of time isotropy; that is, all time directions are not identical. Rather, the direction of time has a real influence on whether energy is being emitted or absorbed.

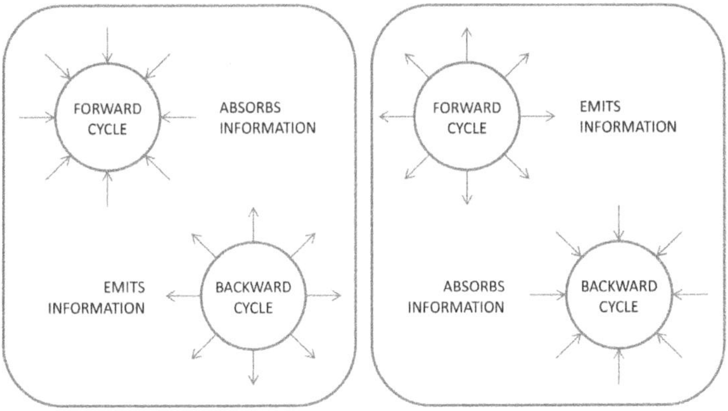

Figure-11 The Conservation of Information

The above description considered only a pair of opposite time instances, which is not necessary. A hierarchical time can also contain several nested time cycles, each being produced from a higher time state with the highest state of time being that of timelessness. Each of these cycles will exchange information with each other. The information absorbed in a higher cycle would be distributed as information addition in the lower cycles, and the information emitted in the higher cycle would be distributed as information reduction in lower cycles. When higher and lower time cycles are in opposite phases of their respective development, more energy would be absorbed and emitted in some systems relative to the other systems.

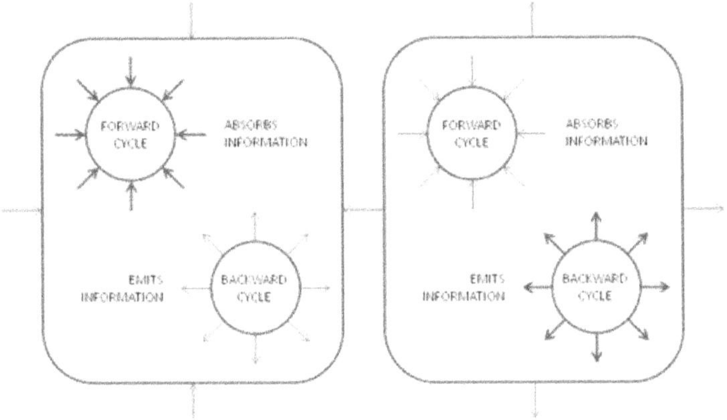

Figure-12 The Behavior of Cycles in Opposite Phases

Similar reasoning can be used for the conservation of other properties such as momentum and angular momentum. Different regions of space, in this case, would represent semantically opposite meanings. Now, it is possible to speak about two kinds of information emission and absorption: the emitted or absorbed meanings can also be opposite. For instance, if some object emits the meaning 'hot,' this would be synchronized with another object that absorbs the meaning 'hot.' Likewise, if an object emits the meaning 'cold,' it would be synchronized with another object that absorbs the meaning 'cold.' The emission and absorption of the meaning 'cold' can be viewed as the inverse of the absorption and emission of the meaning 'hot.' However, for two such objects to exchange meanings, they must be synchronized *a priori*. This synchronization can be achieved if two locations in space are created from emptiness, like two child nodes of a parent node are created by dividing the parent node by a distinction. This emptiness is not the emptiness of space in classical physics where the location always exists although it does not contain a material object. The semantic emptiness is a lack of information, and since this information is identical to the structure of space-time, lack of information also implies that such a location itself does not exist.

In the hierarchical space-time, therefore, all spatial locations and time instances are not *a priori* real; space and time are not continuous and infinitely extended containers. Rather, locations and instances in this space-time are constructed by the addition of information and they can be destroyed by removing information.

The Nature of Time

The universe in this view can begin from a singularity, which is then divided into opposites thereby creating diversity. The division of the singularity into opposites requires zero total energy or information. However, an explanation of whether such a point splits or remains undivided is needed. Similarly, the explanation of when the distinction between multiple space-time locations is collapsed does not violate any conservation laws, but it requires an explanation. While nodes in the semantic tree can represent names, concepts, and things, there is a need to explain how this tree is created and collapsed. This explanation can be attributed to time if time is viewed as the cause of the cyclic pattern of creating and destroying information.

The universe, in this case, would begin from a singularity of an elementary idea, which represents the origin of space. Time, now, would exist in an undivided state where it neither produces nor destroys nor conserves information. The universe, in this state, does not exist in the conventional sense of an extended space and changing time, because both space and time are undivided. This is the singularity from which the universe can spring provided either space or time was to split. If time splits, thereby producing two opposite cycles, then it can act on the undivided space and split it as well. The split in the space would produce semantically opposite locations; we can call them particle and anti-particle. Now, time acts on each of the newly created particles and anti-particles and splits them further thereby creating further particles and anti particles, each of which becomes a different location in the space-time hierarchy. Each successive particle and anti-particle have their own time since time did not exist prior to the split. The split creates time at a new location, and therefore time begins from its origin. Each split creates a new space-time *origin* from which further such splits occur. When the second split occurs, there are two time cycles: the first time is at its second time tick while the second time is at the first time tick.

In the beginning, therefore, the universe would rapidly expand absorbing information in the productive time cycle branch and creating an anti-particle branch from where the information is emitted. The absorption creates more particles and the emission creates more anti-particles. The semantic tree would therefore rapidly grow, thereby increasing its depth. This expansion in the particle branch would be at the expense of the expansion in the anti-particle branch and this process continues until the time cycle reverses

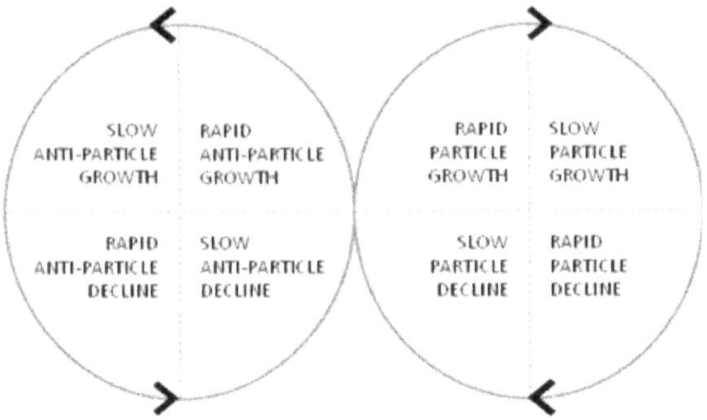

Figure-13 Opposite Time Cycle Behaviors

When the time cycle reverses, the source and sink of information are reversed. Now the particle branch will lose information and the anti-particle will gain information. The gain of particle information in the anti-particle branch is the gain of anti-particle information in the particle branch. Particles and anti-particles are the same information with a time phase inversion. The anti-particle, therefore, looks like the particle, although moving in the opposite direction in time. As the particle branch loses information, the semantic tree begins to collapse. Similarly, as the anti-particle branch gains information, that branch begins to collapse. The build-out and collapse of the tree completes a cycle of information evolution. Particles and anti-particles annihilate each other and create each other. Since these two branches are correlated, they expand and collapse simultaneously.

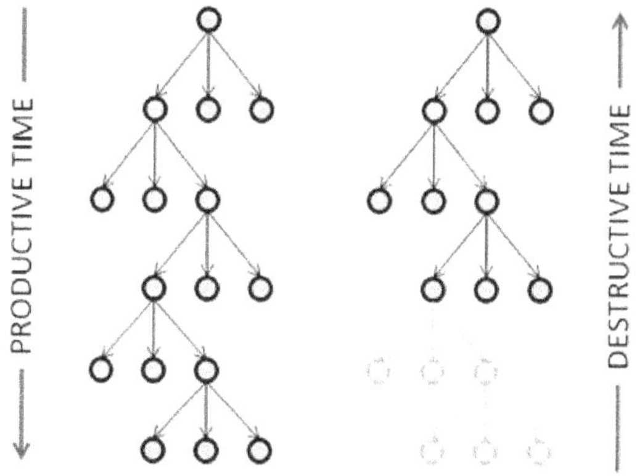

Figure-14 Productive and Destructive Times

The total number of particles and anti-particles in the universe is always equal but they are distributed differently. The particle and anti-particle branches, therefore, look different because the first node in each branch is a particle vs. an anti-particle. All successive elaborations of these two branches also result in different meanings. For instance, if the roots of two branches are 'hot' vs. 'cold,' the elaborations of these branches would also be developments of the ideas of 'hot' vs. 'cold.' The higher nodes in the branch, therefore, have a greater degree of importance in determining the properties of the branch than the nodes that are lower in the branch. As the higher node evolves, all downstream nodes also evolve in concert.

Therefore, the evolution of the universe can be described in an abstract manner by observing the state of the higher nodes. To know the state of the universe, it is not necessary to know the state of all the nodes in the branch. Rather, a qualitatively accurate account of the universe can be obtained simply by observing the states of the higher nodes in the hierarchy. The lower nodes in the tree represent a detailed elaboration of the states of the higher nodes. We might say that the higher nodes are 'controlling' nodes which define and determine the behavior of the lower-level 'controlled' nodes since the controlled nodes are created by detailing the controlling nodes.

The causality in this universe is not in particle properties and changes are not effected due to forces emanating from such particles.

This is because particles themselves can be produced and destroyed. If the causality is in the particles, then the production and destruction of such particles requires another causal agency. If, however, such a causal agency exists then another particle-based causality is unnecessary. Therefore, it is appropriate to say that the causality in the hierarchical space-time view is in the time. More accurately, the causality is in the cyclic nature of time which causes the universe to expand and collapse cyclically. Once time has been created by a split from a state of timelessness into opposite time cycles, the rest of the universal evolution (observations) can be described deterministically.

The Underdetermined Tree

The notion of hierarchical space and time raises some basic issues about the relation between abstract and contingent. The issue is that just as the abstract underdetermines the contingent, the contingent also underdetermines the abstract. The former underdetermination implies that a node higher up in the tree can have many child nodes. Conversely, the latter underdetermination implies that a node lower in the tree can have many parent nodes. In short, the top-down semantic tree construction that I have employed thus far may not always be correct; semantic trees could also be created bottoms-up.

Let's illustrate this with an example. Suppose that we are trying to instantiate the idea of 'tools' into different objects. We might instantiate this idea into the ideas of a hammer, screwdriver, saw, wrench, etc. Each of these ideas can also be instantiated into specific object instances of hammer, screwdriver, saw, wrench, etc., which have some material properties like shape, size, color, weight, etc. So far it seems that the idea of a hammer is an instance of the tool and a specific hammer is an instance of the idea of a hammer. However, once we create a physical object such as a hammer, we can view this object also as an instance of other ideas such as paperweight, weapon, etc. As I drew the hierarchical tree model so far, a parent node could have several child nodes, but a child node always had a single parent. Now it seems that the same object can have multiple parents as well (if we still view concepts as parents). Indeed, most physical theories of meanings start from rooting their trees in the objects rather than in abstract ideas. They claim that there are only things in nature and ideas—such as tools or weapons—are merely *interpretations* of the object. The interpretations are in some sense not as real as the object itself and are thus relegated to the mind.

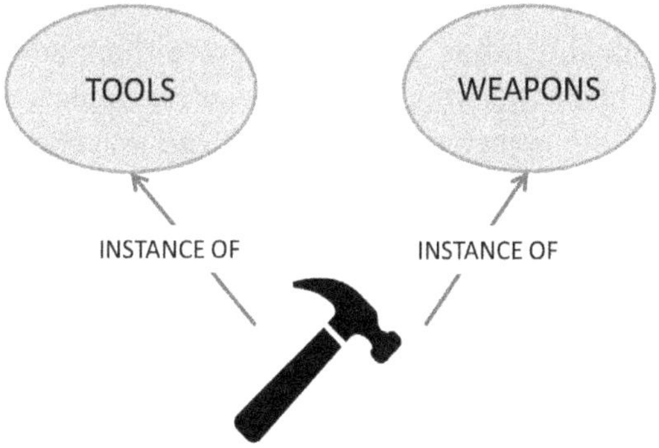

Figure-15 An Object Can Instantiate Many Ideas

We have earlier seen the consequences of trying to derive ideas from things—namely, Gödel's incompleteness, Turing's Halting Problem, and recursion—so this derivation is not logically sound. However, such a derivation seems imminently possible. How do we reconcile the fact that many ideas can be derived from the same thing with the fact that contradictions can be avoided only when we derive things from ideas? The solution to this problem is contextuality. The same thing becomes an instance of a tool or weapon in different contexts. In these contexts, it would also be called a tool vs. a weapon. The physical state of the object alone, therefore, does not determine its meaning. Rather, we must look at the object in relation to its context, or other objects in the context. This fact does not per se invalidate the semantic hierarchical view, although it nuances it somewhat. Now, the same thing is a tool or a weapon in different contexts, and its meaning cannot be known without the context.

An everyday intuitive fact in this regard is that the meaning of a word in language is given only in the context of a sentence. The same word 'address' can represent both a noun and a verb, and only the context determines which figure of speech is actually meant.

However, we continue to distinguish between the universal and the contextual meanings. For example, even if we contextually use the hammer as a paperweight, we will say that we are using a hammer as a paperweight. The hammer in this case is the universal meaning and the paperweight is a contextual meaning. The thing in question has been designed to be a hammer; it has the form of a hammer, and it emulates the ideal hammer closely. The same thing however doesn't have the form of a paperweight and doesn't resemble a paperweight. By the form of the object, we can discern the universal idea a thing represents. However, by the contextual use of that object—in relation to other objects—we can understand its relational meaning.

Contextuality arises because there are two distinct factors involved: (1) the object, and (2) the role in which it is used. For example, I have the bodily form of a man, but in different contexts, I can play the role of a father, husband, citizen, employee, etc. In the same way, material objects can have the form of a hammer, but they can be used as a paperweight. This fact confuses people endlessly because we seem to have a contradiction between universal and relational types of meanings. Since there is a form of the paperweight, but the hammer doesn't have it, by calling the hammer a paperweight, we are creating a contradiction in definitions. The only way to resolve this contradiction is to say that universal and contextual meanings are different categories of meaning. If something is not being used, and we try to discern its meaning just by its form—i.e., independent of the relations to other objects—then we can call it a hammer. But this designation is only a potentiality or possibility. It must be converted into a reality through use. Therefore, if you are an empiricist, you can say that if something is used as a paperweight, then it is a paperweight. If, however, you are rationalist you can say that the object by itself has a form that defines its functionality or ideal types of use.

Factually, there is no contradiction in these two cases, *if* we distinguish between two categories of meaning—universal and contextual. The conflict arises if we think that meaning is only of one type—either universal or contextual. To reconcile the paradox that a parent node in a tree can have many child nodes, and each child node can have many parents (which creates loops), we must say that every child node has only one parent, however, there is more than one kind of tree. When a hammer is designated as a paperweight, we are talking about the contextual hierarchy of relations between things. This is also hierarchical because it arises from contexts, which create *roles* for different things; a smaller role can be embedded in a higher role. When the same thing is designated as a hammer, we are talking about the universal conceptual hierarchy in which the form of the object has been produced from an abstract idea through detailing.

We can also say that a paperweight is the *function* by which we call a hammer in some context, and that function represents a role something plays in relation to other things. But that name is not the true *concept* to be applied to that thing; the concept is given by the *structure* or the form of the object. Both structures and functions are meanings, but one is contextual and the other is universal. In short, the universal notion of a hammer cannot be universally applied. It just indicates the form of the thing, its design, or the structure. But it doesn't forbid someone from using the thing differently. That use constitutes the role or the function to which it has been put to.

Now once we have made a distinction between universal and relational types of meaning, it is much easier to draw a distinction between the universal and the individual. This distinction is easily seen in physical theories where an object's properties are the universals while the object is the individual. For instance, a particle can have many different masses, and the same mass can be present on different particles. Similarly, the concept 'hammer' is the universal, and there can be many identical instances of the concept hammer.

This leads us to three distinct categories, arising from two distinctions—the first between the universal and the relational, and the second from the distinction between the universal and the individual. The fact is that all these three categories are combined in all situations, but they are three different ways of looking at the same thing. For instance, consider the handle of a hammer. It has the universal form of a handle, so it is conceptually a handle. It is also one of the many handles corresponding to different hammers, so it is an individual. And it plays the role or function of a handle in relation to the head of the hammer, so it is also relationally a handle. This is, however, a coincidental case in which the universal, relational, and individual are identical. In other contexts, we distinguish between the concept of hammer and the individual hammer, besides the distinction between the form of a hammer and the use it is put to.

The problem of underdetermination means that we must think of three kinds of trees—relational, universal, and individual. Each of these trees combines in all cases, so everything is an individual, to which we can apply a universal concept based on its structure or form, and everything is playing some role in relation to other things. So, the three kinds of trees or hierarchies represent three ways of designating and classifying each thing, but each of the classification methods can be applied to everything. In that sense, you cannot see separate instances of the three categories; we must rather see these categories in each individual phenomenon. Alternatively, we can say that the three categories are the 'reality' that precede the phenomena, and the phenomena are created by combining these realities.

The crucial point is however this: an object's conceptual interpretation can be changed after the object has been created, although the object cannot be created without some conceptual notion. In that sense, it is wrong to assume that concepts are afterthoughts that come subsequent to the creation of an object. It is more appropriate to say that every object is created with some initial idea, although once the object has been created, its conceptual interpretation can be changed. The creation of objects therefore always follows the top-down semantic hierarchy. However, the same physical entity could also have been created by a different conceptual hierarchy. This physical entity would, however, have a different *description*. For instance, we would call the same physical thing a tool or a weapon.

Two Metaphysical Questions

There are still two fundamentally unanswered questions. First, why are space and time hierarchical and closed? Or why are space and time semantic? As a contrast, for instance, time could also be open and linear. Second, what causes the timelessness to split into opposite time cycles? Once time has split, the rest of the universe can be constructed and destructed deterministically. However, the split in time is itself not predictable just from a state of timelessness.

I don't believe these two questions can be answered from within science. What science can describe is the structure of space-time, which can be empirically confirmed via observations. However, why the universe has a mathematical structure would be a metaphysical question that cannot be addressed within this theory. In any scientific theory, there is always a set of axioms. Hierarchical space-time is the assumption or axiom here. This theory arises from a need to solve the problem of meaning in mathematics—as we saw earlier, the problem is seen as Gödel's incompleteness, Turing's Halting Problem, and the problem of recursion in set theory. These problems can be solved by using a hierarchical space-time structure. To the extent that these problems exist in mathematics and can be stated logically, they are woven into the nature of logic and numbers. The hierarchical space-time theory only describes how these problems can be addressed but cannot answer the question of why the problems arise in the first place. For instance, someone can ask: Why are logic and numbers this way? Why could they not have been different?

These questions, however, are not pointless. For instance, if logic and numbers were different, could this space-time view have been avoided? I think this is a valid question, and it could be answered if we were able to construct a different kind of logic and number theory. I will later describe how this metaphysical question could be understood if there were other kinds of logic and number systems. For instance, different logical systems could be constructed by dropping either or both of the logical principles of non-contradiction and mutual exclusion. These logical systems would produce space-time structures that may not be hierarchical and/or may not be bounded in space and cyclical in time. We can, therefore, in principle, conceive of at least four different logic and number systems that use or don't use non-contradiction and mutual-exclusion. The present universe uses mutual-exclusion and non-contradiction, but there could be other 'universes' that have different logic and number systems. The metaphysical question now is: Why are we in a universe which obeys the logic with mutual-exclusion and non-contradiction?

For instance, in the present world, we can speak about the choice between vanilla and chocolate ice cream, which are mutually exclusive choices. Having eaten that ice cream, the ice cream would not be left behind. But it is possible to imagine a logical system in which you can eat both vanilla and chocolate ice creams at once and the ice cream would be left behind even after it has been eaten. Such a universe would arise by dropping the principle of mutual-exclusion (the exclusive choice between vanilla and chocolate ice cream) and non-contradiction (if the ice cream has been eaten, then it could not be left behind). While such logical systems are imaginable, the reasoning in each such logical system would be quite different. The metaphysical question, therefore, is: Why are we in a specific type of logical system rather than other logical systems? Clearly, it would be nice to be in a world in which we can eat both vanilla and chocolate ice creams at once and still have the ice cream left untouched!

This question is metaphysical because if indeed there are other logical systems, and universes governed by those logical systems exist, the choice of the universe would clearly be a choice of logic. Such a choice cannot be made within the system governed by a type of logic, but it is possible to consider how such choices could be made. The choice of logic is different from the choices that differentiate between different propositions made within a given type of logic. The choice of logic and the choice of a given proposition in that logic are therefore different kinds of choices. The former is a metaphysical question and the latter is a physical or a scientific question..

4

Science and Semantics

It would be possible to describe absolutely everything scientifically, but it would make no sense. It would be without meaning, as if you described a Beethoven symphony as a variation of wave pressure.

— *Albert Einstein*

Information in Nature

The previous chapter described a theory of nature that was rationalistic to the hilt. It made no assumptions about the real world that we live in, nor was its explicitly stated goal to solve any problems of empirical science. It only aimed to find a theoretical model that is computable (avoids Turing's Halting Problem), complete (avoids Gödel's incompleteness), and finite (avoids the recursion problem). The hierarchical semantic tree structure is such a theoretical model. This chapter aims to apply this theoretical model to currently unsolved problems in physics. The model already solves the greatest outstanding foundational problems in logic, mathematics, and computing. Can such a model be a useful description of nature as well?

Recall our previous discussion on the three problems of indeterminism in science: (1) physical theories are predictively incomplete; they don't describe all that is empirically observable, (2) even when the theory is predictively complete, it incompletely describes matter distributions; the theory many permit many distributions but does not pick a specific one, and (3) even if a physical theory completely describes matter distribution, it still does not solve the problem of which observer experiences which part of the distribution. This chapter addresses the first and second types of indeterminism while the next chapter addresses the third form of indeterminism. This chapter aims to apply the semantic hierarchical model to show how the model can form a computable, complete, and finite theory of the events in the universe, and the selection of a matter distribution over these events. This doesn't answer the question of which observer is in which part of the universe, which the next chapter will discuss.

The essential insight necessary for the subsequent discussion in this chapter is that material objects are concretized from the abstract. An abstract object is the possibility of being many different things; for instance, the idea of a car can be instantiated into many different cars. Therefore, if the system exists in an abstract state, it can be viewed as the possibility of being in many alternative states. This is often viewed as the problem of probability, uncertainty, or randomness in science. But it can also be viewed as the possibility that the system is in fact an abstract idea. This abstract idea can be concretized in many possible ways by adding information into it. Like a specific car can be produced by refining the abstract idea of a car to greater and greater detail, similarly, a definite object can be produced from an indefinite object by adding semantic information to it.

The uncertainty, indeterminism, probability, or randomness of science can therefore also be viewed as the idea that matter is the potential for information. As more information is added, the object becomes definite. As information is removed, the system becomes indefinite. There is a limit to the maximum amount of information that can potentially be added to a system, and this limit appears as the quantum of action limit which restricts the smallest possible space and time extensions. The gap between a completely empty and a completely full system is therefore given by the total amount of information that can be added to that system. However, whether the system has reached its state of maximal information or not, it can be described accurately to the extent that it has information. For instance, if some object only carries abstract information about a car, then its evolution would represent the evolution of the idea of a car. If the object represents some more concrete information—such as that about BMW cars—then its evolution would represent the evolution of the design of BMW cars.

Only when the design of the car has been sufficiently concretized to produce an actual car, would the evolution of the object represent the motion of that specific type of car.

Therefore, we cannot describe every material system in terms of motion, but we can model every system in terms of information evolution. A system that represents an abstract concept and can hold more information will not deterministically behave like the motion of a thing. But it will deterministically behave as the evolution of the abstract idea. To describe such a system, we would have to know the idea that the system encodes. To decode these ideas, we must see the parts of the system as symbols of meanings. We also must understand the *order* of these symbols, since the same symbols ordered in a different way would produce a different meaning. The combination of words and order produces a complete proposition, which is also a complete description of the system that encodes the proposition. If the system has been accurately described, its evolution can also be accurately predicted. If a system is inaccurately known, its evolution would still be predicted to the extent of its descriptive accuracy.

The essence of the matter distribution problem is that physical theories cannot predict the actual space-time structure of matter. Physical theories begin in some energy which is an abstract concept. The ways in which this energy can be distributed represent the ways in which the abstract concept can be concretized. The total amount of energy is like a bottle of ink which can be spread on paper to produce many different books. Each book is produced from the ink by applying a specific space-time structure to the ink. Each such space-time structure produces a different meaning in the book. After the ink has been spread on paper, the physical properties of the book (e.g., its total mass) cannot help us ascertain the meaning in the book. Rather, we have to look at the spreading pattern as an act of encoding meanings. The meaning can therefore be objective, and it is represented in the book as a specific space-time distribution structure.

Now, some people may argue that the meaning in the book is not objective because to decode this meaning we need to know the language in which the book is written. If we do not know the language, then we cannot decode the meaning. This is indeed true. However, this is where the hierarchical space-time structure is helpful. The language used to encode the meaning is given in the relation between the book and its environment—the readers, writers, publishers, and the domain for which the book is written. These form the context in which the book must be read, interpreted, and understood. We can therefore completely know the meaning in the book if we know the language in which it is written. However, we cannot know the language by just looking inside the book. Rather, we must also look at the context of the book. The relations in the environment and the content in the book, therefore, play complementary roles. The former defines the language of encoding and the latter, the content.

It is hence not possible to simply look at the book in isolation and know its meaning. We have to rather look at the complete semantic hierarchy to know the meanings encoded in the book. Since the hierarchy involves greater parts of the universe described in more and more abstract ways, the book's meaning can be known, but not without knowing its relation to the rest of the universe.

With this conceptual background, I will begin discussing the problems of physical theories and what they mean. A better understanding of the problem also helps us better understand the solution. I will begin with the problem of indeterminism in statistical mechanics, followed by a discussion of probabilities in quantum theory, and then describe the matter distribution uncertainty in general relativity. Finally, I will sketch the path on which these three theories can be reconciled. The reconciliation of quantum mechanics and general relativity is often cited as the biggest outstanding problem of physics. In their current forms, both theories are linear, and if the resulting combined theory is also linear, it would still leave a gaping hole in our understanding of non-linearity as described by statistical mechanics. Therefore, while statistical mechanics is generally not considered a fundamental theory of nature, I include its reconciliation with quantum theory and general relativity as the route to a complete physical description of nature.

Statistical Mechanics and Information

We earlier saw how statistical mechanics posits the existence of *a priori* real particles, and the distribution of energy in the ensemble is the distribution of total energy into the momentum of each particle. Classically, such a system must always be in a deterministic state, even if we don't know that state. Since a classical system is always linear and reversible, such a deterministic theory could not explain why a thermal system is non-linear and irreversible. To address this problem, statistical mechanics posits that the system is simultaneously in multiple different states. This is of course predictively correct, but it leads to the problem of understanding how a classical system—which is always supposed to be in a definite state—could be indefinite.

The solution to this problem is possible if we can discard the idea that there is a fixed set of particles whose state is uncertain. Rather, we can say that the total number of particles in an ensemble is equal to the number of particles whose state is certain. The particles are thus not *a priori* real. Rather particles are *created* when the system becomes more certain. How does that happen? We can say that a system becomes certain if *information* is added to it. The uncertainty in a system is not randomness in the system. It is rather the total amount of information that could be added to a system before the system runs out of its information-storing capacity. A system into which more information cannot be added has a net-zero uncertainty. Such a system can be likened to a classically definite object. Since the addition of information and the reduction of uncertainty create ever more particles, a classically definite system must have the maximum number of particles that can be packed in a given region.

To adopt this viewpoint, we will have to discard the idea that nature comprises of *a priori* real particles. The particles would rather be *created* only when some information is added to the ensemble to convert the energy in the ensemble into a definite kind of material distribution. Therefore, the particles are not *a priori* real. They are rather byproducts of adding information into an ensemble.

The point of inflection in statistical mechanics is that a classically definite state implies a definite energy in a particle but a definite energy in the ensemble does not imply classically definite states. If we suppose that the number of particles remains the same even if the system state is uncertain, then the system must exist in multiple such states simultaneously. This problem, however, does not arise if the total number of particles equals the definiteness in state. As information is added, the state becomes more definite and the total number of particles (which must exist in definite states) increases.

Classical physics studied individual particles, which have both definite state and hence definite energy. A canonical example of such a particle is a billiard ball which has both a definite energy and a definite state. The successes of classical physics led us to believe that all matter exists as particles in a definite state. Essentially, the universe was modeled as a collection of very small billiard balls. But this is inconsistent with thermal phenomena and we cannot claim the reality in the ensemble is classical. We would still like to retain classical intuitions for billiard balls. So, how do we reconcile the ideas that particles in an ensemble are not in a definite state but the particle as a billiard ball is in a definite state? This is possible if we acknowledge that particles are created by adding information into an ensemble. The billiard ball is a particle created by adding information. However, in an ensemble, much of the information is missing. Therefore, the ensemble must have much fewer particles in a definite state. This means that the ensemble has a much larger potential to create new particles by adding information as compared to the billiard ball. These definite particles would be created only when the ensemble has been encoded with its maximum possible information capacity.

The informational viewpoint explains why an ordered system becomes disordered when it performs 'work.' The 'work' in this case is the act of passing information from the source to the destination. In this interaction, the transfer of information decreases the order in the source and increases the order in the destination. Since order and disorder represent the number of particles, this viewpoint implies that some particles *disappear* in the source system and *appear* in the destination system. However, the exchange of particles does not involve classical motion because in thermal phenomena there may be physical barriers that prevent the motion of particles in a classical sense. The transfer of energy however represents a transfer of information and since particles are created when information is added, the transfer of information denotes a transfer of particles. This notion of material transfer requires a new physical theory.

In this theory, the primary entity being transferred is information, which is currently described as energy. A system with some information exists as a concept with some level of definiteness; for instance, it can encode the idea of a car. When information is extracted from this system, the system becomes less definite and will now encode more abstract information. For instance, the ensemble would now encode the idea of a vehicle, rather than a car. The reduction in definiteness in the system state means that there must be fewer particles. These particles encode more abstract information, which cannot be exchanged with the environment because the environment may already have that information. For instance, we cannot transfer the idea of a vehicle to an object which is already a car. The reason is that the idea of a car includes the idea of a vehicle. We can transfer abstract information between systems only when these systems live on different branches of the semantic tree and the idea being transferred is not already part of the receiving object. An idea cannot be transferred if it already exists in the receiving system.

Therefore, as more energy is extracted from a system, it becomes harder to extract any further energy. This is unintuitive in classical physics where a moving object X can collide with a static object Y and transfer all its energy to Y. After the collision, X would be static, and Y would be moving. In this interaction, all the energy in X has been transferred into Y. Thermal systems seem incapable of doing so. The thermal system can never transfer all its energy. To explain why some energy is not transferrable we must say that that energy does not exist as motion but as information. When information is concretized, it appears as physical things and their motion. However, when the information is removed, it exists as abstract ideas and cannot be transferred as would be the case if it were motion. To correctly describe matter, we should now describe motion as information exchange rather than information exchange as motion. The specific change in the case of thermal systems is that all of motion can be transferred but the information cannot all be transferred.

Unlike classical physics, where the work is performed by a transfer of energy, now the work is performed by the transfer of information. Therefore, the capacity for work in a system is not its total energy, but the total information that can be transferred. While all of the motion in a system can be transferred, all of the information cannot be. The information system does not behave classically because of this difference. The transfer of information depends on the object with which the information is being exchanged. The more informationally similar the two objects, the less information would they exchange. Conversely, two objects that are informationally dissimilar would exchange significantly more information. Eventually, the information exchange stops when the most abstract type of information that a system can transfer is already present in the receiving system.

A disordered system also has energy, but it does not have transferable information and thus its capacity for work is reduced. The fact that work cannot be done unless information can be exchanged implies that work is done by information and not by energy. This is a revision of the idea of work in classical physics where work is done by the transfer of energy and the order of the system transferring this energy plays no role in the amount of possible work. The problems of statistical mechanics indicate that measuring information as energy is like measuring a book on a weighing scale. Lots of books may weigh the same, but they would not be equally useful to us in terms of information. Essentially, when we reduce information to energy, we lose the *type* differences between the semantic particles. Some type differences represent information that can be transferred, while other types denote information that is like the environment and therefore cannot be exchanged. This also means that if we were to bring a system conceptually different from the source of the latent energy, the system would be able to exchange the energy with it.

The problem, therefore, isn't that the energy is not inherently extractable. The problem is that we are not using the correct procedure to extract the energy. Two conceptually different systems can exchange information so long as they are conceptually different. The information exchange ends when the receiving system already contains all the information that the sender must provide. There may still be a lot of information in the sender, but it would not be exchanged because the receiver already has everything the sender can provide. To extract this information, a new kind of receiver must be brought into the interaction which can extract the information. This fact is clearly observed in the use of a thermometer which can measure that the system has heat, even though it cannot perform work.

The inability in the sender to transfer information to a receiver—when the receiver already has the information—cannot be understood in a physical theory. For instance, one computer can keep sending the same type of information to another computer and this transfer of (physical) information cannot be prevented. The receiver can mark this redundant information as 'spam' which is then discarded. But there is no way for the receiver to prevent the sender from sending the spam. In fact, the spammer can find ways to obviate the physical rules that the receiver uses to detect spam. For instance, the spammer could send the same information from a different address and the receiver would not know. Only in a semantic theory can the presence of some information in the receiver prevent the sender from transmitting that information. The inability to send information is a semantic effect, but that effect is visible within matter.

When Claude Shannon formulated communication theory, he used probabilities to describe the *expectation* of some symbols. The idea was that the sender should not send what is already expected at the receiver. Sending what the receiver already expects (and can therefore predict) is a waste of the communication channel. Ideally, therefore, the sender only sends what the receiver doesn't expect. But there is no way in Shannon's theory to *prevent* the sending of information that the receiver expects. A sender may send the same information and the information would be transmitted, received, and discarded. In a semantic communication system, however, it is possible to prevent the transmission of redundant information. There is a sense in which the *expectation* of the receiver is correlated with the *prediction* of the sender and the sender will not transmit what the receiver already knows. Only new ideas would be transmitted.

The perceived non-linearity of the thermal system is a byproduct of the correlation between senders and receivers. These systems are by no means non-linear. However, they are correlated, which allows unique information to be transmitted but the non-unique information to be held back. Ideally, a complete physical theory of nature would have to predict this sender-receiver correlation. If quantum theory were a complete theory of nature, it would predict this kind of correlation, but it does not. This is because quantum theory still treats the senders and receivers physically. The information being sent out is still treated as a quantum of energy (called a photon) but this photon does not represent a semantic *type*. A quantum system—according to quantum theory—thus can keep transmitting information to another quantum system, producing the same kind of prediction that was earlier true in classical physics: i.e., a system can completely transfer all its energy to another system. Current quantum theory violates the basic inability in a system to transmit information beyond a certain point (if the receiver already has the information), and theories of 'quantum thermodynamics' have to be separately formulated to explain the observed non-linearity. This I consider as a flaw in current quantum theory, which can be rectified when the theory treats the sent and received information as meanings.

The hierarchical space-time theory described previously explains and predicts the observed lack of transmission because in this theory the sender and receiver systems are correlated objects produced by splitting an abstract object into contingent objects. The transmitter in this case sends particles (or anti-particles) and the receiver receives these particles (or anti-particles). However, these acts of sending and receiving are not arbitrary. That is, the sender does not send the information and lets the receiver figure out if the information is actually useful. Rather, the sender sends only useful information. If the information is not useful, it cannot be sent.

The emission and absorption of quantum particles are not arbitrary. Rather, quantum systems are correlated in a way that thermodynamics requires although current quantum theory does not yet predict or explain. This is further profoundly related to the nature of light as current quantum theory describes it. Light, in the current theory, is emitted as photons that 'travel' at the speed of light to eventually impinge upon some quantum object which absorbs this light. In principle, therefore, the sender and the receiver of this photon have not *a priori agreed* to exchange information. Rather, the sender is just emitting information and the receiver just happens to be on the path of that information. This is a classical picture of communication as it involves the idea that light 'moves' in space-time like other material objects and it can collide with an arbitrary object. In a quantum theory compatible with thermodynamics, the photon would not be emitted unless the photon carries a unique type of information that is currently absent in the receiver. In other words, quantum communication will not exchange redundant information.

Accordingly, the light we receive from the sun is not just the outcome of a nuclear reaction that happens independently of our receiving it. Rather, the nuclear reaction occurs because a specific object has to receive that information. In a sense, the sun is not just "pushing" out light. Rather, the receiver is also "pulling" in light. Unless the sender and the receiver are correlated, and the communication carries some unique information missing in the receiver, the information cannot be sent. The hierarchical space-time view predicts this, but current quantum theory does not. To the extent that quantum theory is incompatible with thermodynamics—the former is linear, and the latter is non-linear—the hierarchical space-time view can be seen as an advance over current quantum theory. But this advance also involves discarding many ideas that current quantum theory carries. Specifically, quantum objects must be viewed as symbols of information not just lumps of energy, mass, or charge.

Current statistical mechanics is a byproduct of the incorrect classical assumption that the world is individuated into *a priori* real particles. We suppose that each particle must be in a definite state, although we cannot know the state. The idea, therefore, that there are real individual particles is a theoretical and metaphysical assumption. The assumption is consistent with classical physics, but it is inconsistent with observation. In the informational picture, the particles do not exist until information is added. Someone might object: we are able to observe the atoms in the ensemble by doing diffraction experiments. How can we suppose that the thermal system does not have all these particles? The answer is that the diffraction experiment adds information to the system. By probing the system using atomic information, the information is added into the system and the outcome is a byproduct of the information that was added in the experiment. This is further related to the problem of measurement interaction in quantum theory as I will shortly discuss. However, the key point here is that to observe microscopic parts of an ensemble, information must be added to divide the ensemble into microscopic parts that can be observed. The observed outcome of such an experiment is a byproduct of the act of adding information. The classical idea therefore that there are indeed real particles is incorrect.

So long as particles can be added to an ensemble, there is room to add information in the ensemble. These additions will incrementally fix the uncertainty in the state by packing more information. A collection of material particles, therefore, is not always in an uncertain state[1]. Rather, this uncertainty is a byproduct of a shortfall in information in a system. In classical physics, each particle is already in a definite state and further information cannot be added and this corresponds to the state of maximal information in an ensemble.

Quantum Theory and Information

There are several issues in quantum theory that can benefit from a semantic understanding. First, the most well-known problem of probabilities or the inability to predict the next event is a complex issue, as we have seen previously. In the ATM analogy that I discussed earlier, there are several users (detectors) simultaneously drawing cash (quantum objects) but we only measure the presence or absence (a click on the detector) of the receipt of a currency, rather than the currency denomination. The order in which different users receive these events depends on the ATM's internal logic, which is unknown in current theory. The ATM's internal logic issues currency denominations rather than paper tokens, so if we don't bring the denominations into the description, the theory cannot be completed. That in turn requires us to treat quantum objects as symbols of meaning.

Second, we know from quantum entanglement problems that quantum objects are not independent particles. Rather, they are defined collectively as part of an ensemble; so, the ensemble must be invoked as a new kind of quantum object, which is then partitioned into individual objects depending on the measurement setup. The only way to understand this fact is to think of the ensemble as some meaning, which is then *represented* via individual symbols, quite like a total amount of money can be divided into currency denominations. Each denomination is related to the other denominations because they are together meant to dispense some total amount of cash. While we can observe these token notes as objects, we cannot understand them as independent particles; they are part of a bigger whole, which means that the whole must be conceptualized ahead of the parts. This in turn requires us to treat the system *hierarchically*—the whole is the higher node in the hierarchy and the parts are lower nodes.

Third, each quantum has complementary properties—e.g., position and momentum. This can be understood as two kinds of meanings—universal and contextual. The position representation gives us what the symbol means—universally. The momentum representation tells us what the symbol means—contextually. These two representations are complementary in the sense that they are both present but neither determines the other. They are actually existing in two distinct 'spaces'—the first is the space of universals and the second is the space of relations. The space of relations defines the *role* or *function* of the particle in relation to some other particle, which is why we call it *contextual* meaning. The universal space, however, defines the meaning in the symbol independent of contexts.

Fourth, the ability to select an eigenfunction basis based on the experiment can be understood if we say that the experimental setup alters the *language* in which the meaning is expressed. This language defines the symbols or the vocabulary in which the meaning is encoded. Then, during the actual measurement, the order of observed events represents the order of symbols that describe the quantum system. The quantum system is its description; the ensemble has energy because some information was encoded in it. The observed objects are the symbols of information in the ensemble.

Fifth, the uncertainty about position and momentum arises because in classical physics, we thought of particles as infinitesimal points. The fact that quantum objects are extended in space and vibrate can be used to treat such objects as symbols. The vibration in the quantum is like a word or phoneme—i.e., it denotes meanings. In the hierarchical space-time, the periodicity of the wave is the period of the cyclic time and the extension of the wave is the sense in which this particle is a different type of object than the other objects. Recent experiments have shown that the uncertainty principle can be violated by making the quantum state more certain. This is an outcome of the fact that all quanta are not equally uncertain. Rather, some quanta—which are lower in the hierarchy—have greater certainty relative to those at the top of the hierarchy[2]. Therefore, as information is added, an abstract concept is concretized and the new quantum (representing the concretized concept) thus has lesser uncertainty. But the quantum will never be a point particle because then it would be possible to pack an infinite amount of information in a finite amount of space. Hence, if the uncertainty is viewed *classically* as the finite extension of the quantum, then this is indeed a feature of reality. However, if the uncertainty is viewed as the indeterminism of a *quantum* state, then it is false. Thus, physical uncertainty cannot be overcome but information uncertainty can. Even the quantum that represents an abstract concept has a definite quantum state, although this state is classically uncertain. By adding more information, we can construct another quantum state which is equally certain as a quantum state, but more certain classically. Quantum and classical certainties and uncertainties thus must be seen differently.

Sixth, anti-particles are another perplexing feature of quantum theory. The paradox concerning anti-particles is that quantum theory predicts an equal number of particles and anti-particles although measurements find that the particles are in overwhelming majority. Why does the universe have more particles than anti-particles? In the semantic hierarchy, there are equally many particles and anti-particles. However, an anti-particle is a particle moving in negative time. For instance, a positron moving from left to right can be interpreted as an electron moving from right to left. The fact that we don't observe the anti-particles can be attributed to the fact that our part of the universe has a net positive direction of time, given by the fact that the top of the branch has a specific time direction in which the past moves to the present while in the negative time the present would move into the past. The problem is not that there aren't enough anti-particles in the universe. The problem is that we interpret the anti-particles moving in negative time as particles moving in positive time. This problem cannot be solved in the physical view of nature because negative time cannot be given an observational interpretation. In the semantic view, anti-particles represent the semantic opposites. For instance, if the particle denotes 'hot' then the anti-particle denotes 'cold.' When 'hot' moves from left to right, 'cold' moves from right to left. The existence of anti-particles becomes easier to comprehend in semantic time where the quantum spin can be seen as the representation of the opposite parity in time (clockwise vs. anti-clockwise). Quantum spin has no classical counterpart because all directions in time are identical in classical physics. Spin is relevant in quantum theory because it describes symbols that can have opposite meanings. An opposite spin particle is, therefore, an opposite concept, but it is also in negative time. The positive and negative spins can therefore be understood as time directions.

Seventh, the arrival of quanta must be predicted; but how do we predict? In the semantic space-time structure, a quantum state preparation represents the constructive part of a time cycle while the quantum observation represents the destructive part of the time cycle. That is, information is encoded during state preparation while it is decoded during observation. As I discussed in the previous section, thermodynamics requires that energy transfers should be allowed only if the information exchanged in that transfer is novel. Therefore, the repeated arrival of quantum objects is not the repetition of identical information because the quantum arrival cannot be predicted. In fact, based on the above thermodynamic principle, we can conclude that the inability to predict the order of quantum events is due to the fact that the order is non-repeating. If the order has a natural self-repeating pattern, then the transmission would stop[3].

We could now ask: if the sequence of quanta represents unique information which cannot be predicted based on the prior quantum arrival, then how can a scientific theory predict this arrival? The answer is that the prediction can be made in a hierarchical space-time view because the order of quantum arrival is the manner in which the constructive time cycle at the detector is paired with the destructive time cycle at the source. The destructive time cycle unpacks the information that was encoded during state preparation by the constructive time cycle. It is due to the correlation between constructive and destructive time cycles that quantum event order can be predicted. Essentially, the order of quantum arrival must be a function of two things—(a) the information originally encoded in the source, and (b) the manner in which the sink is correlated to this source.

The final aspect of quantum theory that I would like to consider here concerns the finite speed of light. Following Einstein's relativity theory, the constant speed of light is treated as a law of nature and is not given a quantum theoretic explanation. Why, for instance, should light have a constant speed? The notion of speed was unproblematic in classical physics, but it is problematic in quantum theory because space and time are not infinitely divisible and the idea of motion is itself problematic. Therefore, if light actually 'goes' from point A to B, it must hop from point to point. But if it hops from point to point, then for the object moving towards this hopping photon there are fewer locations to hop to (the destination is moving towards the photon). But if that were indeed the case, then the speed of light measured by the moving object would be different; the moving object would detect that the moving photon is moving at a somewhat faster speed. While the photon is viewed as a quantum object, its constant speed has never been understood or explained within quantum theory.

Photons are units of information, but they are not traveling in space. The transfer of energy is necessary to maintain energy conservation but that—in the hierarchical space-time view—is already achieved by having correlated objects with time in mutually opposite directions. In such correlated objects, information is naturally produced or destroyed, and this change happens to be correlated to opposite changes in the correlated objects. Therefore, whether or not the correlated object is moving has no bearing on the time taken to absorb new information. Since the information source and sink are independently producing and destroying information, the time taken in production or destruction is unrelated to the motion of the source or the sink. In fact, we call them source and sink only because they are time correlated in the production and destruction of information, not because information is physically transferred between them.

However, this still doesn't explain why it would take more time for information being received from afar, relative to the information being received from nearby. There are two ways to understand this problem—one semantic and the other physical. Let us begin with the semantic understanding. In the semantic view, far and near have a very precise definition: each location has a definite meaning. Therefore, the meaning being transferred from afar is a different kind of meaning than the one coming from close by. The greater the difference in meaning, the more time it takes for the information to be absorbed. The absorption and emission of information in this case should be viewed semantically as a *transformation*. The greater the change, the more time it takes to accomplish it. The photon coming from afar, therefore, takes a longer time to be absorbed because it brings information that is different from the state of the object receiving it. By contrast, the photon received from nearby brings information that is not so different, and hence the transformation is completed quickly. The speed of light is therefore a function of the time taken to perform a certain amount of semantic change. The speed of light is constant as this time is independent of the other state changes going on in the source or the sink of the information.

Now, let's look at the same problem physically. What we consider the physical distance between things is unreal in the semantic view. Proximity to things is an outcome of their interaction; objects interacting strongly will appear to be closer than objects interacting weakly. Therefore, what we consider a large distance is a weak interaction. Conversely, what we consider a short distance is a strong interaction. Strongly interacting objects—i.e., those that seem to be closer to each other—will transfer the information quicker. Conversely, the objects that are weakly interacting—i.e., those that seem to be farther from each other—will transfer information slowly.

So, whether we look at the problem semantically or physically, the time taken to traverse the distance changes, although the understanding of distance changes. A clarification must, however, be made on what we mean by the 'object'. It is not the physical properties by which we detect the presence of a thing. Those properties are the universals. What we mean by an 'object' here is the *individual* that instantiates the *universal*. We have earlier referred to this individual as a semantic coordinate system, which refers to the axioms and theories possessed by an observer. The strength of interaction—and by that we mean if the objects are interacting strongly or weakly—is to be defined in relation to these coordinate reference frames. They are not moving because the theories and assumptions are not changing. This is very similar to relativity in which the theory remains the same even when the object seems to move in a physical sense. Therefore, even if we see that the object is changing its physical position, the position of the individual remains unchanged, and hence the strength of their interaction is also unchanged. As a result, the time taken by light to reach an object is given by this unchanging distance. When we perform an experiment, we see that the speed is constant. It's not because the speed of light is a 'law' of nature that remains unchanged in all physical reference frames. It is rather that those objects are themselves not moving, although they seem to physically move.

The transfer of light is quantum communication in which the source and the destination are locked, and the information is sent from one object to another, rather than one location to another. Current quantum theory treats this quantum scheme classically and then overcomes its problems by postulating a constant speed of light as a law of nature. In the semantic scheme, light has no speed because it never travels. But light is information, which takes a finite amount of time to be removed and added, and that time depends on the novelty of the information and the strength of interaction between the objects. Intuitively we know that grasping a radically different idea takes a longer time as compared to an idea that we are approximately familiar with. An idea that we are completely aware of, takes zero time, and therefore it is never transferred. Intuitively, we also know that if we are deeply interested in a subject, we can learn it faster, which corresponds to a strong interaction between objects.

In that specific sense, instantaneous communication can never occur in a material system not because light has a finite speed but because to communicate there must be an information difference and instantaneous communication implies a zero difference. Einstein's relativity is correct in postulating the impossibility of instantaneous communication, but it is false in attributing this problem to a finite speed of light, because light never moves. The rate at which information is emitted or absorbed is a function of how fast time 'moves' forward, which can be understood as the duration elapsed in completing a time cycle. This fact is obvious even in physical information processing where the time taken to process information is a function of the clock speed of a computer processor; the greater the clock speed, the faster is the information processing rate. The constant speed of light is therefore not a property of the motion of the photon; it is rather a property of the structure of space-time. In general relativity, too, the speed of light appears in the metric (distance) definition between two points in space-time, and therefore it is viewed as a property of the space-time structure. A quantum explanation of this property is essential to unify quantum and relativity theories.

General Relativity and Information

General relativity posits the equivalence of all reference frames, which I will dispute in the next chapter offering a theory of how different reference frames are possible but not equivalent. The equivalence of reference frames also entails that many matter distributions are possible since we cannot distinguish between the effects of gravity and inertia (caused by acceleration). Here, however, I will discuss two even more fundamental problems which are that the theory begins in the idea that there is an *a priori* set of events in the universe and that the theory involves singularity, both of which violate quantum theory. If the goal of a theory is to predict what happens in the universe (i.e., events) then beginning with events and then retrofitting them with a matter distribution doesn't predict the events. Similarly, the fact that general relativity allows an infinite amount of matter to be packed in an infinitesimal space-time contradicts the quantum principle that all fermions must be in a unique state, which in turn requires finitely extended eigenfunctions in space-time.

General relativity inherits the indeterminism of events from Newton's theory, which could predict the state of the universe only if the initial conditions were defined. How the universe came to be in an initial state was never answerable. Newton's theory is deterministic if the number of particles and their initial state are fixed. Newton's theory is also reversible in time, so if the state at any moment is defined, and the number of particles does not change, then the system is deterministic. The theory becomes indeterministic if the initial state is not deterministic or if the number of particles in the system is not fixed. Of course, the theory is indeterministic in the initial state; in fact, it requires us to presume an initial state quite like Newton's physics. Furthermore, even if an initial state were given, the theory is also indeterministic in the total number of particles. One reason for this is the possibility for particle splitting and combining which we earlier saw in classical physics. However, even aside from these classical problems, there are additional reasons for particles not remaining conserved when quantum effects are applied to gravity.

When quantum effects are applied to gravity, it is expected that in addition to the positive mass of gravitational particles, there must also be anti-particles with a negative mass. Unlike the positive mass particles which are attracted, a pair of negative and positive mass particles would be repelled. A pair of negative mass particles would still be attracted like a pair of positive mass particles. While positive mass has a positive energy, the negative mass will have a negative energy. This means that a pair of positive and negative mass particles can be produced from zero energy. Classically, a particle with a positive mass could split into two or more particles, and the theory could not predict such outcomes, since both splitting and non-splitting are consistent with the theory. However, quantum mechanically, a particle and anti-particle pair can be created from zero energy, making the problem worse. Now, we cannot know the number of particles as particle and anti-particle pairs can be created and annihilated.

Despite its many problems, there is a semblance of sanity in quantum theory because the energy is always positive—even when quantum theory predicts the existence of anti-particles—because the mass is always positive. But this is true only because quantum theory doesn't yet describe gravity. When quantum and relativity theories are integrated, there will be anti-particles of mass and the theory will predict the emergence of positive and negative masses from zero energy. The theory will now be indeterministic because the total energy in the universe would be zero, although there are many ways to divide this zero into positive and negative masses. As the total number of particles changes with positive-negative pair creation, the space-time structure would change as well. Since positive and negative masses will repel each other, these particles will fling to opposite points in space. These parts of the universe can never communicate or annihilate, and the universe can only keep expanding forever. Since the particle production cannot be predicted, the evolution of the universe becomes indeterministic. There is now a need to control the production of particle and anti-particle pairs to have predictability, but there is no way to control the production of such pairs.

The semantic space-time view solves this problem by postulating that the production of particle and anti-particle pairs is determined by the cyclic structure of time. This structure ensures that the universe will not keep expanding forever. Rather, the production and annihilation of matter and anti-matter pairs follows a cycle making the universe itself a process of cyclic expansion and collapse.

There is ample discussion in the academic literature today on the indeterminism arising in general relativity due to various forms of singularity that the theory appears to predict. Black holes and the Big Bang are examples of such singularities, but there are several other types of singularities well-known in general relativity today. These predictions clearly violate quantum principles because a singularity entails an infinite amount of information packed into an infinitesimal region of space-time which is forbidden by quantum theory. Unless, therefore, quantum theory is proven wrong in some fundamental way—e.g., denying that matter is finitely divisible—these discussions of indeterminism are temporary features of current relativity. These issues would disappear when a theory of quantum gravity is formed, although that theory will create new issues.

Part of the reason that current cosmological theories operate without quantum gravity is that quantum theory is viewed only as a theory of the atomic world and not of the macroscopic world. Therefore, cosmologists suppose that quantum theory is important only in the early stages of the Big Bang when matter is concentrated in an infinitesimal space-time. The discussion of black holes is seen as being extremely relevant to the question of the origin of the universe since the singularity at the time of the Big Bang can be understood if the singularity in the black hole were to be understood. The dominant view in cosmology is that about 10^{-43} seconds after the Big Bang gravity takes over and the evolution of the universe can be described quite well without the quantum effects. I believe this view is mistaken because quantum theory is important even to macroscopic phenomena. The classical description of the macroscopic world is false, although the reason for this is not very apparent today; the semantic view explicates the reason: matter holds meanings, which are not just relevant to atomic objects but even more so to macroscopic objects. Therefore, the notion that the conflict between quantum and relativity theories is important only in the very early stage of the universe or only within exotic objects such as black holes is flawed.

Therefore, a deep discussion of the nature of singularities arising from a gravitational theory without quantum effects is, in my opinion, rather misplaced. The divide between quantum and relativity theories hinges on the former describing possibilities *in* space-time while the latter describing matter as the structure *of* space-time. A truly quantum gravitational theory would reduce quantum phenomena to the structure of space-time as well. This space-time, however, cannot be open and linear, because positive and negative masses will fly away to opposite parts of the space making the universe indeterministic. Only when time is cyclic will the universe's evolution be deterministic, and we can accurately predict when the positive and negative masses will be produced and annihilated.

An even more profound revision to gravity and relativity is entailed by thermodynamics. In current gravitational theory, a massive object exerts a gravitational force on every other object in the universe. A theory of quantum gravity consistent with thermodynamics will instead entail that the mass of an object does not exert a gravitational force on all objects in the universe. Rather, the interacting objects must be correlated to exchange unique information. By semantically understanding the gravitational information, it is possible to stop the effect of gravity, quite like information transfer from a thermodynamic system can be halted when the information is no longer unique. When gravity is quantized, the force exerted by mass would be effected due to the exchange of some force particles (these are sometimes called *gravitons*) and these particles must obey the conditions of thermodynamic information exchange. That limitation entails that the effect of gravity can be stopped when the informational difference between the source and destination is over. Since the objects exchange information only with those objects with which they are quantum correlated, the classical notion that gravity acts uniformly on every object in the universe would now be false.

It would now be more accurate to state that gravity acts only between objects that are exchanging a certain type of information that we currently call gravity. This exchange further depends on the correlation between objects, and only the correlated objects will be affected by gravity. Furthermore, the extent of gravitational pull depends on the number of objects to which that object is correlated. In a sense, the gravitational force cannot be uniform; it must rather be viewed as another kind of informational transfer, which must be preceded by the source and the sink of information being correlated. A semantic view of quantum gravity would also entail that the gravitational effect from different cosmic objects in the universe cannot be identical. Rather, these objects emit and absorb different kinds of information which causes objects to alter their states differently. Accordingly, the trajectories around such objects cannot be described assuming a uniform gravitational force in the universe.

Semantic Quantum Gravity

The biggest issues constraining the unification of quantum and relativity theories are three-fold: (1) matter is viewed as a property of space-time in relativity while it is viewed as a probability wave inside space-time in quantum theory, (2) relativity still describes changes as the motion of objects while the idea of motion has collapsed in quantum theory although a new idea of change hasn't emerged, and (3) attempts to unify quantum and relativity with thermodynamics have had limited success; thermodynamic irreversibility is incompatible with either of the theories and has to be added separately.

The hierarchical space-time view shows how this unification could be achieved. In semantic space-time, matter is the structure of space-time. Quantum objects are therefore extended forms in space-time; they should be viewed as vibrations of space-time. The probabilistic view of the wavefunction is unnecessary because the quantum system contains information—which might be abstract—but it is not ambiguous. A quantum system exchanges information with other systems only when the information is unique, and the systems are correlated by the way in which they were split by time.

Material objects are, however, not physical properties like mass, charge, force, fields, etc. They are instead types, which appear as physical properties when the types are described physically rather than through their relation to the collection. To correctly describe an object, we must know the hierarchy of concepts from which it was constructed. Each such concept is a quantum and a macroscopic object is not a classical particle. Rather, the macroscopic object is also a quantum whose meaning is given in relation to higher quanta. The classical description of nature as particles and motion is entirely false; even gravity must be viewed as a quantum phenomenon.

The classical picture of change as motion is false. In motion, the *same* particle moves to a new position, and this sameness is maintained using infinitesimals. A conceptual object on change is never the same. We cannot say that the same object moves; we can say that an object is transformed into another object. This transformation is a partial collapse of one branch in the semantic tree followed by the production of a different branch upon the remaining stump. The earlier and the newer objects are two different types of objects if we look at the entire conceptual hierarchy. However, the differences between the objects may not be very deep: only the last few nodes on the branch may be different. The object, therefore, moves not by significantly altering its fundamental type, but through minor adjustments to this type. Again, the motion is essentially a partial collapse of one branch followed by a different development upon the stump.

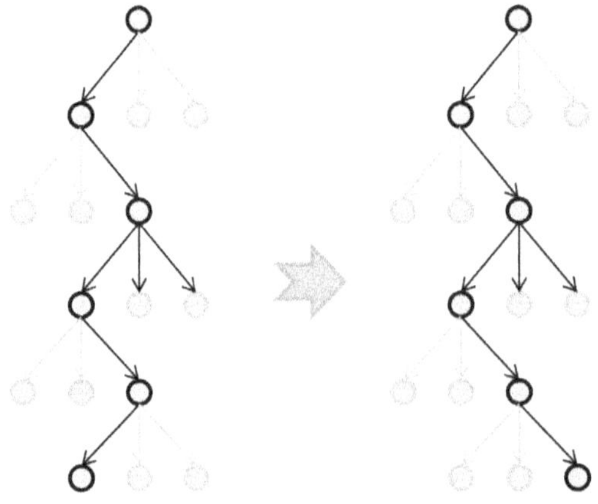

Figure-16 Motion as Tree Transformation

Think of how we would describe the motion of a car. The car is an ordered tuple of concepts: {vehicle, car, 4-wheel drive, diesel engine

...}. When it moves, most of its properties are unchanged; it still remains a vehicle, car, 4-wheel drive, etc. Only some leaves from the semantic branch are removed and new leaves are added. To make this change, the car must absorb some information, or emit some information, or both. Since in the semantic space all locations are different types, it can be said that the 'old' object disappeared, and the 'new' object appeared. The old and the new have a great deal of similarity as far as their deeper tree structure is concerned; however, they have some leaf-level differences towards the end of the branch.

Of course, changes to the tree may not always occur in the leaves. Some deep structure changes could also occur without leaf level changes. These would affect abstract ideas such as vehicle or car, thus transforming the object in a way not apparent as motion. For instance, the car may come to a halt because the engine stops. We can also envision technology that modifies objects in their deep semantic structure rather than their superficial details, thereby dramatically altering the properties and behavior of such objects with only a few quanta. Such a technology would obviously target specific quantum objects rather than a large collection of such objects.

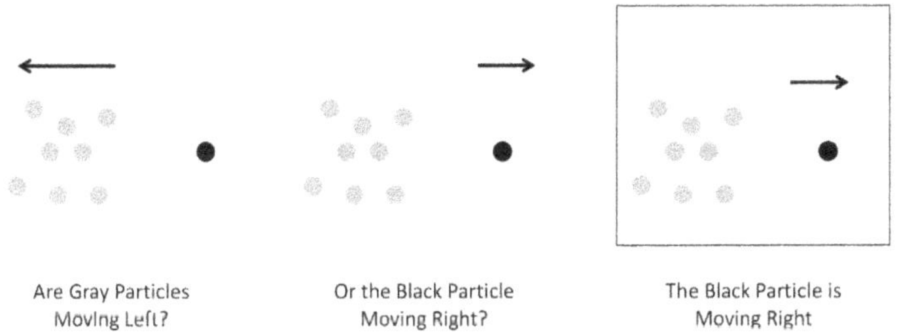
Are Gray Particles
Moving Left?
Or the Black Particle
Moving Right?
The Black Particle is
Moving Right

Figure-17 Ensembles Solve the Problem of Relativity

In physical relativity, it is impossible to decide if the observer is moving forward or the world is moving backward. If this idea is applied to quantum theory, then for a particle to move, it must hop through different eigenfunction states. However, it is hard to say if the change is caused by the particle moving forward or the rest of the particles moving backward. This question can only be answered if we measure the motion of the particle relative to the *ensemble*. If an ensemble exists, then it constitutes the reference frame against which changes to eigenfunction states can be understood. In such a case, the principle of relativistic equivalence would be false.

This clearly helps us see why current quantum and relativity theories cannot be reconciled without discarding either the relativistic principle or quantum entanglement. Quantum entanglement is the outcome of an ensemble boundary which separates the ensemble from the rest of the world. If such a boundary exists, then it is the reference frame and relativistic equivalence must be false. If, however, the ensemble does not exist, then there cannot be entanglement. Relativistic equivalence hinges on the idea of an open space-time while quantum entanglement hinges on the idea of a closed space-time. These are contradictory ideas and thus forever irreconcilable. The ensemble in quantum theory is the space-time reference frame and a correct description of the observed facts can be obtained by aligning the particle's reference frame to that of the ensemble boundary. Of course, this idea would not work if the ensemble itself was changing. To understand the change in the ensemble, we would have to consider a higher ensemble, and so on, until the root of the semantic tree is discovered. That root must be unchanging.

Applications of the Semantic View

Imagine a binary number such as 10011010010. If the last bit in this number is flipped, a small change in the number occurs. However, if a higher-order bit is flipped, a large change in the number is effected. Both changes involve a single flip, but the higher-order bit flips have a greater effect than lower-order flips. Semantically, the higher-order bits are abstract concepts and the lower-order bits are contingent concepts. They are both quanta, but their effect is not based on the physical view of quanta, because in the physical view the order of these bits cannot be known or predicted. By changing the bit order, we could dramatically change the number. Therefore, if these bits represented semantic information, then the higher-order bits would denote abstract concepts while the lower-order bits would represent contingent concepts. A given quantum is abstract or contingent based on its position in a hierarchy of concepts, and its effect on the entire system cannot be understood without the concept hierarchy.

This view of information helps us understand how the mind can influence the body. The mind would modify the higher-order bits or abstract concepts. By effecting a small change, the meaning (and behavior) of the remaining bits would be dramatically altered as well. A common example of such a change is seen in Gestalt perception where the same picture can be interpreted in two different ways. Figure-18 illustrates an example; here, the same picture can be interpreted as either a rabbit (if you observe from the left) or a duck (if you observe from the right). These two interpretations are substantially the same in the details, but they differ in the higher-order interpretation of these details. When you first look at such a picture, you will get either of the two interpretations, and the meaning of the rest of the information is adapted to support that interpretation. In fact, unless you are aware that two possible interpretations exist, you may never shift to a different view of the same picture. This shows that in some sense, the higher-order bit arrives ahead of the lower-order bits. The shift in the rabbit vs. duck interpretations is a consequence of reading the higher-order bits ahead of the lower order bits.

Figure-18 Gestalt Perception

Our perception is organized from abstract to contingent. The abstract, however, has greater importance in deciding the behavior of the whole. In the above example, a small change dramatically changes a duck into a rabbit or vice versa. This seems unintuitive from the perspective of physical information *unless* we also *order* this information. Current quantum theory is unable to order the quanta in observation, and therefore whether a quantum arrives at position X or Y makes no substantive difference to the understanding of the world. However, even if were to order the bits empirically (since the quanta arrive one by one and their order can be measured) it would still be hard to *understand* what the order represents. To convert the order into a meaning, we must view the quanta semantically.

Most human interactions involve a development from abstract to contingent. Studies on human behavior have shown that we form an impression about a person in the first few moments of interaction. Whatever comes afterward is fitted into that impression, unless a huge inconsistency in the later and the earlier views arises. If the inconsistency is small, the aberrant data is discarded as a deviation from the established view. Only if the aberrant data becomes overwhelmingly inconsistent with the previous view, is a more substantive change made. Science is also an example of such a phenomenon. The classical picture of nature that Newton created still sticks around in the minds of physicists and constitutes their pragmatic working hypothesis. Even when aberrant data—such as quantum theory—arrives, it is hard to give up the classical picture. For instance, most quantum theorists would like to believe that the classical picture is true as far as macroscopic objects are concerned. In effect, quantum theory has altered some lower-order bits in our thinking while the higher-order picture of nature based on Newton's view prevails.

The idea that our world is hierarchical and proceeds from abstract to contingent is omnipresent. It is found in the perception of meanings in books, music, art, and science. It is visible in the cognition of the world by observers. It also gives a new way of thinking about matter as hierarchical rather than linear. Science currently describes matter democratically: all locations and directions in space and time are equal, all objects behave according to the same laws, and the universe is uniform across its wide expanse. This science is incomplete in many ways, due to the problem of semantics.

The effects of semantics are palpable in current science as the indeterminism and incompleteness of scientific theories. These effects will also be confirmed in a new science that uses semantic constructs, as they will not only overcome the problems of incompleteness and indeterminism, but overturn many classical held ideas such as causality is force, change is motion, and mathematical laws act upon one kind of object—e.g., the particle, wave, photon, electron, quark, etc. The semantic view will permit infinite types of particles, each having a unique type. The laws of nature would now not be based on mathematical formulae governing a single type. They would rather have to deal in the construction of all types from fundamental types. Such a science needs a reformation in mathematics too, and numbers must be viewed as types rather than quantities. As I described earlier, this requires the set to be logically prior to the objects, space, and time to be hierarchical and cyclic rather than linear. Each of these is a scientific idea, which can be articulated. However, the formulation of a formal predictive theory requires a fundamental shift in practically every assumption held dear today.

5

A Semantic Theory of Morality

One of the principal obstacles to the rapid diffusion of a new idea lies in the difficulty of finding suitable expression to convey its essential point to other minds. Words may have to be strained into a new sense, and scientific controversies constantly resolve themselves into differences about the meaning of words. On the other hand, a happy nomenclature has sometimes been more powerful than rigorous logic in allowing a new train of thought to be quickly and generally accepted.

— *Sir Arthur Schuster*

The Evolution of the Observer

In the previous chapter we noted the three problems of indeterminism in science: (1) physical theories are predictively incomplete; they don't describe all that is empirically observable, (2) even when the theory is predictively complete, it incompletely describes matter distributions; the theory may permit many distributions but does not pick a specific one, and (3) even if a physical theory completely describes matter distribution, it still does not solve the problem of which observer experiences which part of the distribution. The previous chapter addressed the first and second types of indeterminism while this chapter addresses the third form of indeterminism. The key question in this chapter is how an observer hops from one experience to another. The evolution of the observer through discrete space-`time states is like a 'jump' from one branch to another. Nature would be consistent with an observer jumping to many different branches, provided other observers compensated this difference by jumping to branches that were not chosen. How can we predict the succession of experiences for a given observer? In this case, the material distribution may also be changing while the observer is moving from one experience to another, even as the total amount of information or energy remains conserved within the universe.

The theory of hierarchical space-time would describe how the branches of the tree appear and disappear, but it cannot describe which branch *evolves* into another branch. This problem did not exist in classical physics where we could postulate the existence of particles which moved in space-time; the continuity of the trajectory was established by the particle, and it represented the idea of evolution of something that remains unchanged. This postulate of space-time continuity requires an infinite amount of information to exist in a finite amount of space-time, which is impossible. Therefore, when we suppose that the world is discrete space-time states (individual semantic tree branches), then these states must underdetermine the trajectories that could potentially connect these states. It is now imperative to find a mechanism that connects space-time states.

At any given time, the universe exists as a semantic tree, which is the structure of space at that time. Over time, some branches are destroyed, and new ones are created. The evolution of the semantic tree in time can be represented as a *global* coordinate system with both space and time components. However, individual observers can also form their *local* coordinate systems, which represent their own evolution in the universe. The global coordinate system is the objects, phenomena, and theories in the universe. The local coordinate system is the observer who traverses a subset of the global coordinate system and therefore constitutes a trajectory within the universe.

Trajectories create a serious problem in the idea of change. The problem is that whenever something changes, we suppose that something is still unchanged. But what is unchanged? Objects, phenomena, and theories are all changing so we cannot suppose any one of them is unchanged. In what sense are the successive changes in matter, phenomena, and theory *connected* such that we can speak about them as changes of *something* that remains unchanged?

This problem is intimately tied to the notion of an 'observer' which maintains an identity across states. If I walk across the road, my body at each instance is a different branch on the tree. The branches in the past have been destroyed and the branches in the future are yet to be created. Only the present branch is observable. And yet we know that an observer only participates in a small subset of branches. The hierarchical space-time theory can describe the creation and destruction of branches, but it does not answer the fundamental question: which amongst these branches is *me*? Also, if a specific branch is *me* at one time, what would be my next state?

The drama analogy is quite relevant to this problem. Each actor in the drama is a local experience of the reality while the drama is the global reality. Which actor plays which role? And how does an actor jump from role to role? There are two ways in which the evolution of the universe can be described. First, it can be described as the events in the universe, or the drama. Second, it can be described as the trajectories of actors from one role to another. If each space-time state were a momentary observer, which is destroyed once the space-time state is destroyed, then we would not ask how the states are connected into trajectories. Consequently, we would not ask if there is some 'particle' that connects the space-time state order. The problem of observers and trajectories is that it seems that the *same* thing changes its space-time states, so something must connect states.

This problem has two aspects. First, it requires the notion of an observer who traverses through different space-time events; in classical physics, this observer was the particle, but as we discussed earlier, the particle underdetermines the reference frame. The observer must be identified with this reference frame. Like matter is semantic, the events are semantic, similarly, the coordinate reference frame must also be semantic. This reference frame represents the 'goggles' through which the observer sees the world, which include the presuppositions that are later embodied within a theory. Second, it requires a predictive theory that connects the successive space-time states into a trajectory—i.e., experience—of the observer.

The experience of the observer can be understood in two distinct ways. First, the coordinate reference frame remains unchanged, but the material reality and events experiences are altered. Second, the coordinate reference frame itself can be changed. The latter motion is like the change in material states—i.e., it is discrete. So, we can say that the old reference frame disappears and a new one appears. Because these reference frames can change, we are here not talking about a metaphysical 'being' who is transcendent to experience. Such a transcendent being would itself not change its identity. The coordinate reference frame we are speaking about here is a material construct; it can persist through material and event changes, but it can also change, thereby altering the coordinate reference frame.

Two Accounting Systems

To intuitively ground the prediction of the observer's motion across experiences, I will turn towards some new kinds of insights about material transactions different from those used in current science. These insights pertain to financial transactions as different from physical transactions. As I briefly mentioned in the introductory overview of this book, a basic difference between physical and financial accounting is that energy transfers in a physical theory do not create expectations of this energy being returned; such an expectation however often exists in the transfer of information.

In science, when an object moves from one location to another, the total matter and energy remain conserved, and scientific accounting ensures that the total amount of matter or energy is *globally* conserved. On the other hand, when you lend some money to a friend, you are interested in the value being *locally* conserved. This local conservation is achieved by creating an 'account receivable' which exists as the *absence* of the thing that was earlier lent. In scientific accounting, the motion of a particle does not leave a *history*. But in financial accounting the act of lending leaves behind a history, which appears on the accountant's ledger as the expectation of receiving the money back. In other words, financial accounting keeps track of the history of events of give and take although scientific accounting does not.

In current science, causality is mediated by the current states and not states in the past. The universe is supposed to have no trace of the past, and therefore the past seems to have no effect on the present or future. Could scientific accounting be like financial accounting? Can events in the past have a causal role in science?

If the past exists in the present as some sort of "memory," then that memory could play a causal role in influencing the future. Note that the idea of memory here is a metaphorical comparison to our conscious recall. It is, however, not necessary that the memory be conscious. An accountant who keeps track of many financial transactions does not necessarily remember all the transactions. These are rather stored on paper or digitally in computers, outside the accountant's memory recall. The memory of the past, therefore, does not have to be conscious to have a causal effect, if it can exist objectively in us to have causal effects. The existence of observers—and the idea that these observers are moral beings—suggests a different causal model. Specifically, the past must exist in the present and have effects on the future, quite like financial accounting has future effects.

The account receivable does not exist as real money. However, it exists as something that can *become* money. If you have an account receivable, you would still count it as your asset. To make this idea real in science, we would have to describe the *absence* of an object. The absence is different from the notion of anti-matter. For instance, the opposite of 'hot' is 'cold' and these two can be semantically represented as matter and anti-matter. However, 'hot' cannot become 'cold'. By absence we mean the *expectation* or *entitlement* of 'hot.' This idea is obviously clearer in the case of financial accounting. For instance, you may have lent money and therefore you don't have money, but you have assets (because you expect money). On the other hand, you may have money because you borrowed it, which is a liability because that money must eventually be returned. An asset is a positive number while a liability is a negative number on the balance sheet, and these two numbers can exist whether you actually hold any money in your pocket (which is reality). Having money, therefore, is unrelated to whether this money is an asset or a liability. Similarly, not having money is unrelated to assets or liabilities.

The asset or liability is tied to an individual and has nothing to do with the conservation of money itself. While the money is globally conserved (assuming that money is not being created), it is also locally conserved if we expect a return. If you decided to give away money as charity with no expectation of return, the donated money is not an asset. Similarly, if you received money in charity, which you are not expected to return, that money is not considered a liability. In that sense, the creation of an asset or a liability is tied to the manner in which the transaction is done. Some financial transactions emulate the properties of physical transactions because there is no expectation of receiving the money that was earlier given. Other transactions follow the rules of financial rather than physical accounting.

When these intuitions are extended to our everyday experiences, we can formulate a causal theory in which observers participate in events because there are some assets or liabilities pending to be transacted. The observer would be mapped—by a law of nature—into a branch of the semantic tree based on whether such transactions of assets and liabilities would occur on that branch. Again, as the observer partakes in these informational transactions, new assets or liabilities can be created based on how these transactions are being conducted, although the old ones would be considered complete. These assets and liabilities would in turn map the observer into a different branch, where it can transact the new events.

The essence of a natural theory of morality is therefore a new kind of material reality that is created during material transactions, although it is not material objects. This material reality can be called the assets or liabilities of an observer, which map the observer into new transactions, and this cycle of transactions and asset-liability creation must continue until the observer is left with no assets or liabilities. At that point, there is no necessity for the observer to be mapped into any branch. The universe can now be described via three kinds of laws: (1) the deterministic evolution of the universe as events or a drama, and (2) the enactment of that drama through some participating actors, and (3) the individual evolution of the observer who jumps from role to role. The events in the universe are fixed, but the matter distribution over these events and the observer distribution over matter is not. Specifically, the events an observer undergoes can be changed by altering the nature of a transaction—i.e., lending money instead of donating money. Since asset-liability creation depends on the type of transaction, the cycle of give and take caused by assets and liabilities must continue until the transactions are conducted in a way to not create further assets and liabilities.

Different branches of the semantic tree transact different kinds of meanings depending on how they interact with other branches. In such transactions, as one branch grows, another branch reduces. Since time proceeds in cycles, all such branches will increase and decrease over time. The identification of a specific branch with a specific observer, however, depends on that observer's entitlements, which is quite different from the transfer of information on that branch. For instance, if X lends some money to Y, who in turn lends money to Z, it is not necessary for Z to first return money back to Y before Y returns to X. Rather, Y can return money to X even before Z returns it to Y. Similarly, Z can also directly return the money back to X, instead of transferring it through Y. Whether Z returns money to Y or X are transactions on two different branches of the semantic tree. The semantic tree branches fix the events in the universe, but the succession of such events is underdetermined. The observer's trajectory on the semantic tree decides which events he participates into.

Is the Universe a Fair Place?

If an observer could partake into any arbitrary transaction, all observers may want to be on the growth cycles where they will receive information from other branches but don't have to give anything back to these branches. As the branch begins to recede, the observer could jump onto another branch, which is currently into the growth cycle. The information in the receding cycle would then be given away by an observer who happens to occupy that cycle. From an events standpoint, the universe would look perfectly determined, since it periodically transacts information between the branches. However, from the standpoint of an observer, who always happens to be on the receding cycles (because some other observer is always present on the growth cycle) the universe would look *unfair*.

Questions of morality are tied to the problem of whether a deterministic universe is also *fair*. An individual who acquires information must also give information for the universe to be fair. Therefore, the individual must be equally present in both receding and growth cycles. Nature can be a fair place if it ensures that observer trajectories are drawn to ensure a fair distribution of information receiving and information giving transactions across all observers. This is possible only in an informational view of nature for two reasons. First, the notion of matter or energy being returned to the source of that energy or matter cannot be described in a physical theory of nature because physical causality only operates in a single direction. Second, the notion of history as something that exists as the absence of an object cannot be understood physically because physically an absence is just nothing, and the inverse of nothing is anything. If therefore nothingness is conceived physically rather than semantically, then the predictive theory would be indeterministic because when the nothingness is inverted, it will transform into anything[1].

Of course, many modern scientists and philosophers argue that the universe is not a fair place and there is no reason for it to be so. The universe involves competition for scarce resources and the animal best suited to grab these resources wins in the survival battle. In fact, given this competitiveness in the environment, living beings must evolve their capabilities to better compete, and those beings which develop these capabilities better than others survive while the others naturally perish. This idea has now come to be known as a theory of evolution and seems to pose challenges to morality.

One of the key reasons the theory of evolution has had such a widespread impact on modern thinking is that it requires no complicated mathematics, or hard-to-understand ideas, which would make it hard for common people to understand the theory. And yet, the theory suffers from the problems that other theories in physics, mathematics, and computing do. I have surveyed these problems in my book *Signs of Life* which shows how the problems of incompleteness and indeterminism appear even in evolutionary biology.

One specific problem is worth mentioning here because it can be easily understood based on the discussion on matter distribution indeterminism that I highlighted in previous chapters. The idea of evolution requires a boundary between a living being and its environment, although there is no physical basis for drawing such a boundary in nature. The universe—in the physical view of nature—comprises physical particles which exist in an open and linear space-time. These particles can aggregate in many ways—owing to the matter distribution problem I described earlier—and there is no physical principle by which any one distribution could be preferred over another. A set of living beings in an ecosystem constitutes one such distribution of matter. Physical theories tell us that infinitely many such distributions are equally likely, and no physical principle can overcome the indeterminism in selecting a specific distribution.

The idea of natural selection in evolutionary theory talks about the compatibility between an organism and its environment. However, this notion of compatibility has no physical basis for two reasons. First, if the universe is reducible to independent objects, then the idea of compatibility itself does not exist in such objects and cannot emerge from such a theory; the question of compatibility arises only when we can draw boundaries in space-time, and for that to be possible, a new kind of physical construct—boundaries—which cannot be perceived must exist in space-time. Second, even if we grant that matter is organized to be compatible with its environment—like a peg fits into a hole—there are infinitely many ways in which peg-hole compatibility can be constructed. For instance, square pegs would fit into square holes and round pegs would fit into round holes. To create such compatibility, pegs and holes must appear at once, and there are infinitely many ways in which pegs and holes can be designed to be mutually compatible. Which one of these is real?

Another important problem in evolutionary biology is that natural selection depends on the idea of how efficiently a living being *functions* in an environment. For this idea to be theoretically sound, we must distinguish between the organism and its function. The same being in a different environment could perform a different function, and a different being in the same environment could perform the same function. The mapping between an organism and a function depends on the relation between the organism and the entire ecosystem. We would therefore need to define the ecosystem—which again requires the definition of a boundary, and there are infinite ways to draw such boundaries. Which of these boundaries is real?

Yet another problem in evolutionary theory arises from the fact that arbitrary mutations in the genome are analogous to computer programs constructed by randomly ordering bits. Many such programs will be faulty and will therefore crash—analogous to the living beings not surviving. However, there will also be programs that will never stop, because they have internal loops, and these will correspond to organisms that will never die. Studies on computer programs have shown[2] that most of the programs—if these are randomly created—would never halt. Correspondingly, if organisms were randomly created, this process would have created many eternal species. Obviously, the population of an eternal species would only continue to grow eventually consume all the resources. Furthermore, there is no physical mechanism by which nature can know the *age* of a living being, because objects just move in time, but they don't *keep* time. Therefore, even if the living being was very long-lived, no natural process could eliminate such a species, because the natural process could not determine the organism's age. Since the organism cannot be naturally selected, and they are very likely to occur due to random mutations, they must currently abound in nature. Obviously, no such eternally living species is seen in nature at present.

Evolutionary theory suffers from many logical inconsistencies, and I just chose a few examples to illustrate them. The solution to these problems is that boundaries in nature must be conceived as conceptual objects, the object-function distinction requires a theory of relations beyond a theory of matter, and all meaningful programs always halt. The problems of biology can never be solved without a prior solution to the problems of incompleteness in mathematics, computing, and physics. Rather, attempts to create a physical theory of biology would bring us face-to-face with the same problems that exist in other sciences. Much of the debate in biology occurs today without a deep appreciation of its logical inconsistencies, quite like the present physical, mathematical, and computing theories are used with limited effect, although they are ultimately incomplete.

I bring up the relation between biology and other areas of science only to illustrate that the ideas of mutation and selection in biology are not viable replacements for the problem of morality because these ideas are not logically consistent or complete. Only a semantic theory of matter would be logically consistent, but it would still be incomplete in describing the observer evolution. The problem of morality is necessitated not by a need to see nature as a fair place *a priori*. The problem arises from the need to describe observer evolution when the events in the universe are determined. Physical properties in material objects cannot be used to overcome this problem, since the sum total of these properties would determine all the events but not the trajectory of the observers through these events. The idea that the universe might be a fair place—in addition to being a rational place—can solve this problem of indeterminism. By discarding the idea that the universe is a fair place, we have no recourse to solving the indeterminism in the observer's evolution.

In short, the idea that the universe is a fair place is an additional idea over and beyond the determinism of natural events, and the laws by which matter is distributed over these events. This idea is invoked to explain the distribution of observers over the matter distribution. It is thus a solution to the problem of predictive indeterminism. There is, hence, a need to think of the observer as entitlements, which exist, but not as things or events in the conventional sense.

A Quantum Theory of the Observer

Semantically, the absence of something can exist as the *possibility* of being that thing. Scientific theories already describe nature in terms of possibilities; for instance, quantum theory describes nature in terms of probabilities. This probabilistic description of nature in quantum theory is problematic when it is viewed as a theory of material objects because it leads to the view that the world is not objectively real, and reality must be created by 'collapsing' these probabilities. However, the same probabilistic description of nature can be viewed as a correct description of the observer because the observer's experience is not *a priori* real, and it only becomes real when the observer contacts some reality. In fact, this problem can be resolved by saying that both the observer and the external reality are possibilities; the external reality is the possibility of being known, although it is not always known; the observer is the possibility of knowing but it is not always knowing; and the relation between the observer and the observed is also a possibility, as there can be many such potential relationships of knowers and knowns. The combination of these possibilities mutually 'collapses' each other.

We noted in an earlier chapter that every phenomenon is a combination of three categories—the universal, the individual, and the relational. The universal in this case is the external world, or the known. The individual is the observer who knows this world. And the relational is the connection between the knower and the known established at the point of experience, but otherwise a potentiality.

In current quantum theory, we only postulate the existence of the external world, which exists as a possibility, and in the von Neumann interpretation, the observer makes a 'choice' to collapse this possibility. The problem is that the observer too is in a state of possibility; what is to say that the observer 'reaches out' into the world to know the world, rather than saying that the external world impinges on the observer and 'collapses' the probabilistic state of the observer? Furthermore, what decides which observer will know which part of the external world—i.e., establish a relation to which object? Factually, all three of these are possibilities and not phenomena. However, their combination produces the phenomenal experience. Therefore, we should define the observer too in a state of possibility and its interaction with the world via a relation as producing the phenomena. There should hence be no difference between possibility and reality; the world exists—prior to being known—in a state of possibility. So, the reality—as the world exists prior to being known—is a possibility. What we call 'facts' are the phenomena, and these are produced through a combination of three possibilities.

The observer is the possibility of experience which is converted into a phenomenon by adding information. The information is provided by the material objects when the observer contacts these objects. Which observer contacts which external world partially depends on their entitlements; the entitlement is therefore the relational aspect of the observer-observed interaction. The observer's experience can be attributed to the contact with the material world, but that attribution will fail to account for why the observer is in contact with a specific part of the material world. Why, for instance, am I here rather than there? The causal explanation of experiences cannot come from the world because the world is consistent with an observer being anywhere. The explanation can only come from the postulate that an observer enters relations due to entitlements.

John von Neumann presented an interpretation of quantum theory in which consciousness collapses the possibilities in the wavefunction. This interpretation posed the problem of consciousness-matter interaction: how does consciousness interact with matter to collapse the wavefunction? There is however a converse way of looking at the same problem of collapse: matter collapses the possibilities in consciousness. The significant difference now is that consciousness is not something non-material and its interaction with a material level of reality is not hard to conceive. By consciousness here, we do not mean some transcendent observer; we only mean it in the sense of the entitlements of experience. These entitlements represent the meanings that the observer can potentially receive or transmit. The entitlements are thus abstract concepts, and they are converted into contingent concepts. The collapse of the wavefunction is a real physical transaction that converts the abstract into the contingent, but that transaction cannot be described physically. Unlike current physics where the wavefunction is described as the probabilities of contingent alternatives, in the new physics the wavefunction would be described as an abstract entity called entitlement.

A word of caution regarding the distinction between possibility and probability is necessary here. In current quantum theory, possibilities and probabilities are identical, and this is because the possibility is treated physically. In a semantic view, the possibilities will exist, but the probabilities will not. Probabilities are outcomes of the inability to predict the succession of events. Since we are unable to predict, but we suppose that there is indeed an external reality, we postulate that this reality exists as a possibility. In the semantic view, the observer is a possibility not because the succession of events cannot be predicted. Rather, the observer is *ontologically* a possibility even though the succession of events can be predicted. This is because the observer is defined not as a thing but as the entitlement of being a certain kind of thing. The succession of events in the observer's experience can be predicted if we can predict the order in which the entitlements manifest and create a relation between the observer and the world. Possibilities and probabilities are thus not related. The connection between the two is a flaw of current quantum theory which is unable to predict the succession of events. In a semantic description, this flaw can be overcome, although possibilities would still exist. Now, the observer would be defined as the succession of experiences, caused because of their entitlements.

Therefore, when I speak of possibilities, I don't mean probabilities. I mean the sense in which the observer's experience is determined although the observer is not material objects but is the entitlement of material objects. The branches of the semantic tree offer myriad possibilities of information exchange. An observer's possibilities of experience can be mapped onto a branch of this tree. Now, the exchanges of information on the tree's branch (by which the branch increases or decreases) become the mechanism of observer's experience. The observer and the world are not identical, although an observer is mapped to some events due to the entitlements.

In that sense, there are two kinds of determinism pertaining to: (1) the succession of events of the universe, and (2) the succession of events within an observer's experience. The first kind of determinism is entailed by the space-time structure itself while the second kind of determinism is entailed by the previous states of the observer. The next state of the universe does not depend on its history. However, the next state of the observer depends on that observer's history. The individual observer's experience is thus caused by the observer's previous experiences and it can therefore be deterministic.

Free Will vs. Freedom

To better understand the process of entitlement creation, we need to distinguish two aspects of choice which are often easily confused. I will call these two aspects *free will* and *freedom*. The conventional thinking on choice claims that if free will were real then it would have some effects on nature due to which things that could not be predicted by natural laws would be predicted by the choices made due to free will. The problem now is that if nature is completely determined by mathematical laws then obviously there is no freedom in changing the events in the universe. Since there is no freedom to change, we cannot measure the effects of free will—since all such effects would be predicted by natural laws—and the most logical conclusion would be that free will does not exist. The materialist denial of free will rests on equating free will with freedom, and it stems from the idea that if we had free will we would also have the freedom to change the world. If there is no freedom, then there is no free will.

It is, however, not necessary to identify free will with freedom. For instance, if my hands were tied and my body was dragged by force, I may not have the freedom to resist or change these occurrences but, obviously, they are not being carried out of my own free will. The idea therefore that if free will exists then it must have an observable effect is not necessarily true because there are situations in which we may not agree with what is happening, but we simply don't have the power to change it. In such situations we would not deny that we have free will, although we would deny our freedom.

The difference between free will and freedom allows us to construct the following three kinds of causal models about nature:

- PHYSICAL: The world is predetermined by natural laws. There is no freedom and hence there cannot be any free will, because there cannot be any physical *evidence* of free will.
- INTENTIONAL: The world is governed by our choices. The events in the world are outcomes of our choices. We can change the world and the evidence of free will is freedom. If I did not choose to do something, those things would not occur.
- FUNCTIONAL: We don't necessarily have freedom, but we might have free will. The events in the universe may be determined by natural laws, but I have the choice of which events I participate in. The world is a drama whose script is prewritten, but I can choose to participate in different roles within that script.

The question of meanings is closely tied to these causal models. In the physical model, since there is no free will and freedom, there is no choice to interpret the world and, consequently, there are no meanings. At best, meanings must be epiphenomena of physical interactions.

This is, by far, the dominant materialist position today. In the intentional model, the world is totally free to be interpreted; even the idea that there is some order in nature is, in this view, our interpretation by which we formulate some theories of nature. These theories are underdetermined by the phenomena and others could formulate different theories. This is, by far, the post-modernist position. The physical and post-modernist positions exist at logically opposite ends of the spectrum of causality. In the canonical physical position, there is no free will and natural laws govern everything and these laws represent an unchanging fact about nature. In the canonical post-modernist position, there is nothing but free will or freedom and there is no absolute and universal reality; all notions of a universal reality independent of the observer are also free will.

Our real world would not work if we adopted either of these extremes. We acknowledge that there is some reality and order in nature and that we have free will to interpret and understand this reality. The drama analogy I presented earlier reconciles these positions. The script of the drama is events in the universe, which are predetermined while the observers in those events are not. However, to think in this way, we would have to change our causal model and theory of nature from physical and intentional to functional. The observer, in the functional model of causality, is bound in every situation to perform a specific function, although the function would be performed whether or not the observer chose that role. The observer's choice is never about changing the events in the universe; the choice is only whether the observer participates in the events or not. There is hence free will, but there is no freedom in the manner that we equate it with the ability to change the universe.

Even the choice of events can be curtailed by the entitlements, and the succession of experiences is not entirely free. Instead, the choice exists only if the free will is used correctly—e.g., by accepting the true nature of reality—because then the entitlement is never created, and the observer is free of the consequences of his choice. Free will is now the observer's choice of a worldview, and if this view is correct, then there is free will of events as well. If the worldview is wrong, then the free will of worldviews exists but the freedom of events does not. The determinism in nature, therefore, does not contradict the free will in the observer, because free will is not identical with freedom. We can safely say that there is always free will of theories, but never the freedom to change the world; we can choose a different role in the world, but not the script by which it works.

Determining the Entitlement

An observer's entitlement depends on the causal model adopted by the observer, and its difference vis-à-vis the functional causal model. In the physical model of causal interaction, events occur deterministically and because the observer views the world as physical things, the world does not have meanings. The physical treatment of nature, as I have detailed earlier, leads to problems of indeterminism, incompleteness, and incomputability. These problems can only be understood if they were arising from a neglect of meanings. The physical model of causality tries to simplify nature by reducing it to elementary meaningless objects governed by laws that don't require meanings (and would not work with meanings). The entitlement of this model of causality is that if an observer treats nature as determined but physical, then he or she would be faced with phenomena with a complexity that cannot be fitted into the deterministic theory.

The intentional model of causality takes the opposite position: it acknowledges meanings but does not accept determinism. The observer considers himself free to control nature in whichever way he chooses, although nature is determined. The entitlement of the intentional model of causality is that the observer will encounter phenomena that are predetermined such that choices to change the world are not permitted. Of course, the observer who believes in the intentional model may not interpret this failure as determinism. For instance, when things don't go the way we wish them, we may not attribute this discrepancy to determinism; we could also attribute it to the choices of other actors. In the intentional model, therefore, the conflict may not appear to be between free will and determinism; it can also appear to be between the individual instances of free will. These interpretations reinforce the intentional causal model: even though the world does not work according to *my* free will, it still works according to *someone else's* free will. The conclusion, therefore, that nature is determined by some laws may not be easily obvious.

If a theory begins in the idea of physical determinism, then it ends up in physical uncertainty. If, however, a theory begins in semantic freedom then it ends up in semantic determinism. Both positions are logically inconsistent and the observer—who adopts either of the above two positions—can maintain neither physical determinism nor semantic freedom over a period. The entitlements of these theories will subject the observer either to encounters with complexity that cannot fit into the simplistic physical theory or to encounters with determinism that are incompatible with freedom.

Only the functional causal model is consistent and the use of this model does not create the opposite entitlement. The fact that reality is semantic tells us that some meanings must be true (while others must be false) and which meanings he accepts as being true represent his free choice. The fact that the world is determined tells the observer that free will cannot be measured in terms of its effects, especially if the effects were measured in a third-person manner, because all situations will only exhibit determinism. The observer's free will can, however, be known by that specific observer because the observer can hop from one situation to another unencumbered by the entitlements of previous experiences. In effect, the observer is now free to experience whichever part of the universe it wills, although in each situation the universe behaves deterministically.

The deterministic behavior corresponds to the role played by the observer in a context. However, the observer can participate in any role predetermined by the space-time structure. We can now connect free will to the example about the universe being a drama. The roles in the drama and the play as a whole are predetermined. However, the observer—when it uses the correct causal model of nature—can be completely free, not in changing the space-time structure, but in choosing amongst possibilities in that structure.

The essence of free will is that the observer understands that the universe is predetermined and his presence in a certain role is only incidental to the actions and observations being attributed to that observer. If that observer did not participate in those events, some other observer would, and therefore the universe would not be different regardless of which observer participates in those roles from the standpoint of other observers. However, the participation of a specific observer in a specific role is different for that observer.

This free will hinges on the functional model of causality. In the other two models, the causal model is inconsistent with the entitlements of using the model. That inconsistency entails that the observer must constantly alter their understanding of nature's causality. If the observer applies the physical deterministic causal model and encounters the phenomena where determinism fails, he would be tempted to assume that the universe is not orderly, and the observer is, therefore, free to control it in whichever way he desires. This interpretation would now lead to a shift in the causal model from physical determinism to semantic intentionality. As the observer applies the semantic intentional causal model, he will encounter phenomena that are determined. He may then be tempted to conclude that the universe is predetermined and there is no free will. The observer may now return to the physical determinism model, and the cycle of oscillations between the two models would continue.

The oscillation of the observer's causal model is an outcome of the model's difference from the nature of reality. The entitlement of an experience is the difference between reality and its theory. This allows us to define a mechanism for determining the entitlement:

REALITY = THEORY + ENTITLEMENT[3]

In a semantic universe the events are determined automatically by the space-time structure. These transactions are semantic. The physical view sees these transactions as being deterministic but not semantic. The physical view sees the world deterministically and does not attribute choices to any actor. The intentional view, on the other hand, treats these transactions as being semantic although not determined because each actor believes that he or she 'chooses' to perform their actions. The intentional view sees meanings in nature as their interpretation and attributes choices to the actors. The semantic view entails that there is free will in the observer, but the freedom is determined by entitlements. If we use free will correctly, then the entitlements cease to exist. If we use free will incorrectly, then the entitlements restrict and force our interactions.

If nature is described using a false theory, then the consequences of the use of such a theory also must be described naturally. Every false theory has some consequences. For instance, a physical deterministic theory's consequence is indeterminism and a semantic intentional theory's consequence is determinism. In current science, these problems are treated epistemologically and not morally. That is, we suppose that if our theory is false then our technology will not work. We do not suppose that if our theory is false, then we would be *naturally* led into new experiences which can be used to correct the theory. This represents a gap in modern science where we can partly describe the phenomena through an incorrect theory, but we cannot predict the evolution of the theory itself. What is the natural law that governs the evolution of false theories? How can we describe the evolution of science by which it arrives at the perfect theory?

The idea of morality in this picture is that there is a perfect theory of nature, although observers may not have that theory. The conflict between reality and the observer's theories creates consequences by which the theory can be perfected. However, the consequences cannot be understood unless the perfect theory is known. If the entitlement of a theory is its difference with the perfect theory, then to know the entitlement we must know the perfect theory.

Perfect and Imperfect Theories

There has been considerable debate in the philosophy of science about what a theory is about. Is a theory a description of reality or a description of the phenomena? The debate stretches back to the problem of knowing the nature of reality from our perceptions: if we perceive colors, tastes, smells, sounds, and touches, but reality is physical and material properties, then the scientific theory which uses such properties cannot be about experiences; it must be about reality. However, in practice, we have no way of directly observing physical and material properties; our access to such properties is only through the phenomena in the mind. Therefore, the theories in science could not be theories of reality; they must be theories of phenomena. It follows that physical and material properties are only objectifications of phenomena, which we apply back to reality when the theory is predictively successful. This view of the theory is reinforced by the difference between theory and phenomena. If both theory and phenomena are interpretations of reality and they are clearly different then how do we arrive at two distinct kinds of interpretations? This problem reinforces the fact that a theory is not an interpretation of reality but of phenomena, which is observed via the senses. We can now draw three worlds and connect them through *interpretations.* The mind interprets the external objects to produce phenomena. Science then interprets these phenomena to arrive at a theory.

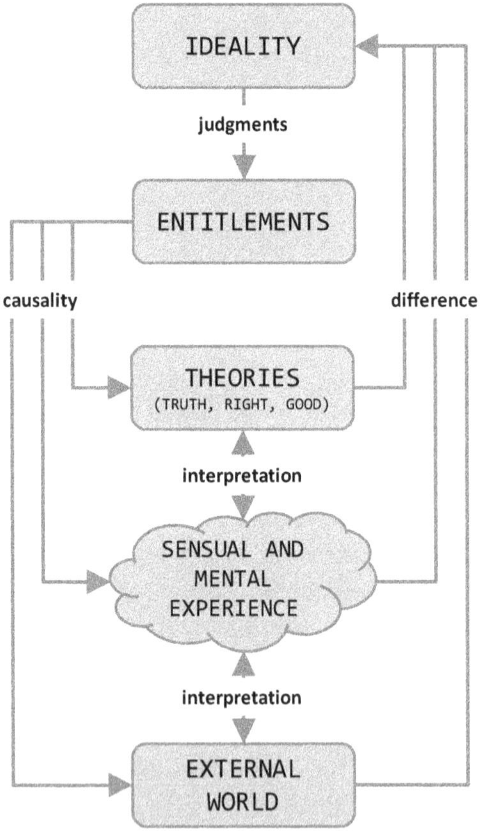

Figure-19 Entitlement - Causes and Effects

Once the theories have been formed, they become our *beliefs* and are used to perform personal *judgments*. For instance, ideas incompatible with a theory would be rejected as false, and effort is spent in collecting facts that invalidate the previous theories or beliefs. What I call a 'theory' is thus not a widely accepted law of nature. What I mean by 'theory' is our personal beliefs; this category includes widely accepted theories too, because many people believe in them. But psychologically we hold beliefs which might not be rigorously proven—rationally or empirically—and yet they are used to judge the truth, right, or good. I have also generalized the notion of a 'theory' to include right and good, besides truth. The reason is that if we believe in false truths, then we also modify the definition of what is right and good. For instance, if we believe that some economic theory tells us the truth about how to achieve prosperity, then enacting what the theory indicates would be considered right, and the actions would be justified on the basis that they are good for the people.

But above and beyond these personal beliefs about truth, right, and good is the *ideal* or the *perfect* truth, right, and good. We might hold false beliefs, and we have the free will to do so. But these beliefs must also be *judged* as being false, wrong, and bad. The entitlements of our beliefs are consequences of these judgments, and these consequences are individual, rather than universal, because the beliefs are individual rather than universal. Judgments can be performed only when there is meaning; as we noted earlier, the existence of something doesn't make it true because false ideas can also exist. To know that they are false, we must look at *meaning* rather than *existence*. So, the existence of meaning is the precondition for judgments.

If nature must perform these judgments, then the *ideals* of truth, right, and good must also be real—i.e., they cannot simply be personal preferences. The entitlements of beliefs, actions, and intentions would follow from an absolute notion of truth, right, and good.

The entitlement is the difference between reality and ideality. That is, if we deviate from the ideal truth, right, and good, then an entitlement that can correct the deviation is created. The evolution of knowledge, for example, is not an infinite process in which we keep speculating and find partially true theories and the process of knowledge gathering never comes to an end. Rather, the evolution is bound by the fact that deviation from the truth will produce an entitlement, which then compels us into experiences by which we can potentially correct the mistakes of our earlier formed theories. Similarly, the understanding of right and good is neither open for personal interpretation, nor is knowing the ideal right and good a never-ending process because the entitlements of our actions compel us into experiences that can potentially rectify our understanding.

The morality of the universe is predicated on the assumption that there are personal and imperfect theories, which drive flawed actions, but there is also ideal truth, right, and good which is used to judge the personal and imperfect theories and create entitlements, which then drive the observer toward greater truth, right, and good. Nature is not just a fair place, but also a *compassionate* place; it gives us free choices, but also creates opportunities to adopt the ideal. Whether we use that opportunity is still a free choice, but the opportunity for utilizing it appropriately is accessible to everyone.

Cause, Effect, and Consequence

In modern science we think that causality involves two factors: cause and effect. To understand entitlements, we must think of causality as comprising three factors: causes, effects, and consequences. These consequences are different from the effects. We can understand this idea through an example. Suppose that a person with a gun pulls the trigger and the bullet hits someone. In this situation, the pulling of the trigger is the cause, and the person getting hurt is the effect. Scientific causality deals with these two things—cause and effect. But in everyday life we also will talk about whether the shooter was performing a legitimate action, and whether he or she should be punished or rewarded. For example, if the shooter was a soldier shooting an enemy then he may be rewarded for performing a legitimate duty. But if the shooter is a criminal, then he may be punished. So, pulling the trigger is the cause, the death of the person who is shot is the effect, and reward or punishment is the consequence.

The reward or punishment coming from the shooting involves another cause and effect. For example, if the soldier is given a medal for his brave efforts, then the cause of the medal is the government of the country which recognizes and endorses the soldier's valiant actions. And the effect of the government action is that the soldier may receive a medal, a commendation, and other types of rewards. So, even when the soldier is being given a reward, there is a cause and an effect. However, this second cause and effect is connected to the first cause and effect of the soldier pulling the trigger. So, when we talk about consequences, we are talking about the connection between two pairs of cause and effect. The second cause is determined by the consequence of the previous action, not by an effect of another cause.

We cannot see this consequence at the time of the action, just like the reward or punishment of an action doesn't come to us immediately. The consequence rather lies dormant for some time, and then it creates a new cause. Many people are going to have a problem with the idea of a third element of causality. They might say that we just have causes and effects, and these are enough to explain everything that happens. How can we respond to this criticism? What is the basis on which we can justify the induction of consequences?

Obviously,` to introduce this idea in the context of causality we must show that the current causality is insufficient. Then the idea of consequences can be used to complete the causal chain. The main reason for the causal incompleteness is that matter is a possibility rather than a reality. If matter existed as a reality then only one cause would act, and the effect would be deterministically defined by that cause. But if matter exists as a possibility then there are many possible causes that can produce many different effects. Which of these causes will actually act is not determined by the laws of nature. This indeterminism is relational in nature; for instance, two objects can potentially interact to produce an effect. But are they going to interact? As we saw earlier, in atomic theory all causes are *quantized*. This means that two objects are not always interacting. To interact, the source must emit the causal particle (called a boson) which must then be absorbed by the destination and the effect is then created. The time at which the source emits a particle, and the destination at which this particle arrives is not predetermined by the interacting objects—these objects are simply the possibilities of action. So, the causality is incomplete because the present exists as a possibility, and we must choose one of the possible causes to create an effect.

In everyday life, we see that the present is not enough to explain the future. There are many things in the present which can change the future in different ways, but we cannot predict which of these things will become real. For example, an employee may work hard in his job, but due to economic downturn he or she may not get the proportionate rewards. We normally attribute this type of outcome to "luck" and we may say that the person was unlucky. But what is luck? Can we understand luck scientifically? This is where we must realize that we need a mechanism to explain how one of the possibilities becomes reality and this needs something additional.

Entitlements of previous actions can serve to fill this causal gap. We must invoke the past and say that some possibility from the present becomes a reality due to the consequence of an action in the past. If we don't invoke the past, then we cannot explain luck; our explanation will only say that some people are lucky, and others are unlucky.

Thus, the tripartite causal model involving causes, effects, and consequences serves to fill a gap in current forms of causality. It is not an *ad hoc* addendum that we use to introduce morality in nature. It is rather a necessary component of causal completeness, which can also be interpreted as the consequences of moral action. Given that alternative ways of causal completeness haven't been found, the tripartite causal model can help us understand the missing causality.

Modern science describes what happens if two objects interact. However, it doesn't fix whether they will interact. Thus, for instance, you could land a high-paying job if you were well-educated. But what tells us whether someone will be well-educated? You can probably trace back education to the prosperity of your family, the type of birth, or other circumstantial factors. But everyone eventually asks: Why me? Why couldn't I be placed in different circumstances? Is it merely luck, that I was born sick, poor, and stupid? Or, can the personal condition—which some call 'destiny'—be explained? The short answer is that once we introduce meanings into the study of nature, then we would also be able to induct judgments in nature. If meanings can be natural, then judgments—based on meanings—can also be natural. You can talk about the truth or falsity of something that is meaningful. You can judge the rightness or wrongness of an action based on the role or function you are performing. And you can judge the goodness and badness of an experience based on your personal preferences about what you consider pleasurable or painful.

These are indeed personal judgments, and if these individual judgments became real in nature, then we could formulate a theory about the absolute or ideal nature of truth, right, and good. If there are no meanings, then personal judgments are impossible, and if personal judgments are not possible, then judgments against the ideal would also be impossible. In that sense, the move from a physical to a semantic viewpoint is only the first step in a longer journey that progresses into personal and then ideal judgments. The personal judgments are based on our imperfect theories about truth, right, and good. And the ideal judgment is that of these imperfect theories itself. Such judgments close the gap that exists in the scientific methodology where the scientific process of experimentation and theory formation is potentially never-ending. Entitlements arising from false theories ensure that occasions for correcting the false ideologies will be available to everyone, whether they choose to use it or not.

The tripartite model of causes, effects, and consequences provides an enhanced understanding of nature, in which the universe is not just something that exists, but is also meaningful, gives us opportunities to judge the nature of truth, right, and good, and if we have a wrong view of this ideality then it also enables opportunities for their correction. The universe is therefore true, right, and good.

The difficulty in this understanding is that the consequences are not *visible*, unlike the effects. Their existence must therefore be postulated as a theoretical necessity. However, the creation of the consequence can be determined by its gaps from the perfect theory of nature, or what constitutes ideality, as we have discussed above.

Three Kinds of Consequences

Since the idea of a consequence is alien to most people, it would help if we delve into it a bit more. I would like to describe here three kinds of consequences that arise from any experience or action. Each of these are outside the physical model of causality because it doesn't explicitly consider conscious observers. Consequences are a unique feature of the causal model as seen in the context of observers. In non-conscious material reality, the consequences don't exist.

The first of consequences is *impressions*. When we experience something, the experience leaves behind an impression, which is the essence of the experience and constitutes the answer to the question: Why is something true or false for me? The impression filters our future experiences as we focus on the things that we have previously judged to be true and neglect other things that we once considered to be false. We don't fully evaluate the truth or falsity of every experience fully every time we encounter something. Rather, by the filtration process, we defocus on things that we consider false. This phenomenon is sometimes called 'echo-chambers' and a person enters an echo-chamber in which his or her beliefs are reinforced by leaving out those ideas or even facts that he or she considers false. Due to filtration you don't even consider novel facts or arguments in favor of the ideas you don't believe in. They may, after all, be true, and your initial judgments about their truth may have been false. However, by filtration you completely neglect listening to those ideas. The construction of such filters which fence your viewpoint and prevent opposing ideas to enter your way of thinking is the first consequence of an experience. Once a filter has been built, any novelty that differs from the established viewpoint is automatically rejected.

For example, followers of a religion will de facto consider other religions false. Followers of a political ideology will de facto demonize other ideologies. People of a race will naturally avoid those of other races. Patriots of a nation will naturally view those of other nations with suspicion, considering them foreign and alien. People interested in science naturally view everything in religion with suspicion, even if the ideas may be useful for scientific progress.

In short, impressions create an *unconscious bias* in our perception. They focus our consciousness on selected and preformed beliefs and domains while moving it away from others. This is a material effect, but it doesn't act on the external world; it acts on our consciousness. Consciousness must focus on something. Filters create that focus by eliminating other things from our awareness. If consciousness is viewed as attention and focus, then these material filters of experience are conceptually very similar to consciousness, but they are not truly the ability to experience. They are simply the restrictions on what we focus upon; the focus is created by removing other things that we consider alien, different, or unfamiliar.

The second type of consequence is *personality*. By personality I mean traits such as introverted vs. extroverted, compassionate vs. selfish, idealistic vs. realistic, innovator vs. executor, thinker vs. feeler, conscientious vs. carefree, leader vs. follower, confident vs. hesitant, trusting vs. skeptic, motivated vs. depressed, etc. Our personality is a certain emotional state that makes us *comfortable*. We all seek comfort in our lives, but different people are comfortable in different ways. The leader is not comfortable following, and the follower is not comfortable in leading. The person who is trusting is disturbed by the constant bickering of a skeptic, and the skeptic is worried about the trusting nature. Those who are conscientious dislike those who are carefree, and those carefree dislike the conscientious. The innovators like to think new ideas and leave the execution to someone else while the executors avoid thinking novel ideas and focus on the stability of the established trends. Some people take comfort in abstract thought, and others seek emotional satisfaction. Some like to spend time with themselves while others enjoy socializing.

Our experiences shape our personality. For example, if you have a bad set of friends and relationships, you will naturally become introverted. But those who had emotionally fulfilling childhood based on love from parents or siblings will be inclined to a social life. If you have failed as a leader, you will prefer to be a follower. But if you don't feel the respect as a follower, then you will aspire to be a leader. If your trust has been broken, you will become a skeptic. On the other hand, if your trust has been confirmed in the past, you will abhor skepticism. Those who have faced difficulties when they behaved irresponsibly will become conscientious. But those for whom things worked out fine even when they acted irresponsibly will remain carefree. Those whose compassion has been abused in the past will become selfish. But those whose selfishness has left them lonely will act more compassionately toward others. Those whose idealism has led to failures will become realistic. And someone whose realism has prevented them from achieving bigger goals will become idealistic.

Our personality is how we feel secure, protected, safe, and happy.

Fear drives our personality in the opposite direction. Everyone is afraid of unhappiness and suffering. So, they seek an approach to life that will make them comforted and satisfied. Like the perceptual filters, our personality also restricts our experience. We shy away from experiences that are contrary to our personality type and indulge in experiences that are compatible with the type.

The third type of consequence is *entitlements*. These arise as a result of impressions that create false beliefs and personalities which restrict our experiences. Due to the personality type, we stay away from right behaviors and due to false beliefs, we indulge in wrong behaviors. The combination of staying away from right behaviors and engaging in wrong behaviors creates negative entitlements. There are also positive entitlements created as a result of the personality when we engage in certain behaviors because they make us comfortable when we possess the right set of beliefs as well.

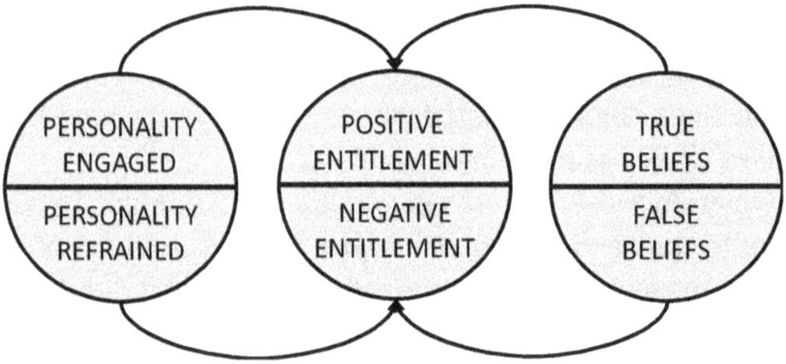

Figure-20 The Creation of Entitlements

An engaged personality that acts under false beliefs creates a negative entitlement. Similarly, a personality refrained under true beliefs also creates a negative entitlement. Entitlements are therefore consequences of behavior. Just having a certain type of personality or a belief system doesn't produce entitlements. We must rather act or behave under the influence of these personalities and beliefs. There are many claims about personality which state that no personality type is better than the other, which are partially true in the sense that every person has a certain comfort zone that makes them safe and secure. However, these claims are also false because personality types force us to refrain from performing the right actions. Similarly, many people claim that all beliefs are equally good because they are just our individual choices, which cannot be judged by others. This claim is also false because false beliefs lead to wrong actions.

The tripartite model of causality brings a significant difference in how effects are created. This difference is caused by the fact that the consequence of action becomes the primordial cause that produces some manifest causes, which then produce effects. The consequence remains dormant and unconscious, but it creates conscious effects, which we deem as the causes of the effects. For instance, when we have a certain type of personality, we formulate goals based on this personality. These goals seem to be the causes of subsequent actions, which are described as effects. However, the goals themselves are effects of the previously formed consequences. Therefore, the consequence leads to the cause, which then leads to an effect. Similarly, when we have formed some beliefs, those beliefs create ideas in our minds which then lead to perception of the world.

	Individual	Universal	Relational
Consequence	Personality	Filters	Entitlements
Cause	Goals	Concepts	Relations
Effect	Happiness	Perception	Actions

Figure-21 Cause, Effect, and Consequence

Our entitlements similarly produce different relations with other individuals and things, where we are compelled to encounter things that may not fit our worldview or may be uncomfortable to our personality. If these relations are compatible with our beliefs and comfortable with our personality, then we will do the right actions. If they are incompatible with our personality, we will try to avoid the right actions, and if we do indulge in the actions under false beliefs, we will produce wrong actions, both of which create negative entitlements. Thus, a consequence becomes a cause, which then produces an effect, which then again becomes an entitlement, and the cycle of tripartite causality continues indefinitely until our beliefs are corrected, and our personality is improved to balance the contrary dispositions, such that we remain equanimous in all conditions.

In the scientific causal model, causes lead to effects, which then become the causes of subsequent effects, producing a cycle of cause and effect. The tripartite model of causality is also a cyclic causality, but it acts on the observer. That is, we are not speaking about someone pushing a billiard ball, which then pushes another billiard ball; this causal model is *externalized* to act on other objects. In contrast, the tripartite model of causality creates actions which then act back on the observer through entitlements. This is not to say that our actions don't produce external effects. It is only to say that those actions are not merely caused by our actions but by their *entitlements*. So, someone not entitled to an action would not be affected our actions. Only those who have the necessary entitlements will be matched against our actions, produced as a result of our entitlements.

Therefore, the cycle of causality, in this case, is totally internalized—i.e., within the observer. An observer's experience shapes their personality and beliefs, which then lead to actions, thereby resulting in entitlements which then further cause new experiences. The result of these new experiences are changes to personality and beliefs. So, the observer remains in a cycle of change produced by their own experience. To study the evolution of the observer, the experiences of the observer are enough; we don't have to know the effects of other things on the observer, or the observer's effects on other things. Each observer is self-sufficient or sovereign in fixing their evolution.

Can We Know Reality?

The central problem of epistemology is to know when the theory is false. This can be determined if the theory can be tested against all possible phenomena, especially those that may not potentially fit the theory. But how do we find the phenomena which do not fit the theory? What guarantees do we have that we will in fact encounter all the phenomena, especially those that contradict a theory? If we begin in a false theory, which seems to work for a limited set of phenomena, but we never encounter other phenomena where the theory fails, then the epistemological problem can never be solved. We would continue to hold on to a false theory which appears true to us because we only test it where the theory seems to work. Unless we find the facts that contradict a theory's predictions, the theory can never be perfected. If nature does not guarantee an encounter with phenomena that falsify a theory, the perfect theory can never be found.

Epistemology proposes two broad methods to knowledge—verification and falsification. In verification, a theory is true if it successfully predicts some phenomena not predicted by other theories. In falsification, a theory is tentatively true until the falsifying phenomena are found. Both verification and falsification are incomplete. Verification is incomplete because of underdetermination—there can be many equally successful theories that predict the same phenomena. Falsification is incomplete because it is not guaranteed that if we have a false theory, we would find the facts that falsify it. We can keep looking for such facts, but we may never encounter them. And therefore, we can never be certain that we will indeed find the correct theory of nature, or even that we have already found such a theory. It may just be that we have so far encountered those phenomena that appear to confirm the theory, but not those that conflict with it. Since we may find conflicting facts in the future, all theories can be potentially falsified. All knowledge is hence tentative. It might be revised in the future, and the history of science illustrates that evolution. Nevertheless, every generation of scientists feels that theirs is perhaps the first one which had a mastery over nature's laws.

The epistemological project is hopelessly incomplete without the moral one. We cannot hope to know the truth unless we are led into phenomena that conflict with the theory so that the theory can be modified. So, unless nature is guaranteed to arrange an encounter with such phenomena, we can never be sure of our knowledge. The moral viewpoint makes it possible to know the nature of reality and the epistemological project is logically sound because nature will arrange an encounter with the phenomena using which a false theory can be updated. Nature is a moral place because it will ensure that we find all those facts that contradict our worldview if that worldview is false. If, however, the worldview is true, the observer is not constrained to enter any specific phenomenon. All such phenomena are consistent with the perfect worldview, and the moral consequences end only when the epistemological project has been completed.

There can never be a complete theory of knowledge if that theory is not intertwined with a theory of moral consequences. Epistemology is therefore perennially incomplete unless it is tied to a theory of the evolution of false theories. This latter theory, as I have argued, represents the moral evolution of the observer by which the observer creates entitlements whenever it uses a false theory. These entitlements shape the observer's future experiences. Specifically, the experiences will illustrate the need to incorporate those parts of reality which were previously missing from the false theory. Nature is therefore a moral place because it will help us find the truth.

The search for the perfect theory ends when the observer has regained his free will. Such an observer can roam to any part of the universe at will. In each encounter, the observer would appear to follow the laws of nature, and yet, the observer is completely free of the laws. The test of knowledge is therefore moral freedom: a theory of nature that fixes the observer's future experiences is a false theory. Only a theory that relieves the observer of any moral obligations is the true theory. The universe is a moral place because it will lead the observer to the correct theory of nature. But if such a theory has been formulated, the observer has the free will to use it as he wills.

Theodicy and Cosmodicy

In the simplest form, the problem of theodicy is the existence of evil in a universe created by an omnipotent and omnibenevolent God. The problem of cosmodicy questions the idea of whether the universe is good. The reader might have noticed that I haven't so far referred to God in the context of morality—I have chosen the path of *moral naturalism* in which the outcomes (good or bad) are based on the individual's choices; they can be viewed as the responsibility of our choices. The problem of cosmodicy, however, has been directly addressed. The universe is a good place because morality helps us close the gap from our ignorance to perfect knowledge by compelling us into those encounters which can rectify the mistakes of the past. Thus, without getting into the question of whether God created the universe, both problems disappear when we conclude that the universe is good.

The key point of inflection in this argument is that goodness is not the only issue that we must be occupied with. Rather, we must look at a broader spectrum of issues, such as whether the universe is a fair and righteous place, and whether perfect knowledge is possible. This is because what would be the point of saying that the universe is good without saying that it is righteous and fair and that our ignorance of reality can be overcome? If people were fundamentally incapable of overcoming ignorance, then by holding false beliefs they could not become righteous. And if everyone is not righteous, then they also cannot be good. In short, true knowledge leads to right action, which then leads to happiness. Of course, happiness is the goal we aspire for. But this goal cannot be achieved without right action which in turn cannot be practiced without true knowledge.

So, the question of whether the universe is a good place begins in the question of whether the universe is knowable. To answer this question, we must formulate a method of knowledge that over time guarantees—subject to freedom of choice—perfect knowledge. The moral naturalism outlined earlier describes this method. There is reward and punishment in the universe through the entitlements we create, which are necessary to modify our outlook of the world. If there weren't rewards, then the correct view could not be reinforced. Similarly, if there weren't punishments, then the false ideas could not be discarded. Therefore, rewards and punishments serve to improve our understanding of nature and take it toward perfection.

With this perfected understanding of nature, we can act correctly toward others, because that action is in our *self-interest*. Moral action—i.e., doing the fair and just thing—toward others is not rationalized by an extra set of rules about how we must act in a society. Such rules are changeable and subjective to the culture and individual perspective. Besides, any argument of doing the right thing that doesn't affect self-interest is ultimately impractical because no one will practice these righteous actions if they are not concerned with self-interest, and we can safely assume that everyone is. Therefore, since times immemorial, wrong action is tied to punishments: we must demonstrate that hurting others is going to hurt oneself. This retribution is not *indirect*; for example, it is possible to claim that if everyone acted wrongly, then the entire society would be worse off, and we as individuals would be indirectly affected by it. It is rather a direct entitlement in which every action is individually rewarded or punished individually (rather than indirect and collective suffering) that makes the connection between choice and responsibility. If we made choices that caused others to suffer and we suffered collectively consequently, there would be no direct relation between the choices and the consequences of our actions. Therefore, tying the moral outcomes to the individual self-interest is necessary.

We can demand that the universe be a good place, but we cannot demand it at the expense of it being a fair place. In short, our individual good cannot contradict the collective good; we cannot become happy by making everyone else unhappy. Therefore, righteous action is a precondition to happiness. When we bridge the gap from the quest of truth to righteous action to the quest for happiness, then can see why the problems of theodicy and cosmodicy are incorrectly formulated: they focus on the goodness and ignore the righteousness.

Most philosophers have kept the questions of epistemology and ethics as separate concerns. We have assumed that there are natural laws that govern matter, but there can be no natural law about our actions. Now this makes the laws of social order arbitrary, and compels us to ask: Why should we follow some man-made laws? After all, if all men are equal, then the lawmakers are no better than the citizens for whom they make the laws. If we reject the man-made laws, then society would become anarchic and chaotic. To fix this problem, religions argue that the laws of social behavior are given by God. Rulers in the past have claimed their rule as a representation of God's laws on earth. Similarly, many governments—even democratic ones—claim that they are doing God's work. But the connection between their action and God's commandments is often hard to establish, as they are often openly flouting the norms of truth and justice for all.

The problem originates in the separation between epistemology and ethics, and the belief that epistemology is only the study of nature's laws, not the laws that govern human behavior. Moral naturalism overturns this claim; now, moral laws are also natural. And following these laws is a necessary precondition to happiness.

The key to the solution of the problems of theodicy and cosmodicy is establishing the causal connection between ignorance, wrong action, and suffering on the one hand, and knowledge, righteous action, and happiness on the other. If nature compels us through suffering to improve our knowledge, which then leads to righteous action, then nature is compassionate, although not a benevolent dictator. There is still free choice in whether we want to learn and act righteously. We need to balance between conflicting demands of forcing the righteous action and the choice of righteous action. When we look at these problems collectively, then the answer is obvious—ignorance will perpetuate wrong action, which will then lead to suffering. Conversely, knowledge will translate into righteous action and thereby bring happiness. A system that pushes us toward correct knowledge—even if that is through suffering—is ultimately good. We cannot see that goodness unless we see the link between knowledge, action, and happiness. That is the goal of ethical naturalism.

6

The Problem of Free Will

Morality is not the doctrine of how we may make ourselves happy, but how we may make ourselves worthy of happiness.
—Immanuel Kant

Underdetermination and Choices

Free will appears in science as the choices of a theory. There are generally several possible explanations for the same observations, but these explanations are not equally good. The deficiency in the explanations becomes obvious as we attempt to use the same theory to describe more phenomena. However, given a certain phenomenon, many theories can *seem* to explain it equally well. This seeming adequacy of different theories rests upon selective neglect of some aspects of the phenomena that may seem irrelevant to the problem at hand. For instance, Newton's gravitational theory describes the motion of planets as point particles by discarding the complexity within a planet. Thermodynamics describes the behavior of gases by ignoring the exact states of individual molecules in a gas chamber. Different theories thus appear adequate for a phenomenon not because they are accurate descriptions of a phenomenon in its entirety, but because they are sufficiently accurate for describing some specific *interesting* aspect of the phenomenon. Which aspect is interesting, depends on the observer's choices. A partial—and therefore incorrect theory of nature—emerges from reality by the selective appreciation of some parts of that reality while neglecting other parts.

Since reality is a sum of a theory and entitlement, whichever part of reality is left out from the theory becomes the theory's entitlement. For instance, if determinism is chosen while choices are neglected, indeterminism becomes the entitlement. Conversely, if choices are chosen while determinism is left out, determinism becomes the entitlement. Countless ways of dividing reality into theory and entitlement can be conceived. These divisions would construe a theory between the extremes of determinism and freedom, and the logical extremes of semantic and physical. They would, correspondingly, also create the opposite types of entitlements. These theories would be based on a selective appreciation of reality.

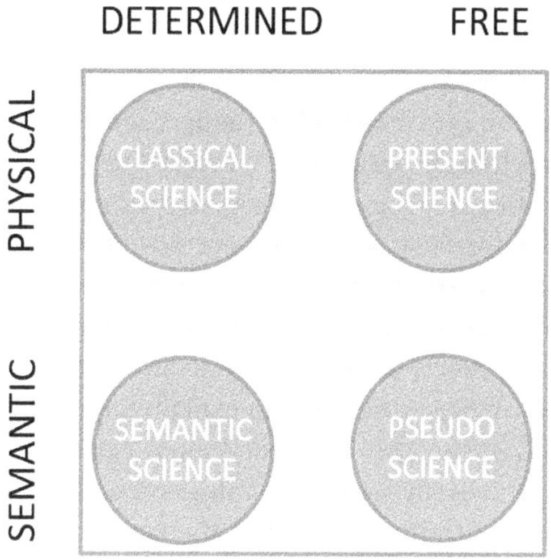

Figure-22 The Quadrant of Scientific Theories

Figure-22 illustrates the space of possible theories that vary along the two dimensions of semantic vs. physical and determined vs. free. Classical physics is physical and determined, and it works for single independent objects quite well. As objects are collected, this theory becomes indeterministic; most present-day theories of science are physical but indeterministic. Many pseudo-scientific approaches argue against the materialism of current science thereby taking away the ability to make deterministic predictions. The present work presents a third alternative of a semantic science that is deterministic and yet not physical. The semantic theory in this case represents the observer's worldview and its entitlements. The observer is free to choose a theory, but the world is determined in its events; as the choices of the theories are made, their entitlements are changed, and the observer moves to a different part of the world. The observer is thus free even though the world is determined; the interaction between the observer and the world is mediated via a theory about the world, which combines the observer's free will and the material world. Each such theory—if it is false—can be produced by limiting the nature of reality in some manner; the true theory must recognize all aspects of reality and should not limit reality within the theory.

Modern science is divided into many different fields—physics, chemistry, biology, computing, mathematics, etc. Each of these fields is further subdivided into many other fields. Each such field limits its focus upon certain limited parts of the world, by defining what is *interesting* to its practitioners. The theoretical models and conceptual tools employed in these differing fields are expected only to be adequate for the purposes of the specific interesting problems.

If we cherry-pick aspects of nature, then many theories can seem adequate for these cherry-picked features. Some theories may even be better than others because they can explain more than one aspect. Eventually, however, the perfect theory must explain all aspects of nature. Thus, when we say that a phenomenon underdetermines the theory, the underdetermination of the theory is a consequence of underdetermining the phenomenon itself. If the phenomenon were completely described or known, then it would single out a theory.

The choice of a theory depends on the selection of some aspects of phenomena. This choice is free in one sense because other observers could pick different aspects of the phenomena. And yet, the choice is not free if the consequences of this choice determine the subsequent experiences, where the previously ignored aspects of nature become prominent and hence can no longer be ignored. For instance, if we look at the planet Earth from afar, then only the total mass of the Earth is important. If we look at Earth from up close, then other phenomena such as living organisms, language, and society are also important. As newer aspects of nature become prominent, the theory must be modified to fit such aspects. However, in the new situation, facets that seemed important earlier may no longer be relevant. For instance, gravity may not play a very key role in understanding language or society. Gravity is important when many details of a phenomenon have been neglected; it is unimportant when those details are reinstated. This makes the search for a theory very difficult.

The problem of theory formation is that all available details about a given phenomenon must be taken into account. Reductionists generally contend that phenomena such as language and society can be reduced to properties such as gravity that appear useful in the description of phenomena which neglect the complexity in language and society. However, this is assumed as a working hypothesis based on faith rather than as an outcome of factual accomplishment in reducing the complexity to the purported simpler assumptions.

There are hence two broad problems associated with the existence of theories—one epistemological and the other moral. The epistemological problem is that a theory may be a selective and incomplete description of nature. The moral problem is that if we happen to choose a theory—by leaving out aspects of natural phenomena—then this choice will have moral consequences. Can there be a natural theory that solves both epistemological and moral problems at once? Such a theory would have to explain all aspects of every phenomenon to address the epistemological issue. Furthermore, since such a theory is also a complete theory, it would also not create moral consequences. The solution to both epistemological and moral problems thus lies in the complete description of nature. Epistemology and morality are not separate problems for us; they are identical.

The perfect theory of nature is the most complete explanation of nature, and this explanation represents the *rationality* of nature. Furthermore, since this rationality frees one from the moral consequences of an action, it is also constituting free will. I had noted in the first chapter that the contradiction between rationality and free will is unnecessary if free will is viewed as rationality. That view entailed that we are not free to construct arbitrary theories, because free will does not equate to falsities. Free will is only the correct choice.

If a wrong theory of nature has been chosen, its consequences will deterministically evolve the theory to other theories. However, since every false theory arises as a partial description of a phenomenon, the evidence necessary for the correction of a theory exists in every phenomenon. The observer may not be interested in such evidence and may ignore it to maintain the false theory. However, every false theory always has at least one alternative—the true theory of nature. The determinism in the evolution of an observer is limited to the encounters with newer phenomena which force an observer to modify the theory. However, the observer could potentially accept any phenomenon in its entirety and thereby form a new theory.

Therefore, an observer's theories can never be constrained to a point where the true theory cannot be an alternative explanation of any phenomena. Every phenomenon can be explained by several false theories and one true theory. The false theories discard some aspects of phenomena while the true theory attempts to explain all aspects. The choice of a false theory therefore depends on the selection of some interesting aspects of nature and represents the misuse of free will, which in turn constrains the possible experiences. However, the possibility for a correct theory exists in all experiences. Therefore, the false theory can be falsified in many phenomena but the true theory would be true in all phenomena. If free will is defined as the choice of the correct theory, then it never disappears.

But what kind of free will is that which allows only one alternative? Isn't the choice of a single alternative effectively a denial of free will? This question needs a distinction between two kinds of free will: the choices of theories and phenomena. The universe permits infinitely many phenomena, but not infinitely many theories. Free will is not the choice of an arbitrary theory, although it is the choice of arbitrary phenomena. Since the correct theory of nature is consistent with all phenomena, the observer with the correct theory can have any experience. The incorrect theory of nature, on the other hand, is consistent with limited phenomena and it restricts possible experiences. Thus, we cannot simultaneously choose an arbitrary theory and arbitrary phenomena; we can only choose one of them. If we choose an arbitrary theory, the phenomena are constrained. If we choose the correct theory, then the phenomena are unconstrained.

The relation between free will and rationality is therefore quite straightforward in this view. The simplification is that nature is a hierarchy whose root is the true theory of the universe; its many trunks are phenomena or experiences, while the leaves are objects. The universe originates in a true theory, which is then exemplified into phenomena, which are then elaborated into objects. Alongside the true theories are also false theories that consider selective aspects of nature and this selective appreciation models the reality to a limited extent. The world works according to the true theory but it *appears* to work according to the false theory to the observer who discards many parts of the reality. Such false theories create consequences. Arbitrary theories of nature would designate arbitrary nodes in the semantic tree as the most fundamental concepts. Anything more abstract than the root of such a theory would be considered false. There may also be attempts to construct such abstractions from the more contingent, and all such constructions will eventually fail.

For instance, think of some hierarchical structure denoted as A.B.C.D...W.X.Y.Z in which A is the root and Z is the leaf. The higher nodes in this branch are more significant than the lower nodes. By changing the higher nodes, we would dramatically alter the meaning of the proposition but changing the lower nodes would only bring minor changes. Therefore, if we were aware of some portions of the branch, we might describe the branch as D.E.F...U.V.W. This is a proper subset of the branch, but its meaning is different because it begins in a different root. The physical view of nature, for instance, begins in the study of objects and disregards the layers of conceptual hierarchy which must exist before any object can be observable. Any theory of nature formulated based on such objects would therefore neglect many higher nodes in the semantic tree, and the meaning of such a theory would be very different. Different such theories would appear to be contradictory not because they are actually inconsistent or false but because we only look at parts of their structure.

In other words, if nature has a unique theory from which phenomena are created, then the conflicts and contradictions between theories, phenomena, or objects are outcomes of a partial understanding of their origin. We are, in effect, faced with the proverbial five blind men and the elephant problem, where the blind men only perceive parts of the elephant and conclude that to be the nature of the entire elephant and argue with each other about their conclusions. The branches of the semantic tree are like the trunk, tail, ears, belly, and legs of the elephant. These parts are connected in the elephant as the root. However, if we see the parts but don't see the root, then we would believe the other parts to be false. A partial understanding of any part would also revise the whole as we move from one part to another. The evolution of the observer's theories is therefore entailed by the ignorance of reality. This ignorance results in false choices of theories, which in turn create entitlements.

Every object is produced from a true theory, although every object is not true. The truth of the theory and the falsity of the object produced from that theory require something that converts the truth into falsity. This falsity is ignorance about truth and it must be associated with the observer. It must perform two functions: (1) make the observer's experience (his mind and body) false, and (2) hinder the perception of truth even in objects that are true. In other words, ignorance has both an existential and a cognitive role. The ignorance is material—and exists as personal theories or worldviews—and it alters the observer's own existence as well as the perception of the reality different from that observer. If this ignorance was removed, it would not only change the observer's own existence but also the perception of the nature of external reality.

Ignorance is a consequence of the fact that we see only parts of reality, different from the root from which they originate. When non-fundamental parts are designated as being fundamental, other parts which differ from these parts are discarded as being false. Every theory of nature obtained from generalizing such parts into the nature of the whole, therefore, results in an incomplete understanding of nature because the left-out parts do not fit in the theory.

The Nature of Consciousness

An understanding of this ignorance requires the postulate of an observer that observes the branches of the tree, although that observer is not any of the nodes of the branch. The observer is, in a sense, transcendent to the nodes of any branch, but becomes aware of certain limited parts of the branch. This limited awareness is the ignorance of the true nature of reality. True knowledge is the awareness of all the nodes on a branch. It is not necessary to know all the branches to know the complete theory of nature; it is only necessary to completely know a single branch as the complete theory is at the root of every branch. The observer is ignorant because it treats a limited portion of any object to be the entire truth of that object.

It is appropriate at this point to speak about the consciousness of the observer which becomes aware of the branch. The free will of the observer is the extent to which he is aware of any branch. The misuse of free will is being aware only of portions of the branch and the correct use of free will is being fully aware of the entire branch. Complete awareness of the branch results in true knowledge while a partial awareness of the branch results in a false understanding of the nature of reality. This false understanding causes entitlements and obligations, thereby constraining the experiences of the observer. The predetermined trajectory of an observer in the universe is therefore an outcome of a limited knowledge of any branch. If the consciousness were extended to the entire branch, it would represent the true awareness of reality and hence entail freedom from the moral consequences which arise due to a partial awareness.

Many modern theories of consciousness define it as *attention* to facts[1]. This attention cannot be defined materially because it is possible to attend to multiple facts at once, although these facts exist individually. In the semantic view, the complete knowledge of even one object[2] requires the awareness of all the nodes from leaf to root. The problem of attention, therefore, is not just that we might partially know many facts at once, which would violate the idea that an object cannot be more than one thing at once. The problem is also that even to fully know one fact we must be aware of many 'deeper' facts, which are all materially distinct and exist as separate symbols within other symbols. For example, if you observe a dog, you also see the idea of mammal and animal within it. The ideas of animal and mammal are higher symbols in the hierarchy, and yet to know the dog completely you must know all the deeper level realities that exist within it.

Of course, as we have seen previously, the semantic hierarchy already addresses this problem because the higher nodes are more abstract than the lower nodes and they, therefore 'perceive' the lower nodes. The sense of seeing for instance represents color which is a more abstract concept than individual colors like yellow or red. Consciousness of the world—if this must know all the facts in the world—must therefore be more abstract than these facts. In so far as all the facts are material, consciousness must transcend matter, because otherwise we could not know all these facts *completely*—we could only know the facts downstream from that symbol.

The necessity for consciousness also arises from the problem of falsities. If the universe is created from a true theory, then how could the experiences created from this theory be false? If the existence of my brain is true, then how could the ideas in that brain be false? How can a true theory produce falsities? The resolution of this problem is that the theory that governs us is the theory that we choose. There is a reality although our theory might not accurately represent that reality. If our theory differs from that reality, it changes our existence and the subsequent perceptions. However, unlike modern science, where a theory must be *formulated* to know the truth, now the truth is already present if ignorance is *removed*. The true theory produces the truth, but ignorance hides parts of these truths to create falsities. The ignorance is material, but more abstract than the material objects and conscious experience. Since the lower nodes develop from the higher nodes, everything produced from ignorance is also false. The extent of falsity depends on the extent of the difference between reality and its ignorance. The ignorance of consciousness is that it is generally aware only of the material objects and their sensations but not the subtle conceptual underpinnings of these objects and experiences. If consciousness were aware of the deeper symbols in the tree, the resulting knowledge would also be truer.

The quelling of this ignorance requires the consciousness to 'rise' up the inverted semantic tree and become aware of higher-order nodes. A consciousness absorbed in the study of material things without the appreciation of its subtle underpinnings is more ignorant relative to a consciousness that is aware of the subtle underpinnings of nature but unaware of the details of material objects. A deeper understanding of the semantic structure of the universe, therefore, entails not just the knowledge of the truth of the universe but also freedom from the laws of nature that constrain free will.

The laws of nature determine which branch of the semantic tree an observer can sit on, and which kinds of information would be transacted, but they don't determine the extent of the awareness of the branch. The laws of nature limit how much of the 'outer' world an observer can know by interacting with the other branches. But the laws do not limit how much of the 'inner' world the observer can know, because it is the branch on which the observer is situated. The knowledge of the higher nodes does not require interaction with another branch and is not constrained by natural laws. An observer is free to fully know the branch it is currently on, including, for instance, the fact that this branch is an offshoot of a non-dual root.

Complete awareness of the observer's own state hinges on two premises: (1) underlying the world of sensations are many layers of abstract conceptual realities, and (2) the observer of these layers of abstract and contingent facts is even more abstract than the facts. Free will is the extent of its attention to all the facts. When free will is misused by a limited awareness of the complete structure of a semantic branch, then free will is also constrained. When free will is correctly used, it results in the complete awareness of the inner world, and the free will to partake in any phenomena is thereby restored. The epistemological project for every consciousness is the complete awareness of reality. The moral project of every consciousness is freedom from the laws of nature. These two are closely interlinked by the fact that constraints on freedom arise from limited awareness of reality, and a complete awareness results in total freedom.

Filtered Experiences

But why should an observer be aware only of limited parts of the world? Why don't we have complete knowledge of things around us? What prevents us from becoming completely aware of reality?

This question is tied to what we mean by consciousness and how it attends to the facts of the world. Some recent experiments in neuroscience—such as the one by Benjamin Libet—illuminate the nature of consciousness. The basic setup for Libet's experiment is quite simple. A subject, whose brain is wired to MRI equipment, is asked to make decisions—for example, to press a "left" button instead of a "right" one. The subject is asked to report the exact point at which she or he decides to press the left or the right button, while the experimenter observers the neurological activity in the brain. The subject's reports about when they decided to press the left or right button are correlated with the neural events. Contrary to the belief that if free will controls the body, then conscious choices should come before the actual action takes place, Libet found that the brain activity preceded the conscious reporting by almost 200 milliseconds.

Materialists who deny free will have jumped at these findings. They suggest that Libet's experiments demonstrate that consciousness is an epiphenomenon of neuronal activity. Like fluidity arises from a molecular explanation of water, the materialists claim that free will is also not a fundamental property but emerges from the neural activity. Since the chemical activity in the brain precedes the conscious reports of choices, the conscious reports must be after-effects of the brain's chemical activity. A study of the chemical and biological activity in neurons would therefore lead us to an explanation of how these epiphenomena arise. Free will is then just a mistake of retrospection where we attribute ourselves free will *after* the brain has already made its decision through chemical activity.

Libet's own interpretation of these experiments was, however, quite different. He did not consider the experiments to be a denial of free will, although he considered them restricting free will's scope. Libet called free will the "power of veto" rather than the power of choice. In effect, there is no free will, although there is a free won't. Consciousness becomes aware of the world by accepting a certain subset of the entire reality. The parts that are not accepted are not known. This is like the 'attention' model of consciousness where we recompense attention to only certain parts of the world, not all.

The problem with Libet's interpretation is that it cannot be applied to experience. For instance, while I might veto certain aspects of the world, and I would then be aware of the veto, many facts that I am unaware of are not because of the veto but because they were never presented to my consciousness for approval. For instance, I'm not aware of the blood circulation in my body not because I vetoed these facts out of my awareness, but because they were never presented for the veto to occur. While consciousness can reject facts being presented for attention, and we would then be unaware of them, every fact that we are unaware of isn't because we vetoed it. Therefore, becoming aware of things that we aren't currently aware of isn't just a matter of discontinuing the veto, since if that were the case, we could easily know everything simply by desiring to know it.

What consciousness accepts or rejects is a subset of what exists. Much of what exists is never presented to consciousness for its approval. In effect, there is a filter before conscious choices which selectively allows only some parts of the world to appear for approval. The free will of consciousness can accept or reject only those things which have earlier passed these filters. It is therefore no surprise that the material changes to the brain are observed before consciousness reports their awareness because the facts in the brain are the events that occur before they are filtered for consciousness. This filtration doesn't undermine free will, because the observer only has a role to veto the facts, and not to create some intended facts. However, the filtration affects the free will because ignorance of the truth pushes us into misleading beliefs, false theories, and improper action.

Overcoming these filters is therefore imperative, provided we can understand their nature. As we discussed earlier, every action has three kinds of consequences—one of which is habit formation. The problem of filtration can be solved if these filters were understood as the *habits* of an observer. For instance, if we habitually block certain types of experiences consciously, and if these habits were represented in matter, they could be used to automatically filter similar types of experiences subsequently. For this idea to be viable there must be a level of material reality that records the history of conscious choices and interacts with the branches of the semantic tree to filter what is presented to consciousness for its attention.

The conscious observer can now be compared to the executive with a limited attention span. This executive has subordinates who know the executive's preferences about the kinds of decisions that the executive would like to make and the ones that he or she would prefer to be delegated to subordinates. The executive's subordinates become the executive's filters about what facts are presented to the executive for decision making. The subordinates would not present to the executive facts in which he or she is uninterested. If the executive wants to receive all information, she must change the subordinate filtering process. Thus, for the observer to know what he or she does not currently know, he or she would have to change the past habits of perception, by developing the new habits that see the world in a new way. The observer may decide to delegate or offload other kinds of decisions to the automated habits, while paying careful attention to the other decisions which he or she is interested in.

This fact is already well-known to most of us familiar with unconscious mechanical responses. These can include defense reactions, standard ways of responding to questions, repetitive acts such as swimming, cycling, or driving, or even routine activities such as bathing, eating, typing, and walking, where we aren't giving conscious attention to things that are happening in our own bodies. These are not presented to consciousness because of the formation of habits in us by which the decisions are automatically taken.

The fact that we are not aware of every aspect of our own existence is an effect of prior such choices. By habit we focus our attention on certain things and take it way from others. The habitual actions become automated and go out of awareness because they are not interesting. There are other things in which consciousness is interested and these are presented for approvals to the observer. The automation of habitual responses helps us see why certain facts about the world are never in our awareness: we have evicted them out of consciousness through prior choices, by focusing on other things.

If an observer's habits are accustomed to recognizing only the sensations—because the observer has habitually blocked everything else—then deeper reality would not be understood, even if it exists. Observers who have the habits of perceiving deeper reality would, however, recognize the existence of such reality. The acceptance of subtle forms of reality, therefore, depends on the observer's habits of perception. To see newer forms of reality, one must develop the habits of perceiving them. To see the complete truth, one must form the habit of seeing the complete truth, by practicing this kind of perception. If such a perception is not practiced, it would naturally be blocked by the habits of perception and would never be visible.

This idea is pertinent to the understanding of the central problem in epistemology and morality. The problem is not just that there are deeper forms of reality which epistemology and morality should uncover but also that we cannot presently perceive these realities unless the habits to perceive them have been previously formed. The habit of perception in this case requires consciousness to be interested in such things and form new habits through practice. We cannot expect to see new kinds of realities unless the habits are formed. Critics of new realities sometimes argue: Can you prove the existence of such a reality? Can you demonstrate that concepts or the mind are real? The problem here is that the critics are trying to perceive subtle reality, but they cannot because these have been blocked due to prior habits of perception. For such observers, the only way to proceed is to postulate the existence of these theoretical entities and then assess their effects on sensations. If theories involving such entities make correct predictions, then there can be motivations to practice their direct perception. Over time, when reality is habitually perceived via a new understanding, the new theoretical entities can be real.

Filtering and Entitlements

The notion about filters of consciousness helps us clarify the mechanism by which reality is divided into theory and entitlement. The mechanism is filters. Reality represents the whole truth. A part of that truth is covered by the filter producing the observer's theory of nature. The remaining part of reality becomes the entitlement.

Since the creation of entitlements depends on the extent to which the complete reality is known, and the extent of this knowledge depends on habits of perception, freedom from the moral law follows the development of the habit to see the complete truth. Clearly, this journey is long, not because such a reality cannot be theoretically described but because it cannot be perceived unless the theory is used to practice perceiving the world in a new way.

The essence of the problem of epistemology and morality is that observers have acquired habits of perception by historical choices. They have learnt to see the world in a certain way, and those habits limit what they can know. If perception was unconditioned by habits, then we could know the complete truth and be free of the moral law.

The problem of epistemology and morality, therefore, exists because the observer's perceptual choices become habits, which in turn block aspects of reality. In effect, consciousness perceives the world through a set of goggles that it has earlier produced through its own choices. These goggles are obviously tinted by our preferences of what we consider to be interesting within the world. The taints on these goggles must be removed before reality can be known. The habit to see the complete truth is also the freedom from all habits that filter our experiences. That freedom in turn entails freedom from the moral consequences of actions. Complete knowledge brings complete freedom; limited knowledge entails limited freedom.

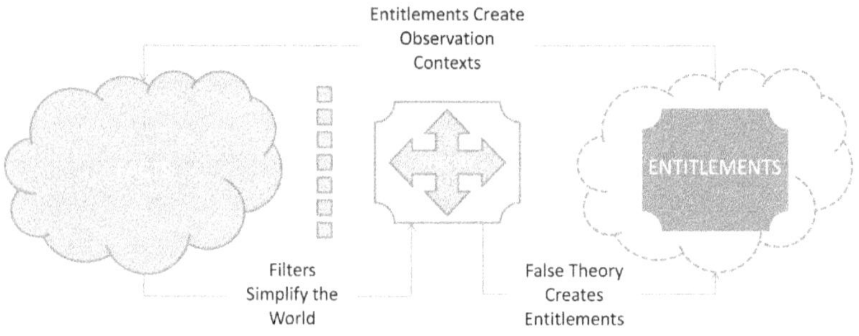

Figure-23 Filters, Theories, and Entitlements

While consciousness is transcendent, the representation of its habits is material and its interaction with reality to create theories and entitlements can be described materially. The habits of perception represent what psychologists often call the unconscious, which makes many automatic decisions and filters what we give attention to. Thus, some individuals may be irresistibly attracted to certain experiences, while others are not. Some individuals may be natural sportsmen, swimmers, artists, or musicians. All these traits are unconscious, but they are material. They can be spoken of objectively although their effects are unique to an observer. There is a huge amount of academic literature on the existence of the unconscious and its effects on conscious experience, so I don't have to repeat it here. The part that is relevant to us here is that if the unconscious filters and amplifies the world for consciousness, and the selective awareness of the world creates entitlements, then the habits of the unconscious are responsible for the observer's evolution.

The problem of epistemology is that our experiences are constructed from the application of filters onto reality. So, what we perceive as 'objects' in the external world aren't necessarily reality. Rather, these objects are constructed by filtering. For instance, physical theories measure object properties by using instruments. An object is defined as the collection of such properties. The outcome of measurement (the measured value) depends on what property we decide to measure, and the choice of that property depends on the physical theory being used to describe the object. Similarly, observers perceive the world through senses such as sight, sound, taste, touch, and smell. The same object can produce different sensations and the object in question is described differently based on the type of sense employed to observe it. Therefore, the 'objects' detected in measurements aren't reality. These objects are rather byproducts of the application of a theory on reality to create experience.

Inevitably, this means that if we had a false theory of nature, which filtered the reality in some way or another, then the objects constructed by such a theory would also only be partially true. Only a true theory's application to reality would manifest all the properties in nature. All other theories would produce objects, but they would not be reality. In that respect, there is a clear difference between reality and objectivity, especially as seen in observation.

Removing the Filters

While the nature of free will—and the fact that it does not contradict determinism—can be discussed within science, recovering this free will requires removing the filters of perception which isn't as straightforward. The problem stems from the fact that filters represent the habits of perception and to change these habits one must form new habits. But if all experiences are predetermined by the entitlements of prior experiences and the effect of current filters, then how can an observer even begin to change the habits? How can the observer step out of the determinism of natural causation?

This problem has a solution in the idea of free will—it must actively *seek* certain kinds of experience. This seeking will cleanse the filters and lead to new kinds of habit. The sincere quest for reality is therefore the key means by which we can find that reality. Of course, nature itself provides avenues for broadening our quest. As we saw previously, if the worldview is incompatible with the reality, then the entitlement of that perception would create a contradiction between the observed facts and the worldview we have entertained.

Once a contradiction has been created, however, there are two distinct ways to resolve it. We might either remove our filters, or create new filters. By removing our filters, we change our worldview, and bring it in accordance with the facts. Conversely, by creating new filters, we block the facts that are inconsistent with our worldview. The inconsistency between the observed facts and the worldview entails a change to one of them, but logic itself cannot determine which one must be change. Changes to either one of them would create a consistent situation. Therefore, these ways remain a choice.

Since the decision of which amongst the two—experience or the worldview—should be changed cannot be made logically, there cannot be a logical theory that predicts which change is actually made. The universe of events is determined logically. However, the inconsistency between a specific observer's worldview and the experience cannot be determined logically. The observer's evolution is determined *if* the choice of the change in worldview or experience can be made. However, this choice is itself not logical. In that respect, there is a crucial aspect of the observer's evolution that is not logically determined, and it can be christened the observer's free will.

Science too adopts a similar approach: sometimes it rejects the theories, when the theories do not fit the experiences, and at other times the scientist rejects the experience as not sufficiently veridical or widespread to refute the theory. Physical theories, for instance, have evolved over time by rejecting the theories in the face of experiences. Likewise, the current physical view of nature steadfastly rejects many aspects of our experience as being epiphenomenal. If the experience is epiphenomenal, then it has no fundamental role in nature and its inconsistencies with the theory cannot result in changes to the theory. If, however, the experience is real, then its inconsistencies with the theory would produce changes to the theory.

The correct use of free will is to regard all aspects of experience as telling us something profound about the nature of reality. However, not all observers treat experience in this way. The early days of scientific empiricism, for instance, rejected most parts of our experience as being irrelevant to the study of reality; this included the notion that the qualities perceived in taste, touch, smell, sight, and sound are irrelevant to the nature of reality. Over time, this rejection of sensations from reality was extended to nearly all everyday concepts (such as 'table' and 'chair'), and anything that seemed even more subjective than the sensations. Physics permitted only a very limited set of concepts—those which could be measured in relation to other objects—as being useful concepts for reality. In effect, scientific theories blocked so much of the everyday experience from the theories that all such theories are now faced with various forms of indeterminism, incomputability, and incompleteness. As we find more and more areas of experience that do not fit with the theory, the tendency is to reject them as being epiphenomena of the currently formulated theories, rather than fundamental features of reality that require a shift in our current understanding of nature.

The current materialist view of science, therefore, represents a misuse of free will which creates filters of perception, refusing to acknowledge reality because it doesn't fit our worldview. Its entitlement is indeterminism, incompleteness, and uncertainty.

Progress in science must remove these filters. This removal must begin with the acknowledgement of taste, touch, smell, sight, and sound as real properties of nature, and proceed into meanings. This doesn't mean that the material world is the *qualia* in perception; it only means that the external world holds *information* about qualia, and its properties were developed by adding information to qualia. The information is semantic and objective and can be denoted by the nodes in the semantic hierarchical structure. This hierarchy in this tree structure represents the layers of perceptual filters that science needs to remove from our current understanding of nature one by one. At every step of this removal, some problems of incompleteness would be solved, making science more complete. Only when all such filters have been removed, and the semantic hierarchical tree culminates in a single root, can science be considered complete.

Free will is therefore deeply connected with the practice of science: When we encounter an inconsistency between theory and phenomena, which of the two do we change? There is no logic to determine this choice because any contradiction can be resolved by rejecting either side of the conflicting notions. Of course, we would imagine that over time, it is harder to continually reject the phenomena to maintain the theory, but this fact is by far the dominant one in modern science. Free will is therefore essential to the method of science because guidelines about how the conflict between theory and phenomena should be resolved need to be formulated. In principle, the scientific method professes falsification: a single fact can falsify a theory. In practice, theories survive and thrive much longer because the veracity of the experience is under question or because whether such an experience confirms or denies the theory is not known.

The problems of incompleteness are notoriously difficult because the theory *partly* works. There is, hence, a tendency to think that incremental additions to the theory would address the problem. As the theory can explain many phenomena partially, it becomes harder to throw away the theory. This happens to be current science's predicament. Even though the problems of incompleteness are well-known, the scientific community steadfastly holds on to the current paradigms. The rational thing would be to accept the phenomena and find the theories that explain them. However, this rationality is not always the logical path in science. Often, when the phenomena do not behave according to a theory, the tendency is to believe that someday these naughty phenomena would be disciplined.

Whether the phenomena are naughty, or the theory is false, is the free will in the observer. Progress in science hinges on it. It is not necessary to use the scientific method as the phenomena to study free will. Rather, as science removes the filters of perception and develops a semantic theory of matter, the newer theory would not just be consistent, complete, and computable, but will also predict new outcomes which are currently impossible due to the incompleteness and indeterminism of current theories. In that respect, the development of newer theories—when described as the choices of filter removal—can in itself be seen as the effect of free will in nature.

The Free Will Debate is Misplaced

This book traced the conflict between free will and determinism to the need to separate an observer from its material 'roles.' The observer is free will together with its theories and its roles are material and determined. The world we see, therefore, depends as much on objective reality as it does on which parts of the world are accepted or blocked by our worldviews. The determinism of the roles does not contradict the free choices. However, for this solution of the free will and determinism conflict to be workable, matter itself must be defined as three categories—universals, individuals, and relations. The difference between the current and new notions about matter is that (1) there are three different kinds of material realities, and (2) matter is semantic and hierarchical. The shift from a physical to a semantic definition of matter hinges upon the need to solve the problems of incompleteness in current science. The book demonstrated how the hierarchical semantic structure solves the problems of incompleteness in science. I had divided the solution into three parts—(1) the determinism of events as the script of a drama, (2) the need to treat matter as information, and (3) the tripartite model of causality.

Filtering the world hinders the development of theories by reducing the kinds of concepts that can be used in a theory: the resulting theory is incomplete. This incompleteness is not just an epistemological problem but a moral one too, since an incomplete theory produces the observer's entitlements of experience. These entitlements can create conflicts between the observer's theory and experience and the observer has a choice: (1) accept the contradiction and do nothing about it, (2) accept the contradiction and reject the theory, or (3) accept the contradiction and reject the experiences. This choice constitutes the free will of the observer. Its effect does not change events in the universe. However, it changes the roles of the observers who make these choices. Morality hinges on the existence of free will and this free will is embodied in the practice of science.

The debate between free will and determinism is therefore false. It stems from the physical deterministic model of nature, even though its flaws are well-known. A revision to the theory of matter can resolve the conflict. This book hopefully described how free will, determinism, and morality can be mutually compatible and can emerge out of a deeper understanding of science and its problems.

The Transmigration of the Observer

Until the observer has found the perfect theory of nature, he must evolve through experiences. These experiences are produced through the combination of three categories—the universal, the individual, and the relational—each of which exists in a hierarchy. We can think of these three hierarchies as three kinds of *real* spaces—i.e., the realities that exist prior to observation. Their combination creates experience. The hierarchical nature of space is closed, and the hierarchical nature of time is cyclic. An observer's consciousness is a subset of these three spaces. That is, the observer is an individual, he experiences some universals, and participates in some relations. The observer's experiential evolution is temporally cyclic, just as the universal evolution is temporally cyclic. If the universal space-time structure were hierarchical but the individual space-time structure was linear, then there would be meanings in the universe but not in the observer. Conversely, if the observer's space-time was hierarchical and the universe was linear, then there would be meanings in the observer and not in the universe. Neither will work correctly.

This fact helps us draw the following important conclusion, which is that if time is cyclic for every observer, then the observers would undergo birth and death repeatedly in a cyclic manner, quite like the universe must expand and contract cyclically. This idea is generally called the transmigration of the soul in Eastern religious philosophical thought, and pervades many current religions such as Buddhism, Hinduism, Sikhism, Jainism, Shintoism, and Taoism.

There are several reasons why transmigration appears false under current scientific beliefs. First, the idea rests upon natural moral causality and science only describes causes physically rather than morally. Second, for some entity to transmigrate from body to body (and mind to mind), that entity must survive the death of the body (and the mind), and such an entity is inconceivable in current science. This is primarily because all entities in material science are temporary: they are created and destroyed, so the notion of something that exists eternally is unthinkable in current science. Third, for the transmigrating entity to inhabit different bodies and minds according to a moral law, this entity must have free will because otherwise its moral evolution would appear unfair. However, free will appears to contradict the scientific belief that nature is determined by mathematical laws and the successes of science are therefore seen entail a denial of free will. I have discussed each of these issues individually through this book, so I will recapitulate them here for summary.

Let's begin with free will. The problem of free will arises when the idea of free will is confused with the idea of freedom. We suppose that if there is free will then the observer must be able to change the events in the world. However, as we have seen, if nature was free in this sense, then it would not be a rational place because anyone could change the world just by their free will and science would be unable to predict its evolution. This also means there cannot be an empirical evidence of free will because free will does not equate with freedom. However, free will can still be defined as the freedom from natural laws, when the law is defined morally rather than physically. The physical law governs the events in the universe while the moral law governs the observers which participate in those events. Free will cannot violate the events in the universe, but it can overcome the moral law when the observer's perceptual filters are removed.

The need for morality arises from the problems of epistemology. We can make false theories, but we cannot know the theories are false unless we encounter the phenomena that falsify them. If nature wasn't a moral place—i.e., if it did not ensure that an observer would encounter experiences which could potentially falsify its theories—there would be no reason to suppose that science would eventually find the perfect theory of nature. The quest for truth would be never-ending and we could never assert that anyone truly knows. We could have any number of beliefs about reality, but those beliefs could potentially be falsified in the future. It would therefore be rational to suppose that if your beliefs are different from mine, then both beliefs are just temporary suppositions that could later change. Morality solves two problems in epistemology. First, it ensures that every observer will encounter experiences that will falsify their theories if those theories are false. Second, it provides the test for true knowledge: if the theory is complete, then free will is reinstated.

The development of science must be driven by a method that can conclude and achieve its stated goals. Current science does not have such a method. Science is defined as the cycle of experiment followed by theory, but the end of this cycle is not guaranteed, because all possible data to be explained by a theory is unknown. As a result, there is also no way to know if the cycle has already ended, so that we can stop the search for the truth and correctly distinguish the falsities from the truth. Science, as it is defined currently, is a perennially ongoing process. How long the process is, whether it even ends, and whether we can know when it has ended, cannot be known. The necessity of morality, therefore, arises from the necessity to define a scientific method that can even in principle terminate, and it should be possible to know when the method has in fact come to an end.

Once the scientific method has been defined in this manner, and morality is central to science, it is natural to seek causality in nature in a way that is governed by morality and not physicalism. This requires a deep understanding of the problems arising from a physical treatment of nature, and how these problems could be rectified by a semantic theory of reality. It is important to understand why only a semantic theory can be logically consistent, complete, and computable at once[3]. This semantic picture would obviously indicate the existence of many abstract forms of reality that we do not currently perceive. While their truth can be *logically* known from the rational and empirical correctness of the theory, their *experience* cannot be guaranteed in this way. To experience such realities, we must ask: What prevents us *now* from knowing that all these realities exist?

This naturally leads us to the problem of developing the observer's perceptual capabilities, and then to the question of what we mean by such perceptual development. All perceptual development, as I have argued earlier, can be reduced to the removal of perceptual filters. The development of knowledge aids in the removal of filtering, but this knowledge must be practiced, overcoming the effects of habits. This removal is under the control of free will, through the pursuit of truth to form new habits of unfiltered perception. Repeated attempts to enhance our vision of reality create new perceptual habits by which the new kinds of realities can be perceived. As false goggles of perception are removed, the moral consequences would begin to cease and the observer would gradually begin to find free will. It can now choose new contexts that it would not have chosen earlier.

The reasons that transmigration appears a flawed idea is because scientific notions about matter, causality, and lawfulness in nature are flawed. The genesis of this problem lies in the fact that science postulates a material reality, but the conception of this reality is incomplete, indeterministic, and incomputable. As this conception finds partial successes in terms of technology, its proponents claim to be discovering the nature of truth. This truth is demonstrably incomplete, for reasons that we have seen throughout this book. But the habits of thinking and perception we have already developed over the centuries prevent the revision of a flawed materialistic ideology.

The problems of free will, morality, consciousness, and transmigration are closely connected to a new conception about matter, causality, and lawfulness. This conception of matter can emerge from a solution to the incompleteness in mathematics, physics, biology, and computing, even without reference to the above problems. But it is worth noting that when those problems have been solved, the picture of reality would be drastically different. In this picture, there are observers who formulate theories of nature based on experiences, and the moral evolution of the observer hinges on the extent to which the theory is true. With false theories, the observer must encounter experiences that can potentially correct the false theory. The transmigration of the soul is simply an outcome of the epistemological project to know the nature of reality through different bodies, senses, and minds, so long as the nature of reality has not been understood.

Epilogue

Cartesian metaphysics separates the mind from the body and brings a slew of problems whose diagnosis has become incredibly hard in science. On the one hand, there is a tendency to disregard the problems of indeterminism, incompleteness, and irreversibility as indicative of something profoundly mistaken about our worldview. On the other hand, there is a need to continue reducing greater parts of the universe to the current materialist approach to nature. These two problems feed on each other. As science is able to achieve some predictive successes with the newer areas not tackled thus far, the materialist proclaims that there is even more evidence that everything is just one type of thing—particles with physical properties. Soon, however, we run into a familiar kind of problem: the materialist theory seems to involve incompleteness and indeterminism.

The greatest hurdle in the solution to the mind-body separation is the problem of free will. In the dualistic view, the body is determined by natural laws, but the mind is free. How can these two kinds of material entities interact? Wouldn't their interaction entail that natural laws can be violated? The dominant scientific belief is that when the mind is reduced to matter, free will would be explained away as an epiphenomenon of material interactions. Some evolutionists can now even argue that those living beings who had the illusion of free will had better chances of survival in an otherwise determined world. When a reductionist sets out to reduce everything to material objects, it is possible to make all such explanations completely *consistent.* However, it is impossible to make the reductions *complete.*

If anything in the universe has an observable effect, it could be reduced to the sensations by which we detect it, so that the subsequent reduction of sensations—as already enshrined in physical theories—can be continued. The only problem is that science is not just about observations; it is also about theories that predict the observations. To predict newer phenomena, we must postulate some new concepts. These concepts are different from sensations; while the sensations can be observed, the concepts in science cannot. Theories, therefore, inject new kinds of entities whose existence cannot be verified by sensation. However, their existence can be inferred by the successes of the theory itself. If the theory makes correct predictions, then everything that it postulates must be true. But now we are faced with another problem—the problem of underdetermination. Even when a theory is quite successful, we cannot know if its theoretical entities are indeed reality because there could be other theories that seem to work equally well. The only way we can prefer one theory over another is if one theory works much better than the others.

In this case, it means that the theory must predict and explain more phenomena than the other theories. Any theory that explains a greater number of phenomena is clearly preferred over a theory that only explains a lesser number of phenomena. Eventually, the perfect theory is that which explains every conceivable experience.

This point is very important because the reality we attribute to the entities in a theory can be false if the theory is incomplete. The limited successes of a theory don't entail the truth of its theoretical entities. So, the argument that science must be true because it works is wrong, if science predicts or explains the phenomena only partially. Here, it is useful to distinguish between two kinds of incompleteness. First, we can take a particular phenomenon and check if a theory fully explains that phenomenon. Second, we can apply the theory to a wider set of phenomena. It is conceivable that a theory may completely explain selective aspects of some phenomena but not all aspects of one or more phenomena. We might then suppose that a different theory would be required to explain all phenomena.

There is, however, an important practical problem that prevents this way of thinking. If theory T explains phenomena X but doesn't explain Y, then T must be modified to explain Y. If T is a minimal and complete theory of X, then we cannot remove anything from T because then T would be unable to explain X. We can only add things to T. However, if we add new ideas to T in order to explain Y, then the theory predicts something additional even for X. If T were a complete explanation of X, then additional predictions would contradict X, and invalidate T. The only way a theory T can be modified to explain Y is if it were already an incomplete explanation of X because to explain Y we must add things to T which would make additional predictions about X, which is permissible only if the previous theory was an incomplete description of X. It now follows that to find the perfect theory of all the phenomena in the universe, it is helpful but not necessary to study an increasingly wider set of phenomena. For instance, if we have a theory T of phenomena X, and it completely explains X, then it would also completely explain Y. If there were a complete theory of anything, it would also be a complete theory of everything.

Conversely, if there were an incomplete theory of anything, it would also be an incomplete theory of everything. The progress in science hinges not upon using one particular incomplete theory to incompletely explain a greater number of phenomena. The progress hinges upon finding the complete explanation of any one phenomenon. If we can even find one complete explanation of a single phenomenon, we would have found a complete explanation of everything. In other words, theories are not underdetermined by phenomena. Many theories seem to explain a phenomenon equally well, only because each theory explains the phenomena incompletely. The underdetermination of theories by phenomena exists only so long as the theory in question is incomplete. When a theory is complete, then there can be only one theory for any given phenomena.

We can now conclude that every misinterpretation of reality—which creates a false theory—must also be an incomplete theory. In fact, such a theory would be an incomplete description of every phenomenon. On the other hand, if there were a complete theory of any phenomena, it would also be a complete theory of everything.

Each observer is one phenomenon. If the observer could formulate a complete theory about himself, then that theory would already be a complete description of the universe. It is therefore not necessary to know the entire universe to know the nature of truth. We can also know the complete truth simply by knowing ourselves. Science is not the exclusive prerogative of those who study the motion of planets, the remote transmission of information, or the way the living bodies work. It is rather the imperative for every person who wishes to know themselves completely. Indeed, all forms of curiosities about nature begin in the questions of our own existence. Who am I? Why am I here? Where will I be in the future? If these were correctly answered, they will also constitute complete theories of nature. On the other hand, if these questions were incompletely answered, then it also entails incompleteness in the theory of anything else in nature.

Present science transforms these questions into the study of everything besides the observer, by separating the world from the observer. It then attempts to bring back insights from the study of the world to explain the observer. Since the world is devoid of the properties in our perception, science attempts to reduce the observer to objective properties, while it denies the truth of perceptual facts in the material world. Both descriptions are incomplete. That is, it is not true that science describes the inanimate world completely and the only remaining mystery is to find a complete description of the observer. In fact, the idea that the world and the observer could be described via different theories is itself false. The way science incompletely describes the observer's experience must also be the incompleteness in the description of any natural phenomena. The incompleteness in the theory of the inanimate world must be intimately connected to the incompleteness in the description of observers.

That fact helps us understand why the incompleteness in scientific theories could be addressed by bringing in the observer. The difference between the current scientific descriptions of nature and the phenomena of the observer is that science describes the world in terms of *quantities* while the observers are known in terms of *types*. These types begin in sensations—tasting, touching, smelling, hearing, and seeing. We perceive the world as taste, smell, and color, which present science aims to reduce to quantities. This reduction is incomplete. It works partially. And the problems of incompleteness exist not just in physical theories, but also in mathematics, and computing. The solution to this problem, as I described in this book, is to find a description of the world consistent with the description of the observer. That is the only way the description can be complete.

One fundamental difference between types and quantities is that types are hierarchical while quantities are linear. Our perception is also hierarchical: it begins in external objects, which then lead to sensations, which are then objectified using concepts, which are then judged as being consistent and complete to form a theory of nature, this theory is then employed as technology to fulfill our goals, and by fulfilling our goals we hope to form a society based on equitable principles. Thus, our perception abstracts from individual objects into broader concerns about the nature of truth, good, and right. There are many layers in our experience which constitute a different type of experience, which cannot be reduced to a single type.

Considering this hierarchy in experience, this book described a hierarchical theory of nature, and how it addresses the incompleteness in science. The cornerstone of that description is a hierarchical theory of space-time. A tree is always loop-free, so it is free of recursion and contradictions. Many modern physical theories aim to overcome the incompleteness by postulating multidimensional theories. String theory in physics for instance postulates 10 and 26 dimensional descriptions of nature. The many dimensions in these theories are, however, linear. That in turn implies that all locations in such space-times would be equivalent. Since these locations can be treated objectively and independently, they would never represent types and the hierarchical structure of types can never be emulated in such a theory. The problem of types is therefore not just that the structure of a theory should be multidimensional but also that these dimensions must also be defined hierarchically. Current physical multidimensional theories are not hierarchical. A multidimensional linear theory of physical objects is therefore not a type theory. If the problem of science is the reduction of types to quantities, then no linear multidimensional theory would ever be able to fix that problem.

In the semantic tree, there are as many dimensions as there are nodes. This is because each location in this space is treated as a distinct type and hence a unique set of dimensions. All locations are therefore distinct types of locations, not just distinct locations. No finite dimensional theory of nature can match the complexity available in the hierarchical semantic structure, because theories with infinite dimensions would also be infinitely complex. The semantic hierarchy also describes how the number of dimensions increase as information is added and decrease as information is removed. There isn't hence a fixed dimensional theory for all possible phenomena in nature. Rather, the number of dimensions required to explain a phenomenon depends on its complexity. Physically, a complex phenomenon is more of a simple phenomenon. Semantically, a complex phenomenon is also a conceptually different kind of phenomenon.

Causality in this picture of nature is the growth or collapse of the tree's branches, attained by addition or removal of information. However, the observer is not always aware of all such informational transactions, although the observer could potentially be aware of each such transaction. The consciousness of the observer is strained through some material filters which make it aware only of certain limited parts of a particular tree's branch. These filters can be called our habits by which we seek only certain parts of nature while ignoring or neglecting other parts. The moral consequences of transactions depend on which parts we are aware of. Transactions that occur without our awareness do not create consequences. Similarly, a complete awareness of all transactions—where the transaction is traced all the way to the root of a branch—also does not produce consequences. Moral consequences are therefore outcomes of a limited awareness in which the trunk or leaf is known but the root is not. Such transactions force the observer into new exchanges.

Freedom from such morality can come about either through the elimination or completeness of experience. In the former case, all facts about the world are filtered creating a state devoid of experience. In the latter case, the experience is extended to the root of a branch, by removing all filters. The former mechanism destroys morality by destroying knowledge. The latter mechanism achieves the same effect, although by completing the knowledge of the world. Morality, therefore, does not exist if there is no knowledge or if there is full knowledge. It exists only in between these two extremes.

The problem of morality involves a deeper understanding of free will, and why it has effects only on the observer's evolution, rather than the evolution of the world. Since free will changes our experiences, the effects are empirical although in a personal sense. Ultimately, this science is not concerned with the intricacies of the evolution of matter but with the intricacies of the observer's existential dilemmas. This existential dilemma—and the associated moral problem—is resolved either through cessation or the completeness of experience. The former ends free will and the latter uses it correctly.

Endnotes

1. THE PROBLEM OF MORALITY

1 The idea that chemical reactions can be deterministically predicted is quite problematic today since these reactions depend on the behavior of atomic objects, which are currently described in atomic theory using probabilities. However, whether probabilities are permanent features of nature or just temporary flaws of the current scientific description is debatable. I believe that this problem will eventually be solved and there would be a predictively deterministic theory of chemical reactions although this isn't the case today.

2 The question of whether science is an invention or a discovery is debatable. Later chapters will show that a true theory is a discovery and false theories are inventions. Furthermore, a false theory is created by omitting parts of a complete theory. The inventiveness of the scientist is therefore only in omitting selected parts of reality. If this inventiveness is discarded, then a complete theory of nature can be known.

3 I am aware that such a line of thinking at the outset will quickly invoke the suspicion that the playwright in this case is God, and the rest of the book will now head into the discussion of how God creates the universe. To those of you who are thinking in this way, I would like to say that the eventual thesis of this book is that the evolution of the universe is due to a peculiar type of generative space-time structure which can be mathematically described and empirically tested. Why the universe must have this structure is connected to some profound problems of incompleteness in science which are solved only when matter is viewed as symbols of meanings. Why the universe must be meaningful is however a question that cannot be answered

within science, although it can be connected to the property of consciousness to seek meaning, and thereby eventually to God. However, that is a topic that this book does not dive into.

4 It is notable that a particle split is the inverse of two particles joining after collision. Both types of changes are called 'inelastic' (and sometimes 'plastic') in classical physics. The inelastic collisions conserve momentum but don't conserve the kinetic energy. Whether they actually conserve energy or not, is not clearly known.

5 Two trajectories or particles that pass through identical events are also identical trajectories or particles. Something is a different particle or trajectory only if it can be distinguished from events.

6 In Newton's theory, for instance, the effect and the reaction of an action are immediate. In atomic theory, the reaction of an action is also immediate and it is the inverse of the effect, caused by the loss of a quantum particle which the effect in turn gains. In general relativity, too, the reaction and effect are immediate although not instantaneous because the loss and gain of energy takes a finite amount of time governed by the finite speed of light.

7 I will describe the semantic notion of space-time in later chapters. Here, for illustration, if the first transaction occurs at a place called 'above' and at a time called 'morning' then the inverse transaction would occur at place called 'below' and at a time called 'night.'

8 It is worth noting that reality in this case is different from the observed facts. All facts are not true, and hence they are not real in the specific sense that they would be temporary. Only the true is real.

2. A HISTORY OF UNCERTAINTIES

1 After energy has been extracted from a system, the remaining energy is in a state of greater disorder due to which it cannot be further extracted. The total entropy of the system increases, even when the total energy has decreased.

2 My earlier book *Gödel's Mistake: The Role of Meaning in Mathematics* discusses the genesis of several logical, mathematical, computational, and philosophical paradoxes and traces them to the inability to hold categorical distinctions in a formal language. These distinctions exist in ordinary language and when language categories are brought into a formal language such as mathematics or logic, various types of contradictions are created.

3 This is also called Gödel numbering which represents the Arithmetization of Syntax rather than Semantics.

4 Stephen Kleene (1952). "Introduction to Metamathematics". North-Holland.

3. A TYPE THEORY OF REALITY

1 We can, of course, describe both the world and the brain as physical properties, but as we saw earlier, this description fails to account for the qualitative perception in the brain as well as the ability to explain concepts. The reduction of the mind to the brain therefore suffers from problems of incompleteness. However, the reduction of the brain to the mind does not suffer from this problem.

2 In the theory of general relativity, the matter distribution is viewed as being equivalent to the coordinate transformations, and the two are sometimes distinguished as active and passive diffeomorphisms. A coordinate transform in the traditional sense of simply renaming all points in space to different numbers is called passive diffeomorphism (since it gives the impression that nothing has changed in the real world except the observer's perspective). A coordinate transform that redistributes matter in a new way is called an active diffeomorphism since it gives the impression of creating a new set of particles which could potentially have different masses.

3 It is essential to distinguish between two notions of real—existence and truth. In the physical view of nature, everything that exists is also true, but in the semantic view, all that exists in not necessarily true. The distinction between existence and truth arises due to meanings: false things can exist; for instance, I can think that the sky is purple and the thought will exist in

my brain, but that thought would be false. When I speak about reality here, I mean it in the sense of existence and not truth. Our experiences exist, but they are not necessarily true; for instance, my mind could be hallucinating or misperceiving.

4. SCIENCE AND SEMANTICS

1 One explanation of statistical mechanics is called the Ergodic hypothesis, which suggests that a system traverses all possible states.

2 There is an important distinction between the classical position and momentum uncertainty and the uncertainty in quantum position and momentum *state*. To understand this difference, imagine an ordinary extended object such as a table. The table has a definite position but we cannot describe that positon in classical physics because the table is extended. In classical wave physics, too, the wave is actually built out of many distinct positions in space because we think that the wave is *in* space. When the wave is space, and the wave is an object, then space is itself not divisible into smaller parts (unless more information is added). Such extended waves are classically indefinite but they are quantum mechanically certain because the locations in space are not *defined* unless information has been added and we cannot speak about an indefinite state unless those locations are defined. It follows that the state of a quantum may be uncertain in the sense that more information can be added. However, if the information has not been added then the state is actually certain! When the information is added, the state would again be certain. In other words, the quantum state is never uncertain in quantum theory, although it appears uncertain in classical physics.

3 Indirectly, it means that a 2-state quantum system can only be measured once because in that one measurement all the communicable information has already been obtained and nothing new is pending.

5. SEMANTIC THEORY OF MORALITY

1 The semantic view also begins in nothingness, but this nothingness is semantic rather than physical. For instance, the origin of the universe can

be described as the number zero which is a form and concept that combines all opposite forms and concepts. The separation of these opposite forms depends on the structure in time and is not arbitrary, and this structure can only be understood when forms denote meanings.

2 Cristian S. Calude, Michael A. Stay (2008) "Most programs stop quickly or never halt". Advances in Applied Mathematics 40, 295–308.

3 I have casually written this as an equation, but it should not be construed as a mathematical addition of two terms in the conventional sense that we define mathematics currently—i.e., as the addition of two quantities. Mathematics itself has to be understood as a description of concepts or types before this equation would represent something predictively useful in science.

6. THE PROBLEM OF FREE WILL

1 Bernard J. Baars (1997). "In the Theatre of Consciousness". Journal of Consciousness Studies, 4, No. 4, pp. 292-309.

2 This object could be the observer's own self, including, for instance, their own body, senses, mind, intellect, ego, morality and consciousness. It is not necessary to understand the world beyond the individual being, if only that being is completely understood.

3 The consistency does not imply that two opposite ideas don't exist in nature. However, it implies that the opposites are defined mutually or not at all. When opposites are defined mutually, they cannot be treated as independent entities, and it requires a fundamental shift not only in our current view of logic but also in how this logic treats concepts. For instance, the logic has to allow the simultaneous existence of opposites because they are only defined mutually. The reconciliation between these opposites is not at the level of those opposites but at a *deeper* level of another kind of reality more abstract than the opposites. For instance, red and blue can be opposites in some context, but they are reconciled at the level of color. Seeing and touching can appear to be opposites in some context, but they are reconciled at the level of the mind. The oppositions end when the semantic

tree terminates in the root. This root must now be viewed as the non-dual and absolute entity that is defined independent of all other entities that emanate from it.

Index

www.ingramcontent.com/pod-product-compliance
Lightning Source LLC
Chambersburg PA
CBHW021924040426
42448CB00008B/901
* 9 7 8 9 3 8 5 3 8 4 0 2 8 *